RIDING THE WAVES

A Memoir of Love, Loss, & Grief

by Katherine Krige

Twin Horseshoes Publishing
www.twinhorseshoes.ca
Ontario, Canada

This publication contains the opinions and ideas of its author and is designed to provide useful information in regard to the subject matter covered. The author and publisher are not engaged in professional services in this publication. This publication is not intended to provide a basis for action in particular circumstances without consideration by a competent professional. The author and publisher expressly disclaim any responsibility for any liability, loss, or risk, personal or otherwise, which is incurred as a consequence, directly or indirectly, of the use and application of any of the contents of this book. While the author has made every effort to provide accurate information at publication time, the publisher and the author assume no responsibility for author or third-party websites or their content.

Cover photo: Leslie McLeod. Inside title page photo: jarmoluk from pixabay. All other photos have been taken and provided by Katherine Krige unless otherwise noted.

Krige, Katherine
Riding the Waves: A Memoir of Love, Loss, and Grief
Includes bibliographical references.

eBook ISBN 978-1-990831-10-2
Paperback ISBN 978-1-990831-09-6

Nonfiction | Biographies & Memoirs | Memoirs
Nonfiction | Health, Fitness & Dieting | Death & Grief | Grief & Bereavement
Nonfiction | Health, Fitness & Dieting | Relationships | Love & Loss
Nonfiction | Family & Relationships | Death, Grief, Bereavement
Nonfiction | Psychology | Grief & Loss
Nonfiction | Self-Help | Death, Grief, Bereavement

2

DEDICATION

To Brad, for starting me on the journey,
and my mom for marking out
the path ahead.

But mostly to my children, Taryn and
Rylie, for ensuring my forward movement,
even (especially) on the days I didn't want
to take another step.

TABLE OF CONTENTS

PART ONE...
RIDING THE WAVES

"You will never know how strong you are until being strong is the only choice you have."

Bob Marley

Chapter 1: Water

I stepped into the bathroom and gently pushed the door shut behind me. These precious few moments would probably be the only alone time I would be able to carve out from my day. The house was full—my mom, stepdad, sister, stepbrother, and of course, the girls, Taryn and Rylie. I turned on the water and waited for it to warm up, before slipping off my robe and stepping under the steaming water. All I wanted was to wash the breast milk from my belly, the smell of hospital that clung to me from my hair, and to indulge in a brief respite before stepping back into the nightmare that my world had become.

The water sluiced through my thoughts and ran rivulets of memories down the drain. How long would I have to stand there to reset the months that had crashed into each other, straining the bounds of normal until all hands had emerged on deck to stem the shock waves that trembled through me? If I inched the temperature to scalding, could I burn the images from my brain of my husband screaming in the emergency room, or worse, lying motionless with a machine beeping softly beside him, the only proof he lived?

Come on water. Work your magic.

I heard the doorknob turn and waited to see the tiny head of my toddler peak through the shower curtain, wondering where I had escaped to. Not today though.

"The hospital is on the phone," my sister said.

Her eyes were dark, as she held the phone out to me. My mother emerged beside her.

No. Not this.

I slammed the water off and snatched the phone from her, my heart already hammering in my chest.

"Mrs. Labravoure?" a voice said. "We're sorry to inform you, but …"

I dropped to the floor naked and shaking, as the rest of her announcement split my life in two. They had warned me this was coming, but with those few words, my surreal bubble burst and I stepped into 'after'.

"Brad passed away a few minutes ago…"

Nothing would be the same ever again.

Chapter 2: This is the Story of a Girl...

As of writing these words, my husband has been gone for 16 years. It feels like forever, but I can also recall moments like they happened just yesterday. I have lived lifetimes since the day he died in 2007. I've learned lessons, shed tears, laughed, and continued on, despite everything. But the darkness that was Brad's final journey lives inside me and always will. The story of his last days, but more importantly MY story inside his—that needs to be told. I have started it many times, never certain that the words were right. Because they aren't. How can any words be right? They can't. They still percolate inside me though. And whether I voice them or not, they exist and will continue to mold me. Those dark days are a part of me. They are also a part of my light. They make the light shine brighter.

Or so I tell myself. Sometimes I wonder though. Sometimes I wonder hard.

Where does this story begin? Hard to say. This version started when someone recommended a book to me. It sounded interesting, even though I knew it might gut me. It was a story about grief. Of course, it would gut me. It always does. So why did I read it? Why put me through that again and again and again?

Grief.

You don't ever get over it. You live within its realm and learn from the lessons, hopefully taking steps to help you heal and start living again. You can't go back to the before with grief. There is no reset. It is a hollow in your heart; a comfort and a weight heavier than any you ever imagined. It is memory and a part of you. Every fiber you have ever been. And my God, it is so much a part of you, there is no cleaving it from your psyche. So why fight it?

Why fight it indeed? This is the story I need to tell. Yes, I have shed many tears, but they remain in my heart like a crazy balm or badge of survival. They are my pain, but also my memory and essential to my healing journey. It doesn't mean there isn't more to me than that, but that loss will always be there. And this story needs to be told for myself, as much as anyone. I know others have the same story; just a variant painted their own. The same grief, only theirs to share. You have your version, but we can see each other in the telling. And in being seen, we gain a little of ourselves back.

I need as many pieces of me as I can get.

For so long, I was unable to look at myself in the mirror. It isn't quite right to say I was scared. I just couldn't. I couldn't look into those eyes so full of pain and disbelief. None of this was real, you know? How could it be? Every day I woke up to the same reality though and it was reflected in the gaze levelled at me. I felt like I wore it as an invisible cloak that everyone could see and in seeing, feel uncomfortable around. It strangled me, so I looked away. I didn't want to be seen. Not like that. Mostly though, I didn't feel like I was seen. That wasn't quite true either though. The person who didn't want to do the seeing was me. I couldn't look at my own pain, my own story, my own hurt. It was too much. So, I looked away.

That wasn't the answer though. It never is. Even if it works temporarily. Avoiding my eyes didn't eliminate the torrent of tears or erase the never-ending nightmare that was my new normal. You know what though? That new normal didn't negate the past. It didn't erase the days before. Before illness, before doctor visits, before first meetings, or hope. The new normal was a harder and softer way to incorporate it all: the tears, fears, anger, relief, and love. They all belong in this tale.

They All belong.

So, as I closed the recommended story — 'A Monster Calls' by Patrick Ness; a story sparked by Siobhan Dowd, a woman who lost her own struggle with cancer — I realized that my story sticks with me no matter where I go, what new paths I wander, and what new truths I choose to explore. If I can still feel the horror of those moments of letting go, but understand the power of telling the story anyway, I need to tell it. I need to write it for me. No punches pulled. No niceties offered. I still cry at other people's pain seeing my own. We hold that story together. So, if I tell my story, then perhaps someone else's tears won't be shed alone. Because we all have stories buried deep inside us. And now is the time for me to tell mine.

Be warned. There will be tears. But hopefully I will find the love too. Maybe I will find another measure of healing again. It is amazing how much understanding and healing a soul needs. But there it is. I still need more. So here goes.

My journey…

The Beginning

Shouldn't every story start in a happy place? I don't know. Not always. I could start the day I met Brad. That was a happy day. He showed up at the lodge I was working at, and we hit it off. We met, fell in love, bought a house, got married, and had a child, all before the phone rang that day…

The story starts before that though. I went to the lodge and met Chip. He told me about a man who had worked there the season before and thought we would hit it off. It was Brad. Chip set forth to work his magic and despite Brad's previously less than stellar experiences there, he convinced him to come back up to meet me. He set the story in motion.

But the story starts before then too. Does it start when I returned from Africa, intent on continuing my travels, with the lodge a steppingstone to flying off to Japan to teach English for a year? Does it start with me being a disgruntled teenager trying to find my feet in a world I didn't feel like I fit in or as a shy child, afraid to open my mouth and speak my truth? Or does it start with the death of my father, his own illness, and the way that closed my mouth from the start. To not disturb. To be a good girl. To do everything I could to change the story at the start.

Where does it all begin?

These are questions I have examined over the years, without truly finding an answer. I'm not sure there really is an answer. I don't know where grief starts, and I begin. It lives in every memory I hold. In every word not spoken; so many words not spoken. In every time I withdraw instead of putting myself out there.

No more. The words need to come. I need to say them aloud, even if it rips me apart. And it will in the telling. But maybe it will also put me back together again. That would be nice. That is the goal. Time to give it a try and see what's the worst that will happen. I make no promises that the story will be linear or easy, but I'm going to try again.

Somehow these stories are always there, no matter how hard I try to block them out. Time to tell them to make more space in my heart. Are you ready to walk this journey with me?

Let's go.

Once Upon a Time

It was a beautiful day. The sun was shining when a 1971 Oldsmobile Cutlass Supreme pulled into the parking lot at Pickle Lake Lodge. Chip had told Brad to come up, promising it wouldn't be like before. Sure, the owners were still there and probably grumpy. Yes, there would be families and customers to cook for and grumble about. But there was also a girl...

That girl was me.

This is where Brad's story and mine converge. I arrived at Pickle Lake Lodge with the intention of spending the summer earning enough money to help launch my trip to Japan—I had signed a contract to teach English there for a year. Brad had worked at the Lodge before and wasn't keen to return, but also didn't have anything drawing him elsewhere. He and Chip were close friends, and he was hard-pressed to let a friend down who was practically begging him to come back up and help. Truth be told, both of us were kind of without a rudder, as despite my goal of heading to Japan, I wasn't exactly sold on the company I was scheduled to work for. The fact that living in a trailer in the woods for a summer felt perfect wasn't lost on me either. Japan didn't feel right, but this did. I'm pretty sure fate was weaving its web in my life without me even realizing it.

So, when Brad caved and came to help Chip for the weekend, the wheels started to turn. Where he had been adamant that he would never return, suddenly that decision softened.

It wasn't just Brad though. Chip worked on me too, telling me how much he thought Brad and I would get along. He was sure of it! So much so, that when Brad did come up, I was already inclined to like him. All it took was a spark.

"Care to join me for a walk?" I asked Brad, as I threw apples and water bottles into a backpack.

"Sure," he replied.

Spark ignited.

For the next few hours, we wandered around in the woods behind the lodge, cutting across glens and hills, and talking about everything and nothing all at once. A little dappled sunlight, care of Mother Nature, set the mood and the music of the wind blowing through fresh new leaves was our background music. My bag of apples gave me the feel of an enchantress spreading a magic spell, but I'm pretty sure I didn't need the fruit's help. Within a week of Brad's return, we were the couple that Chip had envisioned.

Of course, there was still the matter of me going to Japan. The plan was to be gone for a year and the odds of coming home during that time were slim. That didn't bode well for longevity in our budding romance.

In early June I got a call with my placement.

"I just got off the phone with GEOS," [1] I announced to Brad. "They are sending me to Yamanashi Prefecture in Kofu."

"What?" he exclaimed with a little less enthusiasm than I expected.

"In Japan," I added. "They want me there for training for September 8th."

"Oh," he mumbled.

"I have to get ready for shift, but we'll talk more later," I said.

"Mmmph," was all I got in return.

By later though, Brad was blindly drunk and extremely angry. There was no talking with him, but one thing was clear—he wasn't happy about my impending trip to Japan. And honestly, my conversation with GEOS hadn't exactly excited me either.

From the get-go I had had reservations about the trip. It wasn't Japan exactly, although I knew it would be hard going from the middle of nowhere in the near-North of Ontario to a highly populated Japanese city, staying in a tiny one-room apartment. Sure, it would also be nerve-wracking to teach a class on top of that, but I counted it as a new experience that held the promise of living within a new society. Think of the food! Think of the culture! It was exactly what I had been looking for when I came home from my 10-month stint in Africa. But...

There were buts. The biggest one now being that I had a great guy who was head over heels in love with me and not pleased about

---

[1] GEOS - Global Education Opportunities and Services (the company I was supposed to work for in Japan).

the fact that I planned to leave the country for a year. That was a problem. To make matters worse—or better depending upon your view and the outcome—he had felt right all along, and Japan never had. What was I doing then? He obviously didn't want me to go and neither did my gut. But my head still screamed that it was an amazing opportunity to travel the world, experience life, and grow.

The war was now between head, heart, and gut. Which would win? As awkward as it felt, we needed to talk about it. Sober and with honesty on both our parts.

Brad had returned to London, Ontario for the weekend, and when he got back to the lodge, he found me in my room up in the trailer.

"Can we talk?" he asked as he stood in my doorway.

"Sure," I replied tentatively.

This was it. Our summer romance was at an end before it ever really began. He closed the door behind him, as he stepped into the room.

"I'm sorry about the other night," he started. "I didn't handle it well when you told me about Japan. I know you told me right from the start that you were going there, but it actually hit home that you might leave, and I lost my mind."

"I get it," I said shakily. "It isn't fair to you. And I don't blame you. You can walk away now, and I won't hold it against you. Everything has been light and easy, and I don't want to lose your friendship, but also don't want to hurt you or lead you on. I told you from the beginning I was supposed to go to Japan, but I think we stepped over the friend line a while back and I can't fault you for being angry."

"I'm not angry at you," Brad exclaimed. "Far from it! You must know that this was never a summer fling for me though. I don't want to lose you."

His kiss melted me and made me think the exact same thing. I didn't want to lose him either. I wanted more of the moments we had only just begun to build together: talking all night while lying in each other's arms, decadent clandestine meals in the dining room after hours in front of the roaring fireplace, making each other laugh as we slowly paddled across the lake on our afternoons off, and conspiring to snatch joy between the backdrop of petty squabbles of the other staff. Did I want to give that up? Did I want to walk away from him for a life on the other side of the world alone and uncertain all over again?

You know the answer. No way! My knight in grimy apron cooked me steak and lobster, took me for canoe rides along the nearby lakes and rivers, taught me how to drive stick, and wouldn't take no for an answer. It wasn't perfect, but it was love and I liked it.

There were more challenges ahead of us, but by summer's end, Japan was long gone from my plans and life in Toronto with Brad loomed. His plan was to get his official chef's papers starting in January. I threw plans to the wind and figured I would come up with something along the way in my old stomping grounds. Life had a way of sorting itself out like that. My path was there somewhere, I just had to keep my eyes open, and it would present itself. With Brad steering our course, I knew I was in good hands.

Making Plans

Brad and I moved to Toronto that November and spent the next five years exploring our relationship together in Canada's largest metropolitan city. It wasn't Japan, but it was plenty busy enough for Brad and comfortable in a new way for me. I loved living downtown and enjoyed the ebbs and flows of a new couple merging life paths together. For him, that looked like school, followed by work. I followed the opposite path; waitressing at a neighbourhood pub for the first few years, then heading back to school myself to get my Early Childhood Education diploma. We went from a cramped basement apartment to a large two-bedroom unit in a building just outside the core. Every step of the way held growing pains, but ultimately saw us growing closer and more entwined. By the time we had both graduated and set onto our new paths, it was obvious that some decisions needed to be made.

What did we want from life—a house, marriage, babies? Where did we want that to happen and how could we make those dreams a reality? Brad was ever the rational one. He was good at making plans and did everything in his power to turn them into reality. He suggested the move out of the tiny, dark basement into the bright apartment with windows for days. The ink on his Chef's Papers was barely dry before he decided to leave kitchens for driving trucks. The reasoning — restaurant work was typically evenings, weekends, and holidays — and he wanted to spend more time with friends and family when they were available (which was those exact same hours). As much as he loved creating exquisite food and experimenting with new dishes, it meant more if he could do so with those he loved. Not in a restaurant beating him down with its crazy grind and often ungrateful clientele. He could cook and create for me, friends, and family, but ultimately, his vision still held a dream kitchen. One that wasn't located in the heart of Toronto.

The first step to that kitchen was setting up a bank account where we could save for a downpayment for a home of our own.

"Let's go to the bank and see what we have to do to set up a joint account," he suggested one morning after we started our laundry at the local laundromat.

With that step taken, his plan was set in motion. Our account steadily grew, as each payday money came out of both our individual accounts and moved us towards our home ownership dreams.

Once the pot began to grow, the next step was to start house hunting. The question was, where did we do that?

"We can get way more home in London," he said.

"I've lived in London though," I replied reluctantly. "It's impossible to meet anyone. The public transit sucks. And we have jobs here!"

"Okay," he acquiesced. "Let's see what's on the market here then."

A dastardly plan, as he knew perfectly well what we would find in Toronto and countered it with a trip to London for cursory house hunting there too. It was no contest. For a third of the price, we could get three times more home with way more land. Sure, we lost the TTC, but didn't everyone complain about that anyway?

"I've got plenty of friends from my high school days in London," Brad repeated as we returned from our trip from the Forest

City. "My parents are there, and my sister. Plus, your aunt lives there too. We won't be alone."

These were things I could not argue. Nor could I complain about lost restaurants when I lived with a chef who gladly cooked me anything I wanted.

My silence marked his win. He didn't have to point out the fact that he hadn't amassed many friends during our stay in Toronto, nor did he have family there. Brad might have initially moved us to the city, but it was me that kept us there now. Just because I wasn't comfortable with change didn't mean that staying was the right thing to do. And as conflict was never my strong suit, I ultimately relented. I just couldn't argue with practical.

Practical kept on winning over the years. Before I knew it, we left Toronto behind. We initially rented a bungalow from one of those high school friends he had mentioned, who also promised to play real estate agent when the time came.

"Go ahead and plant whatever you want," Ken insisted, as he waved his hand at the front yard on the day we moved in.

There was space for pots on the front porch and room for plenty of blooms in the gardens beside the front door. I immediately started eyeing them up and envisioning colours sprouting everywhere.

"I saw you eyeing those flowerbeds the day we moved in," Brad said a week or so later. "Let's go get whatever you want to fill them up."

I might have missed the hustle and bustle of big city life, but I couldn't resist the therapy of digging my hands in the dirt and seeing things grow around me. He knew that if he indulged this love, I might just warm up to London and our new home a little more. Together, we picked out flowers for the beds, and herbs and tomatoes to put in planters on the porch. He had me pegged from the get-go and I was nesting without realizing it. If flowers would ease the transition, he would buy me all the flowers I wanted. This was just another step in the plan though. Brad still wanted a home we could call our own.

While those early flowers helped, the transition wasn't quite as smooth as he hoped. I found that area daycares only hired supply staff, then full-time from those ranks. By the time I was offered a position, I realized that the pay scale was markedly different in our smaller community, and maybe that wasn't where I wanted to be anymore. If I didn't work in childcare anymore though, where did I want to be? It took a while to figure that out, with lots of moody days and soul-searching nights, where Brad did his best to not push me. But when I found myself at an autobody shop again debating this turn of events, he stepped in.

"You can do this," he said when I immediately proclaimed my ineptitude. "It's a new system, but you will figure it out."

"But I don't know anything about cars!" I cried in frustration.

"So," he answered. "You'll figure it out."

I didn't really want to, but his encouragement persuaded me to go back in for another day. And then another. Until I was charming clients walking in the door and ordering parts like I knew what I was talking about. In the interim, he found a promising driving job in a Monday to Friday gig through a temp agency. No evenings, no weekends, no holidays. We were making it.

Once we both had full-time jobs, and it didn't look like I would bolt back to the Toronto area, the next step was talking to a mortgage broker. Life felt so far from traipsing around the globe like I had envisioned a few years earlier, but also right where Brad wanted us to be. And this was about us now.

Despite a few more hiccups along the way, by the time we had lived in London for a year, we had purchased our first home and started in on renovations. I learned how to sand floors, was introduced to a table saw, got better with a paint brush, and planted way more flowers. When he wasn't working on the bones of our new home, Brad was off to a local high school with my aunt for woodworking classes. Where Cassie was building an elaborate new dining room table, Brad created a cabinet to replace the linen cupboard he ripped out, then moved on to a coffee table and end tables for our living room. Where I had gardens, he nested by constructing furniture. The bonus was building stronger bonds between our families too.

Brad wasn't content to leave it at that though. As my 30th birthday struck, he had another surprise up his sleeve that changed things all over again.

We planned to have a housewarming/birthday party for me. Family and friends were invited to help us celebrate, plus see the progress we had made on the home thus far. As the weekend of the party arrived, I picked up groceries on my way home from work, all while tabulating a mental checklist of to-dos to complete before people arrived.

I pulled into our driveway. Brad immediately drove up behind me in a cloud of dust. We had graduated to a two-vehicle household: no more public transit complaints. I gathered an armload of groceries, then turned to see if he was coming to help, but he was nowhere in sight.

"Bugger," I grumbled.

I slung a few more bags through my fingers and muscled my way to the house.

"Hey," I called as I clumsily thrust my way inside. "Where'd you go?"

I stopped as I spied our dining room table. An exquisite bouquet of delicate flowers had been hastily thrown into a vase. Brad was still nowhere in sight though.

"Awww," I crooned, instantly forgetting my irritation.

I dumped the groceries on the floor in the kitchen, then went back to sniff the heavenly flowers.

"They are beautiful," I murmured to myself. "Now where is he?"

I noticed the back door open and saw him lounging on the deck outside.

"Hey," I cried a little more affectionately from the doorway. "Thank you!"

"Grab a drink before you come out," he called over his shoulder as he heard the screen door creak open.

He didn't move to greet me other than that, so I set myself to putting the groceries away and mixing a cocktail. I was in no hurry, as it was finally the weekend and the rest of it would be about friends and family. The prep could wait a few minutes more.

"Thanks for the help with the groceries," I joked as I finally slid into the chair beside him outside. "And for the flowers. They are stunning!"

Without a word, he handed me a box. A small box that looked decidedly like it might have come from a jeweller.

"What's this?" I asked.

"Open it," he replied.

I had a sneaking suspicion about what I might find inside but wanted to draw the moment out. I turned the box this way and that, flipping it upside down, and staring at it from all angles.

"Just open it," he said again.

"Okay, okay…"

I caught my breath. Inside lay a beautiful white gold ring with a stunning ruby, offset by two small diamonds on either side. My eyes sparkled with the hint of tears, but I fought them off trying desperately to come up with more witty banter to tease him with.

"So," Brad said.

"So, what?" I answered as I held the ring up.

He sighed heavily as he rolled his eyes. God, he was insufferable at times, but right then I was more in love with him than I could imagine. And no way was I going to let him get out of not asking me directly.

"So, will you marry me?"

I couldn't keep up the aloof posturing anymore and flung my arms around his neck with a kiss.

"I guess," I finally replied with a laugh. "It's beautiful!!"

"You have to put it on me though," I insisted, as I held it out to him.

"Wait," I stopped, as a thought struck me. "You can't give me an engagement ring on my birthday! I'm turning 30! That's a milestone birthday. You are sneaking your way out of a present!"

"So, is that still a 'yes'?"

I laughed, as I pulled him close to kiss him again.

"Silly boy," I murmured into his neck. "Of course, I'll marry you."

He slid the stunning ring onto my finger, and we clinked our glasses to celebrate.

"You spoiled it," he explained, as he finally relaxed into the moment. "I was going to tuck the ring into the flowers. Like your first birthday up at the lodge."

"Oh!" I exclaimed as I remembered that day six years earlier. "Aww, I'm sorry. That is so romantic!"

"Right!" he replied. "But you got home before me, and I didn't have time to set it up."

On my 24th birthday, I had waited tables as usual up at Pickle Lake Lodge. My boss' birthday was the day after mine and he had chosen to eat in the dining room that night to celebrate with his wife. A woman at the next table had one too many drinks and came over to talk to Friedrich and Martha, refusing to leave, despite my best attempts to coax her away. Friedrich eventually got up and stormed away, but proceeded to give me royal shit once I made my way back into the kitchen again. The other woman hadn't been my table, but he didn't care. He berated me anyway. On my birthday.

After dinner service was done, I moved on to bar service and didn't stop until close to midnight. By the time my shift finally finished, my fellow staff encouraged me to go change and rejoin them for a drink. I dragged my battered soul up to the trailer and fumbled with the table lamp in my room to brighten the space so I could see to change. In the dim light, I could tell something was on the table, but had no idea what until light filled the room. The lamp illuminated a bouquet of flowers that I instantly leaned in closer to sniff, only to spy a delicate antique bracelet hanging from one of the stems.

Six years later and Brad had done it again. Well, almost. But the thought was there. He was so far from romantic any other time, but in the moments that counted the most, he took my breath away.

The rest of the weekend was a happy affair. I gleefully showed off my engagement ring to everyone who rolled through the door and the party lasted into the wee hours of the night.

So now we had the house, an engagement ring around my finger, and wedding bells in the future. Brad had a plan and ticked off the boxes every step of the way. And I was more than happy to leave him in charge.

After throwing several ideas around for wedding plans and venues, we settled on a quiet ceremony with just immediate family the following April. All told, we had 16 people, and the day was perfect. We were married at a local historic inn, had a delectable lunch at a hotel which had doubled as an armoury at the turn of the last century, and were on our way to Costa Rica for our honeymoon by late afternoon. Two weeks later, the next building block slid into place, as we came home and promptly discovered we were pregnant! Now we had nine months to plan the next stage in our lives. Family life was just beginning.

Does that sound too good to be true? Maybe. It wasn't a whirlwind romance by any stretch—we met in 1997 and didn't get married until 2004—but Brad now had the girl, the house, and a baby on the way. It was every man's dream, right? Pretty much. Of course, there were home renovations that didn't always go according to plan. Pregnancy made me forgetful as all get-out, and the mood swings were shocking at times. And now I wanted him to help pick out baby names? Was that really what he had signed up for? Yup. He secretly loved it all and I know he wouldn't have wanted it any other way.

Now it was time for another chapter…

And Baby Makes Three

Nine months flew by in a whir of sawdust, paint fumes, and midwife appointments that changed everything. By the time I was sick and tired of my swollen ankles, heartburn, aching back, and overall, hugely engorged body, it was time to meet the newest addition to our family.

But what about that name?

"How about Emily?" I asked.

"No," Brad answered. "I dated a girl in high school by that name."

"Jade?"

"Sounds like a stripper name."

I rolled my eyes but continued.

"Sarah?"

"Eh…"

"Do you have any suggestions?"

"Not really," He answered, as he flipped channels on the TV.

I went back to the baby names book.

"What about Aurora," I said a week later as we drove to my mom's trailer. "Or Leslie, Kennedy, Sharon…"

These were all roads and towns we drove by.

"Not a chance," he answered without missing a beat.

"Okay," I changed tactics. "How about Davis, Franklin, or Alexander?"

More road names, but for boys this round. I didn't get any further ahead there. Not that either of us anticipated having a boy. I had girls upon girls on my side of the family and they outnumbered boys on his family tree too. We tentatively tossed around a few names, but just knew a girl was in the works. She might not get a name, but I still threw names in the hat to see if anything would stick.

Finally, my due date arrived in February, with us no closer to agreeing on anything.

"Taryn is going in for a Caesarian today," I announced as I read an email from my Aunt Linn in South Africa. "They don't want her to go any longer with the twins. She beat me to it by the looks of things."

"Taryn," Brad replied with a cock of his head. "That's a nice name."

No mention of my cousin's wife whose pregnancy had mirrored mine on the other side of the world. But I jumped on it just the same. We finally had a name and I loved that it tied me back to South Africa once more. Now all we had to do was get her out of me so we could meet her. I was more than ready.

I tried hot food, hot sex, and even hot exercise—all folk tales said to induce labour, to no avail. Every day Brad would call home from work checking in on me to see if anything had started yet.

"No," I glumly answered, as I finished folding tiny baby clothes, wash cloths, and diapers.

My maternity leave was timed with my due date which came and went with no fanfare. The midwife examined me daily, but despite a small dilation, nothing was happening.

"Once you hit 10 days past your due date, you will have to get induced," the midwife declared at my appointment when I was eight days late. "We can sweep your cervix, but the hospital will want to start you on oxytocin. The problem with that is that it brings on labour right away and it can sometimes be more jarring than going naturally."

It didn't sound pleasant. I rubbed my belly as we left the appointment and gave my own little pep talk.

"Come on now," I encouraged. "We don't want to get induced. It is far less enjoyable for everyone, and we don't want that. You've got one more day and then Eve's hands are tied. Let's do this!"

A trip round and round the mall that afternoon was my last resort but seemed all for naught. I returned home still waddling along, with no contractions in sight. This baby was a stubborn one already. Content to take things on her own timeline and not be rushed about it.

After all that though, the threat might have worked. Or the exercise. Regardless, I got up to use the bathroom in the middle of the night—a regular occurrence with the baby squashing my bladder—and when I returned to bed, a cramp flared across my belly. Seven minutes later, another tightening twinged me back from the edge of sleep. Then eight, seven and a half, nine, seven… it appeared that it was finally time to meet the newest member of the family!

She still wasn't in a hurry though. After lying in bed for an hour, breathing through random contractions, Brad rolled over.

"Are you in labour," he asked. "Because if not, I need to sleep. I have to go to work tomorrow."

I breathed out slow and steady as another contraction crested then fell away and turned to him.

"Sorry," I remarked dryly. "Am I disturbing you? Do you want to meet your baby? Because I think it's finally time."

"Have you called the midwife?" he asked, instantly worried and awake.

"No, she said to wait until contractions were five minutes apart."

"And where are they now?"

"About seven mostly"

"So, what do we do?"

31

"Nothing," I answered. "At least you don't have to do anything. Maybe I'll go sit on my birthing ball and see if I can bounce this kid out of me."

I rolled over and waddled my way to the baby's room where everything was ready for the new arrival.

Life was about to change. In a matter of hours, a new baby would be in my arms, and I would be a mom. Brad would be a dad. Neither one of us really knew what that meant or would feel like, but it was coming down the pipe fast and there was no stopping it now. That pipe being my vagina. And there was no way I wanted to stop it now. I wanted this kid out of me so that I could get my body back. Yes, I was that naïve. Just as naïve as we both were when a few months later a doctor told us that he had gotten all the cancerous areas when he removed the mole on Brad's leg.

For now though, life was exciting and new, and everyone was thrilled to meet our beautiful baby girl who was born 22 hours after my labour began. Taryn made our small family a little bigger. And now we were three.

That made for a big change in everything.

Have you had a child before? For those who haven't, you are instantly caught up in a new world order. Newborns typically only sleep a few hours at a time. They eat every few hours too. And pee and poop constantly.

As new parents, we were overwhelmed with what we should do, what we shouldn't do, and how to balance that with how our parent's generations did things. It was all different and invariably at points you felt like you were doing it all wrong. We weren't though.

Brad was amazing. He cooked. He cleaned. He got over his fear of babies and held little Taryn without breaking her. Babies aren't near as breakable as inexperienced folks believe.

I, on the other hand, got the pleasure of feeding the baby. I had gone through the delivery drug-free and was determined to do everything right. No disposal diapers to fill landfills. No soothers to ruin her teeth. No leaving her to "cry it out" in her crib to learn self-soothing. Breastfed was best, and my cloth diapers were at the ready. I was going to be the model mother.

Says every new mother ever. Until…

"Go to sleep," I begged. "Go back to sleep!"

Every time she drifted off to sleep and I gently tried to lift her into her crib, Taryn's eyes fluttered open, and she started to mewl again. I had been at this for over an hour. Fed her from both now empty breasts. Burped her. Changed her. I had nothing left. My frustration mounted, as that perfect mother image tilted dangerously on its axis.

"Come on!" I insisted a little more vehemently.

"Give her to me," Brad said suddenly from the doorway. "Why don't you go back to bed, and I'll give it a try."

I hesitated, not wanting to cut into his sleep when he had to work the next day.

"We'll be fine," he said, as he gently lifted her into his strong arms. "Get some sleep, hun'…"

I looked up, ashamed to have failed. Distraught that I had woken him on a worknight. And crushed to be dismissed. But I was also at my wit's end and Brad had heard that. As much as it signaled weakness in me, he was offering respite and help. It was his daughter too and just as much his responsibility to soothe her. But tears filled my eyes as I handed her over. This was just one example of how things didn't always go according to plan.

Brad won that night, and I learned a hard lesson. We aren't perfect and no amount of wishing and wanting changed that some days. I also lost on other fronts when a soother was introduced at Easter and Taryn loved it. Then my mom showed up with disposable diapers to lessen my laundry load. Of course, I had to use them, so they didn't go to waste. My resolve to do everything by the book was weakening at an alarming pace, even as sleep took its toll on my good humour. What I hadn't counted on was just because the baby was now outside my body, didn't mean that I got it back. I carried Taryn everywhere, breastfed her, and changed the lion's share of the diapers. Nighttime was usually all me—Brad argued I could sleep in, and he had to work. And everything was shifting all over again in my stretched body.

By the time Taryn made it to her eight-week checkup though, things seemed to be turning around. She slept six hours at a go. She rarely cried and was easily soothed when she did. New people were welcome in her books, and everyone loved up the newest member of our growing family.

"I think we've got the hang of this," I whispered to her as I rocked her back to sleep at night after taking her first round of immunizations like a champ.

A week later though, this brand-new world that we were just starting to get the hang of changed once more. This change proved the hardest one yet.

Chapter 3: The C Word

The Phone Call

I wish I could end this story here. Right here in this beautiful moment where Brad and I fell in love, bought a house, got married, and had a baby. It was everything he had planned for. More than I had ever dreamed of. And yet life has a way of throwing curve balls at you. I certainly didn't see this one coming.

"Can I speak with Bradley La-Lah, bru…?"

I sighed. Obviously, it wasn't someone who knew him. Labravoure really isn't that hard to pronounce, but it's amazing how many people mispronounce names. Not that I had changed my last name when I got married anyway, but that was a moot point for this conversation. Plus, Taryn was in a good mood, so my acceptance for name gaffes was tolerable.

"He's not available," I replied.

"This is Dr. M's office calling."

They immediately had my attention. Dr. M was a physician at the walk-in clinic where Brad had had a mole removed recently.

"Brad's at work," I said. "I'm his wife. How can I help you?"

"Hi," she said. "I am calling with Brad's test results from his recent biopsy."

She then went on to read the microscopic histology, "Sections show a malignant melanoma with a Breslow thickness of 4.7 mm, Clark's Level IV. Ulceration and focal vascular space invasion are identified. There is no evidence of regression or satellite micro-metastases."

She might as well have been speaking another language. Do you know what that means? I certainly didn't. I did, however, catch one word — malignant. Malignant meant Cancer.

"The doctor needs to see Bradley to discuss the pathology report as soon as possible. He will need to get the area re-excised."

My heart stopped.

"We have an appointment for him on ..."

I scrambled to grab a pen and paper to write down the date, while my brain grappled with the information I had just heard. Breslow thickness? Some kind of Level? What the hell did that mean?!

CANCER, CANCER, CANCER...

My hands shook as I put the phone down. It wasn't the first time I had known someone with cancer. Plenty of my mother's friends had been diagnosed. Walter died of lung cancer. Shirley died from ovarian. My own father passed away from prostate cancer at the ridiculously youthful age of 40. No one died from prostate cancer at that age. At the time, he was the youngest patient diagnosed with the disease at the hospital that treated him. They didn't think to look for prostate cancer in a man in his thirties. It was an old man's disease. By the time they realized what they were dealing with, it was too late.

CANCER, CANCER, CANCER...

People die from cancer. Two out of five Canadians will be diagnosed with cancer in their lifetime.[2] One in four will die. Those are staggering statistics that I wish were fake news, but sadly are not. Odds are that either you or someone you love has been touched by cancer. It can strike anyone, regardless of age, gender, or nationality. When it does, your life will never be the same again. It is an awful, wasting away disease that steals people's health, life, hopes, and dreams. And a faceless secretary had just informed me that my husband was one of those statistics.

OH MY GOD!

My brain went into overload.

Brad couldn't have it. He couldn't die on me! We had a brand-new baby! Oh my GOD! He can't die!

Tears rushed out of me. What should I do? What could I do?

I picked Taryn up from her sling back chair and squeezed her into my chest.

NO NO NO NO NO...

Her sleeper absorbed my tears, as she struggled to push away from my tight embrace with a tiny mewl. My baby. How could we do this alone? She needed her Daddy. I needed him!

Death. Cancer. Death. DEATH!

My brain swirled around the words, what they meant, and what I had to do.

[2] Canadian Cancer Society. (2022). Cancer statistics at a glance. Retrieved from Canadian Cancer Society, https://cancer.ca/en/research/cancer-statistics/cancer-statistics-at-a-glance

I had to call Brad.

Wait… How could I call him? How could I tell him what the clueless receptionist had just told me over the phone? It wasn't true. It couldn't be true! What did it mean? What could we do? In my experience, cancer equaled death, but he couldn't die! Oh my God.

And I spun again. Who could make this right?

I don't know if my next phone call was harder or easier.

"Mom," I said through tight lips and trembling thoughts. "The doctor's office called. Remember that mole you saw on Brad's leg before Christmas? They said it's cancerous."

I couldn't get anything else out for the torrent of tears that engulfed me.

"Oh Katherine…" she replied.

There weren't any words. She couldn't make it better. She was all too familiar with where my head space was. She had lived the self-same horror of receiving a cancer diagnosis for her husband many years before. At the time, she had two children under five. Her story ended in loss and a painful journey into a new reality. What would my future days bring?

My brain jerked in erratic circles. Nothing could stop the spinning. Shock, denial, horror, disbelief—this couldn't be happening! Brad couldn't have cancer. He was 32 years old. We were just beginning. Life was supposed to be about our baby, home renovations, about us… NOT cancer. That wasn't part of the plan…

Cancer doesn't follow the rules though. Cancer is all about being outside of the norm. It is a series of abnormal cells that the body should destroy, but somehow misses. Those abnormal cells grow and multiply, often at an alarming rate. I had done a project on it in grade school. All I could remember were the graphic pictures of black lungs and nasty statistics to back up why we should be good little children and never smoke.

This was different though. Brad had malignant melanoma; a particularly virulent form of skin cancer. It had nothing to do with smoking, which he had incidentally just quit. And while many skin cancers were due to sun exposure, Brad had never been a sun worshipper. When I met him, he never even wore shorts. Wool socks stretched half-way up his calves under full-length jeans winter, spring, summer, and fall. He was a pasty white boy with hair that held a hint of red in certain lights. Therein lay his crux.

Dr. B summed it up for Brad when he went to see him for follow-up treatment at the Walk-In clinic the following week. Brad walked in confident that he was in the clear after hearing that the initial surgery had got it all. That confidence wasn't quite as strong by the time he walked out.

"Cancer is like a dandelion seed head. When you blow on it, it goes everywhere. You need to track down every single seed head— every cancer cell—to ensure you get them all or else they begin to grow and reproduce once more."

"But you said you got them all," Brad countered. "It was completely excised."

"That is what the pathology report suggests, but a re-excision is strongly recommended. Not doing follow-up is like shutting the barn door after the horses have fled. It doesn't get the horses back. We have to re-excise the area to make sure we didn't miss anything. What would be the point in not treating you, if there is a risk that we missed even one cell? Those cells will just begin multiplying again. We need to collect the horses first—make sure we've got all the cancer cells—then we can safely shut the door on cancer. Until then, we live in fear that just one of those dandelion seed heads might have escaped and is floating around in your body. We have to be sure. Another surgery will tell us that."

First things first though, Brad needed a doctor. The walk-in clinic couldn't refer him to the specialist he so desperately needed. Only a family physician could submit a referral. Did he know anyone?

He didn't, but I did. I was at my GP's office the very next day.

"Please," I begged through tears. "The walk-in said he needs a doctor. He needs specialists. I don't know what to do…"

What else could she do in the circumstances? I was a mess, pathetic in my urgent need. She agreed to take Brad on.

"But I have to meet him in person," Dr. K gently said. "I can't refer him to anyone until he is officially a patient."

We were back at her office two days later to sign the official patient enrolment form. And with that signature, we started to reel in the horses.

Reeling in the Horses

Are you a horse fan? I like them well enough, but not the runaway kind. They are wild and unpredictable. Just like cancer.

The journey Brad and I now started on was like that. We had no idea what was to come and had to desperately hold on for the ride, hoping not to get bucked off in the process. The horses we had to reel in were doctors; specialists who could diagnose and treat the disease we now faced together. First things first, we started with a GP, then threw our net further afield to collect more professionals for Team Brad. After Dr. K, it was a plastic surgeon with a specialty in melanoma.

"Dr. T is the best plastic surgeon to be had," Dr. K said when Brad and I went to see her. "I will set up the referral for you. Her office should be in touch within the week."

They were. A few days later they called and set up an appointment for Brad to meet Dr. T to go over his case. His appointment was within the week. The speed at which things started was alarming to say the least. It spoke of the urgency of the situation, although we were still clueless as to what exactly that was.

"When is the appointment?" I asked Brad when he got off the phone.

"It's at 9:30 a.m. on Friday," he replied. "But you don't have to come. There's no point dragging Taryn along to this appointment It's a consultation and they'll probably want to do a physical exam She'll just get in the way."

"I guess," I reluctantly agreed, despite feeling like I should be a part of the process.

He was right though. She would be a distraction and it didn't make sense to take her along. This was about Brad and the focus needed to be about diagnosis and treatment. It didn't make sense to take her, therefore, unless I found a babysitter, I wouldn't be a part of that first meeting either.

I argued with myself on why that was best.

It isn't my body that has cancer cells multiplying in it. I don't have an unruly mole, swollen lymph glands, or other symptoms to diagnose. There is no need to poke and prod my body or field a barrage of invasive questions.

I didn't feel any better. This was the beginning of Brad's step into the oncology world, and I vaguely recognized my quiet slide into the wings. This was his journey to make. I was merely the bystander.

So, off he went to meet Dr. T.

"Do you have any other moles of concern?"

"Does it hurt to pee?"

"How's your sex life?"

So many questions and forms to fill out. Followed by stripping down to a paper gown so Dr. T and her many interns could inspect, push, and squeeze every square inch of Brad's body. Specimen B up for inspection and useful as a learning tool. It was unnerving for Brad, but I had no part in it.

I know that plenty of people detest hospitals. They make them uncomfortable and nervous. You would think I would have been happy to avoid this trip then, but when Brad returned home, I peppered him with questions which he just couldn't answer. He described the impersonal exam and announced a date for his first surgery a month hence. Beyond that I got nothing. He hadn't asked questions, and they hadn't volunteered much. My questions only served to irritate him, which didn't help matters.

"Dr. T wants you to come to my next appointment," he stated, effectively ending the conversation. "You can ask her all the questions you want then."

The matter was dismissed.

It wasn't though. In addition to the originally removed mole, Brad also had swollen lymph nodes in his groin. That inferred that the cancer had spread to his lymphatic system. Not that anyone really said that yet. At that point, they were still trying to diagnose and assess where things were, so they could create a treatment plan. We weren't a part of that decision making. Or I wasn't anyway.

As for Brad and me, he tentatively googled malignant melanoma on the computer and I did my best to breathe through the panic that refused to abate. Brad got quiet while scrolling, but I wasn't ready for the pictures and stories. When he went to work, I whispered to my mom and sister on the phone about what was to come. It was like the volume on life had been turned down. But it crackled back to life when I joined Brad for his next trip to see Dr. T. I quickly learned why people preferred not to visit hospitals.

"Wait for me inside the doors while I find parking," he said before driving away.

Stepping inside the building alone was daunting. Brad materialized a few minutes later and steered me and the stroller down a long hallway and into a busy waiting room. We signed in at the main desk of the Hand and Upper Limb clinic, then turned to look for a seat. While plenty of seats filled the extensive waiting room deep in the bowels of the hospital, finding two together was a challenge, let alone space for a stroller too. A wall to lean against had to do.

I couldn't help sneaking glances at the people who filled chairs and walls around us. They had varying degrees of ailments; some with bandages or slings on arms, others with splints on hands. We were a listless mob, quietly awaiting our turns with the doctors within. The only movement came when patients were called and those standing were able to fill the vacated seats.

"Brad Labravoure?"

After the better part of an hour, it was finally our turn. We followed a quick-moving nurse down a series of hallways. It was an exercise to keep up, as I never would have found my way in the labyrinth alone.

"Here we go," she finally said with a smile as she ushered us into a small exam room. "Any cough, cold, or flu-like symptoms? Any new aches, pains, or other issues to report?"

These questions would become standard, but I was numbed into silence. Brad took charge.

"No," he replied. "All good."

Once she ticked off the rest of her intake questions from her clipboard, she left saying "Dr. T will be with you shortly."

More waiting, but at least we both had chairs now. I released Taryn from her car seat so she could stretch her little legs. Her happy gurgles made for a good distraction from the antiseptic quiet in the room. This wasn't how I expected to raise my baby.

"Brad, how are you today?" Dr. T exclaimed when she eventually swept into the room in her starched white lab coat. She turned to me with outstretched hand, "You must be his wife? And this is your daughter?"

"Yes," I said quietly. "This is Taryn. And I'm Katherine. Nice to meet you."

She was a pretty woman about my age. Her open smile set me at ease, but it was her professional demeanour that gave me the shot of confidence I needed. We sorely needed to place our confidence somewhere. She was the team captain I wanted in the fight against Brad's cancer. There was no shirking that duty.

"Our first step is to re-excise the area where the original mole was removed," Dr. T said. "Before we do that though, we are going to perform sentinel lymph node mapping. It is a relatively simple procedure, but it helps us see where things are at. Where the cancer might be."

"Before the surgery, you'll go to Nuclear Medicine. They'll inject radioactive tracer dye near the sentinel node. The sentinel node is the first lymph node, or nodes, that cancer typically spreads to. The blue dye lights up any infected lymph nodes to show how far the infection has spread into the lymphatic system. I'll use the images they take to remove the sentinel node once I have you in surgery."

It sounded worse than it really was. He would have two surgeries in one: the SLN biopsy and a re-excision at the primary melanoma site. It was considered outpatient surgery, therefore in and out in one day. Someone would need to drive him home though. That was me. Time to pull strings for a babysitter...

How do you ask for a babysitter so that your husband can go in for surgery?

"Can you do me a favour? No biggie?"

It was a biggie though. This was surgery. The first major step in Brad's cancer journey, if you didn't count the walk-in clinic visits. It was beyond a little freezing and a minor pinch. This surgery would include slicing back into the area where the original mole was, removing skin from his opposite thigh for a skin graft, and the lymph node biopsy at his groin. Three separate areas. Plus, anesthetic. He would be groggy when he came too. Hence the need for a driver. I still didn't know the half of it though.

Did I mention that I hate asking for favours? Sigh… It hasn't gotten any better over the years either. But sometimes you have to suck it up and this was one of those moments.

"Faye, can you take Taryn when Brad has his surgery?" I asked my best friend when we had a date for the surgery.

"Of course," she said. "Don't worry about a thing."

Now we waited for the date to arrive. Time stretched and folded, distorting normal everyday existence, but finally arrived on the date marked on the calendar. I wasn't sure whether I should be relieved or dread the day, but it came regardless.

At 7:00 a.m. we packed Taryn into her car seat with everything she would need for the day; diapers, change of clothes, soothers, a few toys, and a hard-earned bottle of breast milk to tide her over until I returned. She wasn't keen on bottles, and I failed to express much milk, which made childcare difficult. She needed me. But I needed to be with Brad. So, she would have to make do.

"She'll be fine," Faye said as I squeezed in a last quick feeding before Brad and I headed to the hospital.

"I'll call you as soon as I hear anything," I said through tight throat. It felt like I couldn't make anyone happy, but it couldn't be helped.

"Come on," Brad nudged. "We've got to go."

"I know," I replied as I reluctantly turned away from my baby and best friend.

I knew Taryn was in good hands; Faye's daughter was one week older than Taryn and she had plenty of milk, if push came to shove. But I struggled with overwhelming feelings of failing everyone. Logic played no part in the rationale.

Once we reached the hospital, we made our way to Nuclear Medicine.

"We'll need you to change into this gown," the admitting nurse said, as she handed Brad a blue package. "There are change rooms over there. Put your valuables into this bag and keep them with you. We'll call you when we are ready for you."

I found a set of chairs for us to sit in and began the wait. Brad came out with his gown tied around him, wool socks and runners conspicuous under the robe. This was the beginning of my time spent in hospitals. There would be many more days to come, but on this day, I felt fragile and skittish. I had no idea what was to come.

An hour later, Brad returned to me after the dye was injected.

"How was it?" I anxiously asked. "How do you feel?"

"Cold," he said. "The dye was cold going in. It didn't hurt though. I'm fine..."

He was always fine when I felt like I was falling apart. I compensated by asking questions, questions, and more questions. Not that understanding made much difference.

"What did they say?"

"Nothing."

"What do we do now?"

"Go meet up with Claire."

"But..."

"I'm fine," he repeated a little more forcibly. "Let's go."

Maybe he wasn't as fine as he claimed to be, but I knew enough to let it go for the time being. We reported to the next station for the subsequent steps in the day.

"Brad Labravoure?" a nurse asked. She confirmed his birthday, checked the hospital bracelet he had been tagged with, and ushered him to a hospital bed. "I need to take your blood pressure, then we'll put in the IV. If you need to use the bathroom, it is just there."

I quietly hovered beside the bed watching.

"Let me get you a chair," she said with a smile, turning to me before starting her preparations.

"Yes, thank you," I said gratefully.

"You can keep his personal possessions until after the surgery is complete," she said. She handed me a pamphlet on what to expect post-surgery. "When we take Brad for surgery you can wait in waiting room C. Dr. T will come and see you there after the surgery."

"How long do you expect the surgery to take?" I asked.

"It will be a few hours," she replied. "There is a volunteer in the waiting room. You can check in with them to see how progress is coming along. They will be able to advise you when Brad is out of surgery."

I nodded as I clung to the edges of my worn seat. Brad returned from the washroom, but the sounds from the hospital around us filled our waiting minutes. Too soon, they came to take him into surgery.

That left me to wander the hospital, sit in a sterile waiting room, stare through dated magazines, and attempt to read the book I had brought to fill my time. None of it helped. Minutes dragged into hours, and I wavered between anxious wandering and fitful reflection in the small, windowless waiting room. The kindly volunteer occasionally tried to smile in my direction, but my vision was internal. My thoughts lay in what the future might hold.

Several painful hours later the newest volunteer stood from their small desk in the corner of the room. "Family of Brad Labravoure?"

He was out of surgery. Dr. T would be there shortly to discuss the operation.

Twenty painful minutes later, Dr. T arrived.

"Katherine," she said.

I stumbled over myself to rush to her. She ushered me into the hall.

"Everything went well. We re-excised the area around the original mole; took more tissue to ensure we got everything. I took a skin graft from his left thigh to cover the wound on his right calf. He will need to keep it covered for the next 10 days—no shower and if he has a bath, he needs to wrap the bandages in a plastic bag to keep it dry. As for the lymph nodes, I removed one, but suspect the infection has spread further. Once the pathology report comes back, we will know definitively. If I am correct, it means we will need to go back in and remove the rest of the system."

"Oh," I managed. "When do you want to do that?"

"He will need to recover from today's surgery first," she replied. "Like I said, I have an appointment scheduled to see him in 10 days. Until then, he needs to keep his leg elevated for 22 hours a day. We'll also contact CCAC[3] to take care of his wound management. They will come in to change the dressings on the skin graft site. They should be in touch with you later today and be out to see him tomorrow."

"Okay," I said.

She handed me a pamphlet with the appointment time on it and turned to go.

"Dr. T," I blurted before she could leave. "Where do things stand? How bad is this?"

---

[3] Formerly known as Community Care Access Centres, CCAC now operates in Ontario as Home and Community Care Support Services, an in-home community-based health support system of nursing care.

She paused before replying carefully.

"This is very serious Katherine," she said frankly. "The cancer has spread into Brad's lymph system, which makes treatment more difficult. We need to be extremely aggressive to stop the spread of the disease. We need to take things one step at a time, but there will be other treatments we will need to take to further suppress the cancer cells. Brad is a very sick man."

I don't even know how I found the words to ask, "What is his prognosis?"

"Fifty-fifty."

I reeled. It was impossible to stop the trickle that instantly sprang up, then coursed down my cheeks. Fifty percent. She was talking survival rate. All the air in the universe disappeared, as my brain shrieked inside my head.

OH MY GOD! OHMYGOD, OHmyGOD, Ohmygod, oh....

Dr. T stepped into the waiting room before I could come up with anything more coherent to say.

"Thank you," I whispered, as she returned and handed me a box of tissues.

"I'm sorry," she said as she turned away. "Brad will be in recovery in 20 to 30 minutes. The volunteer will let you know when you can see him "

"Thank you…"

What does one do in that situation? Cry? Scream? Pray? Laugh? I suppose it depends upon you. Praying does not come naturally to me. The hospital didn't seem the place to scream, but that's not my go-to reaction anyway. I know some people laugh when they are nervous or faint when faced with bad news.

Nope. Nope. Nope.

I stood in the hall and sobbed. The trickle turned into a flood that needed release. I gave those raw emotions all the space they needed so that I could pull myself back together before seeing Brad. I could fall apart for a moment, but ultimately needed to be stronger now more than ever. Brad needed that from me and so did Taryn. The luxury of tears was just a mere drop in the bucket—not near as long as I wanted them.

"Okay," I whispered to myself through catches in my breath. "I need to stop. This is about Brad. Pull yourself together. Time to buck up and let people know what's going on…"

I grabbed a few more tissues to wipe away the last of my tears, then went in search of a phone. I had to call Brad's parents, plus Faye, to tell them where things were at and when we could leave. It was time to refocus, so that I could take charge once Brad was released. I would be our chauffeur until he could drive again. Realistically, I would be our everything with his restricted schedule—22 hours a day with an elevated leg. That was little more than bathroom breaks.

I ticked off the items I would have to tackle; move the TV into the bedroom for him, cook all the meals, 100% of all the childcare for Taryn, all the driving, all the everything… No matter, I had to stay positive. It was the way it was. Suck it up.

"Family of Brad Labravoure?"

It was time.

Breathe...

Are you okay? I have relived this chapter so many times and know it is triggering. Anyone who has been here knows how hard that moment is. You are told staggering news and have to process on a dime. And keep going. Keep going. And going.

Reading that chapter might remind you of your own surreal moment. God knows I cried myself silly so many times on this journey. I felt alone then, and it only got worse in the days to come. If you are nodding your head though, Stop.

You are most definitely NOT alone. You might look around and see responsibility and chaos and trauma, but there is so much more there. There are so many more people who you might not even see. People you haven't met yet who will join your journey and be your strength when you need it most. They could be friends, family, strangers, doctors, support groups, therapists, social workers, or maybe a cherished pet. It might look like a hug, a coffee, a long walk where nothing is even said, but there will be moments that fill you back up again so you can face another tomorrow. If you can't see them yet, keep your eyes open. I promise you someone is thinking of you right now. And I want you to be okay, even if my story feels like too much. We can do this together.

Are you ready? Time to dive into the heart of my cancer journey with my husband.

Anger and Bargaining

I thought it was a big deal when I had a baby. And it was. Having my adult husband reluctantly step into the role of invalid felt almost worse though. Who am I kidding? In a lot of ways, it was worse.

Brad was angry; his go-to reaction that his family always seemed to lean into when other emotions threatened. I overcompensated; my family were talkers and we delved into all the feels to process. Together, we grated on each other's nerves. Where we should have been a united front supporting one another, it felt like living in an armed camp. I was the stereotypical Mother Hen, trying to do it all with little help. And burning out fast.

But first, I had to collect Brad from the hospital.

I wound my way through the labyrinth of lettered hallways until I found Brad resting in a hospital bed. I rushed in to hug him and promptly jostled the IV that still dangled from his wrist.

"Watch it," he said gruffly as I smothered him in a hug.

I reluctantly pulled away. He was groggy and my hug felt more like burden than balm. He didn't see my need in it—and lord, I really needed it—but it wasn't the time to push. I could survive without this comfort for the time being.

"How do you feel?" I asked tentatively, as I pulled away.

"Fine," he replied curtly.

I stood staring at him, afraid to say more.

"I've got a metallic taste in my mouth," he added.

"Oh," I answered, uncertain what that might mean: if it was something to be concerned about or not. My thoughts refused to come up with the appropriate analysis and questions that might make sense of this nugget of info, so I dove into the more obvious.

"Um, your leg. How is it?"

He pulled the heavy sheets to the side to inspect his right calf. It was bandaged from below the knee to just above his ankle.

"Can't tell. It's numb."

He covered the calf and peeked down at his left thigh. Another bandage covered his leg from the top of his thigh to halfway to his knee. He was a patchwork of bandages.

"Claire really did a number on me."

Talking about the physical lesions was easier than opening up about emotions. For both of us. I sat there reigning in all the words that I wanted to say and reminded myself to be strong instead. He didn't want to see my tears any more than I wanted to share them surrounded by nurses and orderlies.

As if on cue, a nurse materialized.

"Here to check your blood pressure," she announced cheerily as she wrapped the cuff around Brad's arm. "You are looking better. No more nausea? How is your pain on a scale from 1 to 10?"

"It's fine now," Brad answered. "Maybe a 4."

"You were nauseous?" I asked as my eyes swung from the nurse to Brad.

"Yeah," he said. "But I'm fine. It passed."

He looked at me directly and firmly reiterated, "I'm fine."

Fine. Me too. Trying to be, anyway.

I fluttered between wanting to be there at his bedside and feeling like I was in the way and wanting to flee while the nurse took stock of her patient. As much as I wanted to protect him, I also wanted to escape and leave them to it. They knew what they were doing. They could take better care of him than me. I shouldn't be interfering. I shouldn't be making their job harder.

The nurse must have sensed my panic and vacillation and said, "Let me get you a chair."

I meekly nodded my head and whispered "sure".

"Sit down," Brad said, as I lingered at his hand.

I tried to remind myself again that he was the patient. This wasn't about me. I shouldn't get in the way. I shouldn't interfere with what the doctors and nurses needed to do for my husband. I was just there to drive him home. Brad was already miserable enough. I didn't want to make things worse. I needed to be strong and get instructions for what Brad would need when we left. That was my job. So, I sat silently while the nurse checked the IV, bandages, and his chart.

"Okay," she finally stated as she looked up at us with a smile. "I'll come back in a minute to remove the IV and give you the prescription from Dr. T. If you are ready, we can release you after that. How does that sound?"

"Good," he answered.

"Great," I echoed.

I tried to keep the panic I felt out of my voice, as my eyes darted to Brad's leg.

"Oh," the nurse said as she turned back to us at the edge of the curtain. "Did you bring crutches with you?"

She looked from Brad to me expectantly.

"N-no?" I answered.

"Well, we'll see what we can find for you to borrow temporarily. You'll need them to get around until you are back up on your feet again."

"Yes," I answered. "Thank you."

"What does she mean?" Brad asked me as the nurse left once more.

"Didn't Dr. T tell you?" I asked. I didn't want to be the one to tell him about the new constraints.

"Tell me what?"

"About the restrictions?" I tried again. The look on his face told me he knew nothing of what I spoke.

"She told me you had to have your leg elevated 22 hours a day. No weight bearing. She plans to reassess you when you go back to see her in 10 days."

"What?!"

"I'll see if I can get the TV upstairs. You won't be able to…"

"No," he snapped. "I am not lying in bed for two weeks. We aren't putting the goddamn TV upstairs, and I refuse to be an invalid for you to fuss over."

"But the bathroom," I spluttered. "It's upstairs. And you have to keep your leg raised…"

"I don't care. I'll manage. I am not going to be a shut-in."

And he shut down. Discussion done.

My hands twisted around themselves. How was I going to manage with him at home? I had Taryn to take care of already and now Brad. He wouldn't be able to drive, walk, or even stand for any period. That meant that all the meals would be on my shoulders, as well as everything else: childrearing, laundry, cleaning. What would happen if he fell? If the stitches started to bleed? If he needed help to get up the stairs to the bathroom? How was I going to be able to do it all? I would have to figure it out as we went along…

The nurse returned with her artificial cheeriness and the promised crutches. Brad nodded politely, but I could tell he was seething. They were meant for someone shorter than his six-foot frame, hence awkward at best. There was no way he was going to complain though, even though I could see his frustration simmering just below the surface.

"If everything is in order, why don't you bring your vehicle around," she said to me. "I'll bring Brad down."

I gladly fled, spurred on by purpose. As promised, the nurse wheeled Brad to the front door. When I pulled up, he sat glowering in the wheelchair.

"Up we go then," she said as she helped Brad hop from the chair into the passenger seat. "Take care!"

And with that, I was in charge. I scrambled back to the driver's seat, Brad's prescription safely in my purse. Once he was settled at home, I would fill it. Faye would bring the baby later. And then the fun would really begin.

This wasn't what any of us signed up for, but that playbook had been tossed aside for the time being. It was time to hold on and see what life had in store for us over the next little while.

Hold tight folks. This might get bumpy.

The next day, a knock sounded on the door. Reinforcements.

"Hello," said the woman standing there. "I'm here to see Brad?"

"Yes, of course," I replied. "Right this way. Brad is in the living room."

The nurse from CCAC entered with her bag of medical supplies. She was there to check Brad's wound. Not the calf yet, just his thigh where the skin graft donor site was. The calf needed to stay covered until Dr T saw it. It needed a chance to heal. Water could make the delicate skin tear and then the operation would be for naught. But the nurse didn't know any of this.

"So, what do we have here," she asked with a smile, as she pulled out a thermometer and cuff to take Brad's blood pressure.

"Take a look for yourself," Brad replied before the thermometer was popped into his mouth.

"He had the operation yesterday," I answered as I scooped Taryn up from the floor. "There is a wound on his right leg, but it needs to remain covered until he goes back to see the surgeon. The skin graft is on his left thigh."

Brad shot me a quick glance that spoke volumes.

"Anyway," I mumbled. "I'm sure you have that in your notes."

I wanted to sink into the floor. I had fluttered around him until he wanted to strangle me. Or at least that is what his glare said.

I was so far out of my element; I didn't know what to do with myself. I was used to taking care of the baby. This was infinitely different. Brad was a grown man and used to being entirely self-sufficient. He cooked more of the meals, was quicker to grab the vacuum, and tended to grab the keys to the vehicle before I ever did. I might have had more words at my disposal, but they didn't make the experience any easier. And his frustrations at the limitations were already rising. It had only been a day.

The nurse didn't know any of that though.

"No, no," she said as she removed the cuff from Brad's arm. "It's good. They don't always give us many details before we see new patients. It's good to get a bigger picture of what to expect and what we are dealing with."

She took the thermometer out of Brad's mouth and jotted down the number in her workbook. "Good," she said. "Your blood pressure looks alright and no fever. So, how are you feeling? What is your pain on a scale of 1 to 10?"

Back to the scale. It would become a much-asked question over the years to come. It made me anxious already though. The answer helped me gauge Brad's mood, his level of displeasure. And I felt like I was at the center of it. I was hopeless to control the number or the temper that might come with it.

"Two."

Oh, thank God...

The nurse jotted down his response in her book once more.

"Okay, let's take a look at the leg then, shall we?"

She carefully pulled back the gauze that covered his thigh. Pink skin glistened underneath the bandage.

"Not bad," she said. "Looks clean."

I stared, as I clutched Taryn to my chest. A rectangle of skin had been peeled from Brad's thigh to cover the unseen wound on his right calf. Essentially, it was like taking a potato peeler and gently stripping thin layers of tissue off to transplant elsewhere. Each miniscule layer carefully stripped and moved to his opposite leg. Brad was too thin to remove the flesh from anywhere else. A flabby stomach would have been a godsend here but that wasn't in the cards. So, his thigh gave up precious epidermis to make him whole again.

The question that remained unspoken; what did his right leg look like? We wouldn't know until we saw Dr. T.

Once she had re-covered the skin graft with a fresh bandage, she packed her tools back into her satchel.

"I'll be back again tomorrow," she remarked. "Is there a time that might be best for you?"

"We don't have any plans," Brad said dryly.

Oh, man. This wasn't going to be easy. How could it be though? How do you transition your headspace to playing patient when you are used to being independent? When you are used to moving freely, wherever and whenever you desire.

In case there was any question, Brad didn't take well to playing invalid. He pushed himself. True to his word, he clomped downstairs every morning and took up a post on the couch where the television set blared all day long.

"Can I get you anything?" I asked as I breezed by with Taryn on my hip.

"I'm fine."

Definitive. No arguing. No questioning. He was fine. Okay then.

"Can you watch Taryn while I throw a load of laundry in?" I asked a few minutes later.

His grunt was enough for me to slide her into her chair and position her beside him at the couch.

"I can't pick her up you know," he stated, frowning at me.

"I know. I just want to get a load going. It will only take a minute. You don't have to do anything. Just keep an eye on her to make sure she's alright."

He might have been relegated to the couch, but that didn't mean he still couldn't parent, despite the limitations. But yes, it was my job to clothe, diaper, feed, carry, and mostly entertain our child. There wasn't a lot of choice in the matter.

"Take some chicken out while you are at it," he called as I walked by a few minutes later with the dirty hamper.

Micromanaging from the couch. Fair, as that was his usual complaint anyway. I often got so wrapped up in tending to the baby's needs that I forgot to tend to ours. More than once, Brad had asked— almost begged—me to just take something out of the freezer so we would be able to eat that night. He could make dinner if something was thawed, but I didn't always remember even that. It's amazing how hours slid by with nothing accomplished beyond me keeping her and I alive.

Now though, I didn't have the option to sit back and just mother. Brad couldn't vacuum, clean the toilet, or carry anything more than himself to the bathroom when needed.

After running by him another time, his patience finally frayed. He stood up from the couch and made his way to the kitchen off the living room.

"Where are you going?" I asked in a panic.

"To make myself a sandwich," he replied curtly.

"I can do that," I said reversing direction to head to the kitchen.

"No," he said. "I can handle making a sandwich."

"But your leg," I replied meekly.

"It's fine," he said dismissively. "Take care of Taryn."

I acquiesced but stayed close in case he needed me. He pulled sandwich meat, cheese, lettuce, and tomato out of the fridge, and deftly pulled a massive sandwich together. He returned items to the fridge and grabbed a beer to wash it all down with. The problem was, he now had a plate with a sandwich, a bottle of beer, and the single crutch he had used to maneuver his way to the kitchen from the living room. Normally it would have been no issue, but there were too many items to balance now. And he wasn't used to this new realm yet.

He took a few steps, then watched the sandwich slide off the plate onto the floor in the doorway.

"Fuck!"

"It's okay," I exclaimed as I rushed in to help. "I'll get it. I'll clean up."

"For fuck's sake," he stormed.

"It's okay," I said again as I plucked lettuce off the baseboards.

The words weren't for him though.

None of this was okay. He didn't want me waiting on him. He didn't want to have to ask for help with the simplest of tasks like making and carrying a sandwich to a table. Not only could he not do simple tasks or even help, but now he was a burden on me as well. It did not sit well with him.

And me? I pushed myself. I didn't have a choice. The baby was fully dependent on me for everything. I was getting used to that. She was now four months old and at least smiled and giggled to make life seem more bearable. My family constantly called to offer emotional support however they could. Brad's parents invited us over for Sunday dinners, freeing me up from mealtimes at least once a week. I had driven since I was 16, so driving wasn't a bother.

But the stress was getting to me. I was wound tight and walking on eggshells around my understandably grumpy husband. He had cancer! He earned the right to have a difficult day or two. The least I could do was step up to help while he was unable. I just had to learn to make the best of it.

Visits from the CCAC nurse helped. Trips to the grocery store or out with Faye gave me moments to refocus. Knowing that we would return to Dr. T's office shortly helped too. She was key to getting Brad back on his feet again. And that appointment couldn't come soon enough for Brad's sake.

"Let's take a look to see how things are healing," Dr. T said cheerily when Brad's follow-up appointment finally arrived.

Brad sat on the exam table in a paper gown. Taryn sat in her car seat at my feet. While a torrent of words wanted to spill from me, my lips remained sealed tight. This was about Brad. The doctor was concerned with his health, not mine. She peeled off the tape and gauze that covered his right calf. This was the moment of truth.

"That looks great!" she exclaimed.

I wish I had her eyes. It looked the furthest thing from great to me. My brain reeled in horror.

Oh my God. That looks like hamburger. It looks like she took an ice cream scooper and hollowed his leg out with it! How can she think that looks great?!

"The margins are healing nicely," Dr. T continued. "It doesn't look like there is any infection…"

Blah, blah, blah. I couldn't hear what she was saying anymore. I stared at the finally exposed leg and was horrified by her

65

version of 'good'. She admired her handiwork on his left thigh too, but that was far less dramatic. The small incision where the lymph nodes were removed was healing well too. In fact, the CCAC nurse had removed the staples from there a few days earlier.

I felt weak. How was this my reality? How was it that we were sitting in this doctor's office having this surreal conversation about a surgery that removed more life-threatening tissues from my husband's body?

"The test results came back from the sentinel lymph node biopsy," Dr. T was saying now. "As we expected, it was infected. We'll have to do another surgery to remove the rest of the lymphatic system at the site. I want you to recover a little longer, but I am going to go ahead and schedule the next surgery for later in July."

Another surgery.

"Unfortunately, this one won't be day surgery. You will need to be admitted for a night or two."

It was getting even more serious. How the hell was this happening?

"I will go in to remove more nodes at his right groin. Take anything that is infected, then a few more to ensure we get everything."

Jesus…

"I'll meet with you before the surgery though. We'll schedule another appointment for next week to see how your leg is healing. Until then, you get another hour of freedom. Keep your leg elevated for 21 hours a day until I see you next."

One extra hour. Whip-dee. It still amounted to nothing more than pee breaks. I foresaw more sandwiches falling to the floor, more frustrated arguments between Brad and I, and more tension all around.

"Good," Brad said.

Not good at all. Fuck, nothing was good. Nothing was fine. Nothing was the way it was supposed to be. But yes, good thanks. Great.

We're All Fine

Some moments are crystal clear, and I can almost taste them, they are so close. They slow down into painful slow-motion stop gaps that you swear you will never get out of. And then you blink, and all those moments are gone, and you are left with only the wisp of them. Doctor visits, once painful, become a bittersweet melancholy that you wish you could hold in your hand just one more time. Even in the semi-horror of hospital visits, there is comfort too in all the players at the table. Oh, to touch those players once more…

"I hate hospitals," Cassie remarked as we made our way to the cafeteria.

It was July 19th and Brad was back in hospital for his next surgery. Cassie had agreed to stay with me this time, so I wouldn't have to wait alone. It was a longer surgery, and I needed the distraction. After Dr. T's devastating talk with me after the last surgery, I couldn't stomach being alone again.

"Poor Brad is going to look like he has been to war," I said trying to make light of the situation.

67

"Yeah," Cassie agreed. "He doesn't have enough meat on his bones for this shit. Think of the stories he'll be able to tell though!"

I couldn't imagine Brad looking back on these moments with levity, but I was losing my ability to see the future at that point. Everything was in the moment.

"How about this table?" she said as she set her muffin down in a sunny spot in the cafeteria.

Any spot would do. We had several hours ahead of us before Brad would be through. Time enough to talk about gardening, antics her friends got up to, and Taryn's latest accomplishments. Anything to pass the time and distract us from the moment at hand. Thankfully, we've never struggled with conversation. We had six excruciating hours to fill.

Amazingly, the hours dispersed into the day.

"Family of Brad Labravoure?"

I jerked around to look at the volunteer. We had returned to the waiting room an hour previous. "His surgery is complete, and they have him in recovery. The doctor will come to speak with you shortly. Once Brad is in his room, we'll let you know so you can go see him."

"Thank you," I said to the volunteer, then turned to Cassie. "I need to call Joan to let her know. I should check on Taryn too. Hopefully, she hasn't given Gramma and Pup a hard time."

"Ha," she said. "Hopefully, she has. Anyway, I think I'll take off then if you're alright. Brad won't be in the mood to visit. He'll be groggy and probably a little grumpy if I know him."

She was not wrong.

Dr. T came a few minutes later to outline how the surgery went and Cassie took the opportunity to slip away.

"Everything went well. I removed the string of lymph nodes from his right groin area and suspect a few of them were infected. The pathology report will confirm how many, but we like to err on the side of caution regardless. He will probably have some swelling, so you should get a compression stocking. It will prevent edema."

My blank look let her know she was talking a foreign language to me.

"You can get compression hose at any major drugstore. Because we removed Brad's lymph nodes, the lymphatic fluid doesn't drain properly. The stockings help to reduce the likelihood of swelling in the area. We will have Occupational Therapists (OT) work with him while he is in the hospital but will also arrange for someone to come to your house to continue working with him once he returns home."

"Okay," I replied. "How long do you anticipate he will need to stay in hospital for?"

"Probably a few days. We'll see how he recovers."

More concessions. More professionals. More procedures. We were in a whole new world that I knew nothing about. There was no going back though. I just had to learn where I fit into this new domain. If anywhere. In the interim, I waited.

An orderly finally came to take me to see Brad. The scene wasn't pretty. He was in worse shape than after his first surgery. Tubes snaked out of him, as he lay buried under a mound of rough cotton blankets. A metal bowl sat on a tray beside the bed.

"Hey, honey," I tentatively said as I inched into the room.

Brad's eyes fluttered, but he struggled to keep them open. A morphine pump loomed over him on the IV stand: a guardian and sentinel preventing my getting too close. He managed a weak grunt, but his eyes didn't win the battle to focus.

I stood, uncertain about what to do or how to proceed. Should I sit? Should I leave? Was I strong enough not to break down and cry right then and there? I wasn't certain about anything, let alone the last point.

A nurse swept into the room and began to check his vitals.

"Hello," she said brightly. "Are you Brad's wife?"

I nodded weakly.

"Go ahead and put his things down for now," she said as she attached the cuff to his arm. "We'll put them away shortly."

"Thank you," I mumbled, then pointed to the stainless-steel bowl. "What's the bowl for?"

"He was sick," she said. "It's from the anesthetic. It's pretty common, but he should feel better once it works out of his system."

Brad eyes fluttered open.

"Hello Brad," the nurse said. "How are you feeling now? Any more nausea? Any change in pain level? On a scale of $1 - 10$, where is your pain at now?"

Brad's eyes flickered with a wince. He still wasn't winning the battle, but he was trying valiantly.

"Six or seven," he managed, as his eyes slipped once more.

"Remember," she said as she adjusted the plastic bags hanging from the pole. "You can press the morphine pump any time you feel like the pain is getting worse. It is better to stay on top of it. Mind you, doing a tap dance on it won't do you much good. You will get a measured dose but won't overdose. It only releases so much over the course of an hour. But if you are in pain, we can certainly do our best to make you more comfortable."

I sank quietly into the chair beside Brad's bed taking everything in: Brad's pain, the medical equipment, the nurses tending to his needs. There was nothing I could add to it. Nothing I could say or do to make anything better.

As I watched, Brad slid back into a fitful sleep. He was nauseous and in pain. Time and sleep were what he needed. Not conversation with me. I felt useless, but also tethered in place. I was in the way, but how could I leave him in this state? Would he be mad if I left or irritated by me hovering over him?

I sat, twisting my hands around each other, but a decision became obvious. Taryn was 5 months old and exclusively breastfeeding. While I had left a bottle for her, my body reminded me of my responsibilities. My breasts were heavy and becoming painful. It was time to feed my child.

I leaned in and kissed Brad's cheek.

"I'll be back soon," was the only whispered reassurance I could offer.

That reassurance might have been the right thing to say, but it didn't sink into my own heart. Looking back now, I wish I could be kinder to that young, frightened woman who was doing the best she could and doing a mighty fine job of it. Brad might not have wanted all kinds of people fawning over him, but my presence alone showed my love, let him know he was not alone. No words would have made a difference to cut through the physical pain, but I had his back and that was the best gift I could give him.

It didn't make leaving the hospital any easier though. Leaving alone was the hardest thing I had ever done up to that point. I walked out blindly and slid into our van, then sobbed, hands gripped hard around the steering wheel.

How could I leave him there? I held so much guilt, so much fear. Forward motion was the only thing that drove me, so when the sobs ebbed, I slid the key into the ignition and used it to push me back into the day. There was more to be done before I could rest and no comfort in any step I took. Each one, excruciating.

Oh, but I wish that step was the worst. I would return to this hospital and many others plenty more times though.

"Hey honey, look who's come to see you."

I raised Taryn's car seat as we walked in the door, so she could see her daddy.

"Hey baby," he said as he waggled fingers at her.

A good sign. The anesthetic seemed to have finally worn off. He was less groggy and hopefully in less pain, making his mood potentially that much better.

"How are you feeling?" I asked. "Can I get you anything? I brought a couple of magazines, some socks, a pair of pj pants; not sure if you are allowed to wear them, but thought if you were, you would want them…"

"I'm fine," he interrupted.

Shoot. He wasn't fine yet. His classic response always signaled annoyance.

"Thanks though," he added when he saw my face fall.

I nodded. We both knew how hard this was. The go-to response his family had always fallen back on was stoic silence. He hadn't learned any different. Yet.

"So, has the doctor been in yet today?" I asked as I slipped Taryn out of her car seat and fussed with her for a moment. I didn't trust myself to make eye contact yet and potentially increase his annoyance level.

"No, but plenty of nurses have been in. They don't leave you alone."

As if on cue, a nurse walked into the room.

"You must be Brad's wife and daughter," he said with a smile. "He told me you'd be in today. I just need to check Brad's vitals and then I'll leave you to visit."

He turned to Brad, "How's your pain levels currently?"

Brad went through the process like a model patient: polite, unobtrusive, doing his utmost to not cause trouble to those around him. The process made him crazy.

He hated being there. Nurses constantly checked on him day and night. An Occupational Therapist visited to start the process of rehabilitation, introducing exercises to reduce the edema that threatened. Dr. T and her entourage of interns would breeze through at random moments for tiny windows of time. And the food? It was edible, but not the caliber he was used to. It was all too much, and he just wanted to go home. But the morphine that kept his pain at bay also gave him crazy, wicked dreams and didn't help his digestive system. He was not in a happy place, and I didn't blame him. Like so many others, venting that frustration often fell to those closest and safest— me.

"What's that?" I asked when the nurse finally left.

Brad pulled the sheet aside to look at the new tube that exited his body.

"Mary had to put a catheter in last night, because my stomach was swollen."

"Oh," I replied in alarm.

"They took it out as soon as they drained me, but a few hours later, I was in agony again. The swelling put pressure on my wound, which they don't want. So, they put the catheter in again and decided to leave it for the time being."

"Oh," I said again.

I didn't know what to say. I had no suggestions at the ready, no stories I could share to make it better or empathize. I held Taryn on my knee and tried not to let my brain shriek in alarm. It was fine. It would be fine. He was in the hospital. They were taking care of him. They knew what to do and everything would be alright.

Everything wasn't at all right.

"Here," he said sensing my tension and looking for a way to diffuse it. "Give her to me."

Taryn happily slid into Brad's hands and reached for his nose. Thank God for her boundless love that shone into the darkest places. She was the bright spot that helped lighten the other days.

Surprisingly, the ones that followed got easier. Brad couldn't leave until the catheter came out and Dr. T wanted him to have a few more sessions with the OT before heading home. Another one would be assigned to us through CCAC once he came home, but the good news was that he was beginning to walk again. Despite the additional pieces removed, he was healing. The morphine pump disappeared and after several painful days in hospital, I was shuttling the van around again to bring him home. No more surgeries planned.

"We are setting up an appointment with an oncologist for later in August," Dr. T announced on her last visit before Brad was released. "Next steps are treatment."

"What treatment?" Brad asked. "I thought you got everything."

My brain went back to the horses that had been released from the stable. They still needed to be corralled. But that treatment would come after Labour Day. Between this moment and then, we needed to heal, both mentally and physically. All of us.

Brad left the hospital that day in a wheelchair, but was walking before we met the newest member of our growing team a few weeks later—Dr. J. In between, there were nourishing moments; family dinners, road trips, baby firsts, and a little much-needed reconnecting between husband and wife. It seemed so long ago that we had met on that hillside at Pickle Lake Lodge. Too long and too far removed from our present.

The Cure

"Brad?" a woman called with a clipboard in her hand.

We gathered ourselves up to follow her. Blood had already been taken and processed. Dr. J had outlined the process Brad was now to undertake. Interferon was the next step in the game. It didn't feel promising.

Interferon

"Adjuvant therapy is secondary cancer treatment, given after primary treatment with surgery, to help delay or prevent the recurrence of cancer.

Immunotherapy is treatment that stimulates the body's immune system to detect and kill cancer cells. As a systemic treatment, it travels through your bloodstream to reach all parts of your body.

Interferon is a type of immunotherapy patients receive as adjuvant therapy to reduce the risk of melanoma relapse." [4]

"You are young and relatively strong, so should withstand treatment well, but the side effects can be difficult: nausea, vomiting, headaches, fever, chills, lack of appetite and energy. You might have trouble sleeping. You will probably experience weight loss. Also, don't

---

[4] Melanoma Research Alliance. (2021). Interferon (Intron® A or Sylatron™). Retrieved from Melanoma Research Alliance, https://www.curemelanoma.org/patient-eng/melanoma-treatment/adjuvant-therapy/interferon-intron-a-or-sylatron#:~:text=or%20Sylatron%E2%84%A2)-,Interferon%20(Intron%C2%AE%20A%20or%20Sylatron%E2%84%A2),detect%20and%20kill%20cancer%20cells.

be surprised if you have issues with mood swings. If you do, we can introduce antidepressants."

Holy, mother of... what?

"I won't need antidepressants," Brad stated firmly.

"It is a symptom of treatment, but we will deal with that if it becomes an issue," Dr. J reassured us.

Now that treatment was set to begin, which of these symptoms would we see? We were surrounded by old people; grey and washed out from too many days spent at the Cancer Clinic. Vitality stopped at the door. Would we look like that by the end of the month too? Brad's treatment was scheduled to be Monday through Friday for the month of September. Would treatment leave him a shell of a man, like those who now surrounded us? It just seemed wrong that we were there.

"Follow me," the smiling nurse said on his first day of treatment, as she led the way to the yawning mouth of the chemo ward.

People lined the labyrinth of rooms that snaked off the central hub. Hospital beds parked beside windows, while lounge chairs sat in rows along inner walls. IV poles were everywhere. The only evidence that spoke of family were the stiff looking chairs squeezed in beside patients' beds.

"You won't be able to stay," the nurse said to me, as she stopped at a large chair for Brad.

"Oh," I exclaimed looking from her to Brad. "Um, okay. When should I come back to pick him up then?"

"You can check back in about an hour," she replied, as she began the process of checking his vitals.

His damn vitals. He was alive for fuck's sake. I was not though. I was a ghost in the machine. An unwelcome visitor to the cancer realm. I didn't belong and obviously shouldn't be there. What was I thinking?

"I guess I'll be back later then," I said, trying to exude a false sense of cheeriness; the farthest thing from what I felt as I pushed Taryn's stroller back the way we had come.

I didn't know where to go, but at least I had the stroller to hold. And Taryn when I couldn't take the cold comfort of the hospital corridors any longer.

This was day one. We had a month to go.

Over the weeks that followed, the story remained the same. I would drive us to the hospital, wait while Brad had blood tests to see how his body was tolerating the interferon, sip at insipid Tim Horton's coffee while we waited for him to be called in for treatment, then be politely barred entry to the inner sanctum of the chemo ward. Taryn didn't care. She charmed people everywhere we went. She lit up faces on many of the others who also waited their turn for a spin in the chemotherapy beds and chairs. At six months old, she was full of smiles and had no comprehension of the emotional pain that surrounded her, whether it be strangers or her parents.

"What an angel," ragged people would remark, as she pulled off her socks or stuffed crinkle toys in her mouth.

She made the whole world a little brighter on a lot of days.

Once Brad passed through the chemo ward doors with a stiff upper lip, I couldn't take their weak smiles though. My head kept screaming *"we don't belong here!"*, as I wandered through the hours ahead of me. I was 32 years old, pushing my infant daughter through the bland maze of medicine. No bouncy castles or ball pits to be seen. No other young mothers to commiserate with. And a few other things decidedly lacking as well.

Today, you can find change tables in most public restrooms. Certainly, in women's bathrooms, but increasingly in men's as well. Heck, washrooms come in family and gender-neutral varieties nowadays too. But in 2005, in the Cancer Clinic at the local hospital, I couldn't find a change table anywhere. That first day, after pushing along random corridors and alternately sitting watching fish float in soothing tanks, I stood to take care of a mundane, but necessary task— Taryn needed a diaper change. I located the nearest washroom but was disappointed to not find the plastic fold-down tables found in so many other public restrooms. Perhaps another bathroom would accommodate our needs? I looked but didn't find any that day. Eventually, I pulled out our travel change mat and quickly and discretely changed her diaper on the floor.

It wasn't just the diaper change though. I also needed to feed Taryn. A baby blanket thrown over Taryn's head hid her from view, but she disliked the cover and would pull the blanket from her face before finishing. We never used them at home, so why would she like them anywhere else? It divided us during this bonding time, but I knew many were uncomfortable seeing a woman nursing in public, so I tried to hide us. Taryn would have none of it. And I felt increasingly despondent at how conspicuous I felt.

I railed against it all. We didn't belong at the Cancer Clinic. Our family was so much younger than everyone else there. They didn't have facilities for families, and I struggled to ask for accommodations for our needs.

"Ask to borrow an exam room when you need to feed or change her," one nurse suggested.

But I didn't want to bother anyone. We shouldn't be there. I didn't belong. But Brad did. He had just as much right and need to be there as anyone else who walked through the door. Just not me. At least that was how I felt.

Instead, I fought Taryn with blankets draped over her head. Or fed her while sitting on a toilet in a cramped cubicle. Or wandered outside to find a measure of privacy beyond prying eyes. Like there was privacy when the parking lot was still in sight.

"There is a lovely water garden down the end of the hall," a kindly old woman mentioned to me one day.

She could see my struggles. She must have sensed the tears that were always on the verge of spilling over.

"Someone pointed it out to me the first week I started coming," she said kindly. "It helps you forget where you are for a few minutes."

"Thank you," I replied. I couldn't manage much more for fear that I would lose the battle against tears.

Thank you to all the strangers who tried to make those moments better. Kindnesses gutted me when I couldn't manage to ask for the simple favour of borrowing an exam room for 15 minutes. Those gentle words were a lifeline for my heart that was terrified and felt like it was shredding in fear. If only the escape she pointed out could have lasted.

The garden was beautiful. A Zen oasis filled a tiny pocket of concrete where you could sit and listen to the burbling fountain or stare up into the heavens looking for answers as to why any of us were there at all. It was a mainstay of my days after that. Even better, it got me to thinking.

"Maybe there are other niches to discover? Or something else I can do with my time while I wait for Brad?"

From then on, I walked.

I finally discovered changing tables in the public washrooms in the main part of the hospital. Not surprisingly, they were close to the maternity ward. I also found another garden outside with lush expanses of lawn where I could lay a blanket and pretend we were on a lovely picnic. I suppose it was a picnic for Taryn, but it did my spirits good too. Garden beds buoyed me up as colourful flowers nodded their pretty heads in the warm September sun. That was all I needed in that moment. Those moments were fragile, short-lived things though.

Invariably, as soon as we crossed the threshold back into the hospital, gloom settled back into my heart. Brad was inside having poison pumped into his veins. The interferon was tasked to attack any last cancer cells that might be floating around in his system, but it also attacked anything it came across. Over the course of the month, he became pale, grey really. His appetite disappeared. So too did any good humour he had built up during his convalescence that summer. Words dried up. His patience too.

"I'm going to ask my sister if she can take me to a few appointments," Brad said one afternoon after he pushed away another lunch with barely a bite taken out of it.

"Why?" I asked startled. "I can do it."

Didn't he want me there? I already felt like I wasn't welcomed by the hospital. Now he didn't want me hovering either.

"I thought it would give you a break," he said. "Not have to drag Taryn to the hospital…"

"I don't mind," I countered hurriedly, then paused. "But if she wants to, I guess that's okay."

And it was okay. His sister probably needed to feel a part of the process too. We were all scared and looking for ways to help. But letting go of any little thing felt like losing control even more. So be it.

Tracy took over a shift. And Brad's dad did too. I know Brad suggested it for me, for them, but my God, I had no filter to see that at the time. Instead, I stayed home and tackled laundry. Or vacuuming. Or squished crayons into Taryn's hands so she could draw Daddy a picture for when he came home.

I wanted to support my husband—my family—but my brain reeled every step of the way. He was the patient, and I was in the way. I made life more difficult for everyone. All I wanted to do was help, but my presence alone felt like an inconvenience. Mother and babe didn't have a place.

Fine, but damned if I would let go of the one thing I could do, which was drive my husband to his treatments. So, while his family took shifts, I remained the primary driver. No one needed to see the tears it cost me to walk away from Brad in the chemo ward every day. I was fine.

The days crept slowly along. Every day I pulled together dinner, only to have most of it remain on Brad's plate. My appetite wasn't exactly ravenous either. I countered by introducing Taryn's first solids to her; at least someone was eating. Mealtimes were my desperate attempt at capturing routine and some semblance of normal in the day. By Sunday, we all got lighter for the few days break from our hospital visits, but Monday always loomed on the horizon.

"Morning, Brad," another smiling nurse said at the start of our fourth and final week of intensive interferon treatments.

I stood tentatively, as Brad helped to gather the diaper bag up for me.

"You can come with us to see where Brad will be today," she said as I waffled listlessly debating which direction to head that day.

"Thank you, but I've been told I'm not allowed in," I quietly replied.

"Oh no," she said. "It's not that. It's just the baby. She is more vulnerable because she is so young. If there was ever a spill, she would be at a much higher risk. There are so many strong drugs in use for the many different chemotherapy treatments going on inside. As adults, our bodies would tolerate it, but she could get very sick from the strength of the chemicals used. Not that we anticipate a spill, but it is a necessary precaution. It is just safer for her not to be exposed to anything. But you can come in to help Brad get settled. And please feel free to come check his progress whenever you want."

I wanted to cry. I had spent the better part of the last month feeling rejected. Feeling like I didn't belong, like I was a burden and inconvenience to be tolerated. But this nurse changed the tune with her moment of compassion. She recognized the family. She saw me.

The hospital was protecting me, protecting my daughter from the poisons meant to bring health to those who desperately needed salvation. They were doing all they could to keep Brad alive; to fight the disease that threatened our family. We belonged there as much as anyone, but yes, we were an anomaly. More people got diagnosed with cancer at later ages, but not all. Way back on our first day there, we passed a teenager—rebellious in ripped clothes and spiky hair—lying in the bed beside Brad. She wasn't a visitor. She too was a patient. And when I took the time to look around, I saw that many of the people who looked old and grey, were actually not so old, rather withered from treatment and doing their best to still own tattered dignity.

Stupid cancer made us all old. It sapped the colour from all our lives and left everyone fighting to hold on. No one was immune to the abnormal cells that greedily streaked through bodies. And sadly, I was far from alone in that, as alone as I felt in that moment. I was not the patient, but I was part of the story.

I was part of other people's stories too. I know other people saw the young family sitting in the cancer clinic. I'm sure other people guessed why a woman with a baby randomly wandered the halls of such a specific location. They didn't know my story, but it was safe to assume I was there for a reason, and that reason was cancer, same as their own. Our stories were different but held the same thread. Cancer brought us all there and made of us a family struggling along our own parallel paths. Some of our journeys were harder or easier at times, but in that moment, we were all at the same crossroads. Cancer touched us all.

But it didn't own every day. And we had light at the end of our tunnel.

"Congratulations!" Dr. J said when he walked into the exam room where Brad, Taryn and I sat. "Today is your last treatment. Well, in hospital anyway."

"Yay!" I declared.

"It is definitely worth celebrating," Dr. J's nurse agreed. "Do you have any plans?"

I turned to look at Brad. It felt weird celebrating anything with all the drama of the last month. We had been at the hospital at least two and a half hours every day from Monday thru Friday. The days when he needed lab work were longer. Brad had lost his appetite, some weight, and any good spirits he had mustered over the summer. But we were done with this portion of the treatment and that was enough.

"We are going to my aunt's for a family dinner on Thanksgiving," I replied.

"That sounds lovely," she said. "Enjoy!"

"Yes, it sounds nice," added Dr. J. "Now, about the next steps. Your subcutaneous injections start next week. We'll arrange for CCAC to come out to show you how to do it. Essentially, instead of receiving the interferon through IV in hospital, you will inject it yourself at home three times a week; more or less every other day."

Not through yet, but at least we wouldn't have to be at the Cancer Clinic every day.

"How are you feeling Brad?" Dr. J asked. "How has your mood been?"

Could he read my thoughts? Brad had been a bear, but I wasn't about to say that.

His curt response of course was, "I'm fine."

"I just want to remind you that if you start to feel sad, depressed, angry, or just not yourself, there are things we can do."

Like having cancer wasn't bad enough, the side effects from treatment were punishing. Brad was the one to make the call as to how he was managing things though. As per usual, I swallowed my thoughts and busied myself with the baby. I didn't want to be the one to tattle on him and his short fuse, potentially opening up another emotional can of worms.

"Let me know," Dr. J said, before moving on to the last lab results and the plan for the day.

When we walked out of the hospital three hours later, the warm sun was a blissful gift. It wasn't like we wouldn't be back, but one awful stretch was finally behind us.

Chapter 4: The Upward Turn

Putting Life Back Together

Putting life back together again isn't always easy. When you go through traumatic events, mental scar tissue is left behind. Nerves are frayed and tempers sometimes quick to break. Just because the intensive treatments were behind us, didn't mean that everything went back to normal. How do you define 'normal' after staring cancer in the face? The best you can.

"Don't know why they need to send someone to show me how to give myself a needle," Brad grumbled the next week. "It's not like I can't figure it out. Stab away…"

"Yes…well, there is the where of it," I replied, as I wiped mushed peas off Taryn's chin. "Just be nice."

"I will!" he snapped.

"I know."

It was our usual repartee. He hated the attention. Taking medication wasn't something he liked either. It all sat badly with him, leaving him frustrated that other people were telling him what to do and him with no say in it. He had to go along with it, regardless of his wishes and wants. And I quietly watched on in the background of his drama.

"What time is the nurse supposed to be here?" Brad asked as he flicked between TV stations.

"Here comes the airplane. Open wide!" I urged Taryn, as I wiggled a spoon at her and answered over my shoulder. "She'll be here in half hour."

"Hmmph."

"Daddy better be as good as my baby girl is when the nurse gets here," I sing-songed to Taryn, as I swooped another bite towards her.

I got no response but could feel him glare at me. I didn't care though, as I was still lifted from Thanksgiving. Everyone was there, including my very pregnant sister. She was due in less than a month but waved off everyone's concerns about her driving that far so close to her due date.

"And miss out on turkey farts? Not a chance!"

"One good fart and you might squeeze out the baby," Cassie laughed.

Laughter was the medicine I needed, so I soaked up every ounce of it. It seemed far too fleeting nowadays. Time with family was always healing though. And its aftereffects meant that I could handle Brad's scowl, as he waited for the nurse to show up. Good thing too, as once she arrived, he was nothing but polite. I could see through it but was glad that he was always nice to the people around us who were there to help.

It was funny though—not in a truly funny way—every time a CCAC nurse showed up, we had to share the story all over again. They didn't know who they were scheduled to see and what their issues were. Cursory details sure—wound management, medicine administration, respiratory therapy, or whatever was required—but they never knew *our* story. We had to start from the beginning every time. And there were an awful lot of doctors and nurses we met with.

"Hi," the cheery woman said as I let her in. "I'm from CCAC. Here's my ID. What are we in need of today?"

I handed her the binder that the nurses signed into when they arrived. It was steadily growing.

"Brad has malignant melanoma. They excised a mole on his right calf, then went back and re-excised the area about a month later and took a skin graft from his left thigh. He also had lymph nodes taken from his groin. He just finished the intravenous portion of interferon treatments. Now he is starting the subcutaneous portion of it. You are supposed to show him how."

"Thank you," Brad said from where he had risen from the couch. "I could have told her myself."

"I'll go get it," I mumbled, as I retreated to the kitchen chastised.

Why could I never remember that this was about him? He was right there! He was quite capable of sharing his own story. It was his story after all. I was forever forgetting and being reminded of the fact that I was not the patient, not the star of the show at all.

I brought the package back and placed it on the table between Brad and the nurse, who had moved on to checking Brad's vitals; temperature, blood pressure, checking his pain on a scale of 1 – 10.

I picked Taryn up and retreated to the far loveseat. After Brad's rebuke, I folded back into myself. I wanted to disappear with Taryn but was torn; I also wanted to stay close to watch what went on. Even though it was Brad's story and not always my place to tell it, I often found myself having to share the tale. While I could just leave him and the nurse to it, I might also need to know how to administer the interferon at some point too. We had been told he had to get injections three days a week. For how long remained up in the air, but it would be for the foreseeable future anyway. If the injections knocked him out as bad as the IV portion did, I might have to step in to help at points.

So, I stayed. Whether I recognized it or not, I was part of the story. I might not be the patient, but I helped Brad get to appointments. I weighed in on treatment plans. I asked questions that he often didn't think of and was a second set of ears to make sense of what the doctors told us along the way. If friends or family members asked how things were going, the story came pouring out. And many days I needed to get that story out to make sense of it myself.

"You need to inject it into the muscle," the nurse continued, as she looked at Brad.

I might have had my hands full with an 8-month-old, but she glanced my way too. Did I need to step up for this part of the treatment? Could I handle another load on my plate? I didn't have a choice. I sat watching and listened to every word she said; observed every step of the process. And she smiled kindly at me when I walked her to the door when she was done.

"I'll be back in two days," she said as she left.

A day's reprieve in the middle. And as much as Brad was right about doing the injections himself, he needed that extra day of recovery. The injection was straightforward. He tolerated a few more lessons from a few more nurses, then took over the job himself. My role was to stand sentry and watch. To mark passage of time and stand witness to the journey. He might not need me to stab him, but somehow, I needed to be there regardless.

Days turned into weeks and somehow time marched on. Brad was stoic. He learned that the injections made him nauseous, so timed them accordingly. On the days he had them, he ate almost no dinner and looked like death. But his days off balanced that. And that had him itching to get back to work.

"I talked to Don," Brad announced one afternoon. "I told him I want to go back to work."

"Oh," I said, slightly surprised.

"Not full-time," he added. "He figures he can put me to work in the warehouse. Pick orders and stuff. Push paper about. It will suck having to hang out with Steve all day, but I need to get back."

"Do you think you can handle it?" I asked tentatively. "You've always said those cylinders are heavy…"

"Nah, I'll be fine. Don won't get me doing anything too crazy. And I can probably still do circles around Gene…"

Somehow, I doubted that. And I didn't love the idea of him pushing himself physically. If I was honest with myself, I didn't want him doing anything at all. What was I going to do without him at home? He might be grumpy at times but having him home was now the norm. And as he was generally feeling better, he was becoming more pleasant. Plus, he had talked about starting work on the laundry room. What would happen to that project?

Ultimately, it wasn't my call. He didn't need to go back. He wanted to—for the mental and social stimulation. I understood, regardless of my wishes and wants. It didn't prevent me from trying to keep him home a little longer though.

"You always feel shitty on your shot days though," I wheedled. "And what about your doctor appointments? You have one with Dr. J next week. What are you going to do about that?"

"It won't be a problem," Brad answered. "Don knows I have appointments. He understands my circumstances. He's not new. I just have to talk to HR and adjust the short-term disability."

"I need to go back," he added with a pointed look at me.

Well, that was that then. He wanted to get back to normal and I couldn't blame him. If I could erase the last six months, I would, but everything about my world had changed. I had a baby. Our world had turned on a dime and now revolved around doctor appointments and the effects of the myriad of medications the doctors plied on Brad. His mood teetered depending upon the day of the week. And I just had to roll with the punches. I didn't even recognize the eggshells that were scattered everywhere in my mental minefield. I was just trying to clutch onto the positives that flitted past as best as I could. Having a happy husband at home to help with the baby on a full-time basis wasn't something I could get a grip on though. As per so many other things in my life, it wasn't my call. And I was getting used to feeling powerless.

"You should think about it too," Brad continued reading my thoughts. "Have you found a daycare for Taryn yet?"

Kick me when I'm down! Something else to let go of and lose just when I was getting used to our new normal.

"Not really," I murmured. "I thought about going to visit the one by the grocery store…"

"Good," he said.

It didn't feel good though. Taryn was a mere 10 weeks old when her daddy was diagnosed with cancer. For the last six months, she had spent more time in hospital entertaining cancer patients and doctors than doing all the cute things babies were supposed to do; tummy time, bouncing in her jolly jumper, madly scribbling crayon masterpieces with little ham hock hands. When was there time for that?

I wanted to be the uber-mom using cloth diapers, making homemade baby food, encouraging early literacy by reading her a never-ending stream of books. The cloth diapers sat unused. My mom plied me with enough disposable diapers in the early days to help mitigate extra tasks, like laundry. We did read plenty of books waiting for Daddy to come out of treatments, but the crayons were still mostly intact. The only reason why her baby food was homemade was because Brad still reigned in the kitchen and looked down on the nasty jarred food on the market. Leftovers were scooped into the blender, then popped into ice cube trays. She was a gourmet foodie in the making.

But daycare? I wasn't ready for that. I wanted to raise my daughter myself. The idea of handing her off to strangers was wrong. I felt like we had lost too much time to hospitals already. When was our time?

Wait lists were a thing though and if I wanted to find someplace decent, it behooved me to get her on one of them sooner rather than later. My maternity leave wouldn't last forever. We couldn't afford for me to stay home. Stalling wouldn't change that. So, when Brad happily packed himself off to the "real world", I glumly fired up the computer to see what my options were for nearby daycares. If I had to leave my baby with someone, at least it would be someplace with decent programming and a welcoming feel. My ECE training refused to accept anything less than the best.

In the interim, I threw myself back into 'Super Mommy' role. Taryn and I went to Mom and Baby Yoga classes. I took her to drop-in playgroups. Playdates filled mornings that Daddy was gone. And I tried to plaster on my biggest smile and encouragement when he walked in the door gray and dishevelled after dragging himself to the half days.

You couldn't hide the days he took his shots though. He might have thought no one noticed, but his temper got shorter and shorter as the days went on.

"Steve fucked up the order for ..."

"I almost dropped a cylinder when I was helping Troy unload his truck..."

"Fucking Ray..."

There was venom there and it was growing. I couldn't help but remember the warning that Dr. J had cautioned months previous— that depression was a possibility. Brad had immediately dismissed it, but his mood was black, and nothing seemed to lift it. Not even tackling another home reno project.

"Hand me those screws," he demanded when I went down to check his progress on the laundry room he was working on.

"So, how's it going?" I asked as I scooped a handful of screws from the box across the room for him.

"Fine," he snapped.

So, not fine. Time to tread carefully.

He measured the ceiling under the stairs, then moved to the drywall propped against the wall and grabbed a fresh sheet. Another cut piece lay beside the main pile.

"What's wrong with that piece?" I asked.

"I cut it wrong."

"Oh."

I looked from the space he had just measured to the drywall in his hands.

"Umm, is that the right angle?" I ventured cautiously. "Shouldn't it run in the opposite direction?"

He paused and stared at the drywall, then glanced back to the ceiling.

"Fuck!" he stormed. "For fuck's sake…"

He dropped the drywall in frustration and threw the measuring tape over his shoulder. It narrowly missed my head, as I flinched away from his words and actions.

I was right and he knew it. Me, who had the barest minimum handy skills was telling him what to do and it enraged him. Not that I was right, but that he was wrong. And that he had almost wasted another sheet of drywall on stupid mistakes, like making a dyslexic cut. Again. He hadn't seen the mistake himself and had no one to blame but himself. But that didn't excuse his outburst and he knew it.

"Seriously dude!" I exclaimed, as I headed for the stairs. "That almost hit me! I'm sorry you're frustrated, but you need to chill the fuck out."

He let me go, but the air hung heavy in my wake.

The next day, Brad came home in somber spirits.

"I'm sorry about yesterday," he said from the doorway of the kitchen where I prepped dinner. "I lost my temper and realized I've been losing my temper a lot. With everyone. Steve might be stupid and deserve it, but that doesn't excuse me throwing shit, especially at you. I'm angry all the time and can't control it anymore.

I talked to Dr. J about it today at my appointment. He's going to get me a referral for a psychiatrist."

I knew how challenging that epiphany was. He needed help. Asking for it was the hardest thing in the world to do though. That's not how he was raised and so far from his comfort level. But he had done it. For me, for his family, but most importantly, for himself.

"Oh hun'," I said as I turned from the stove. "I think that's a great idea. You know it's not your fault but admitting it still must have felt so hard. But Dr. J warned us that side effects from the interferon might be depression or personality changes. Hopefully, a psychiatrist can help."

What did help right off the hop though, was owning that he struggled. It wasn't his fault, but he still needed to acknowledge his response to the turmoil. He needed to accept that coping with it on his own was beyond his capability and sometimes extra support helped. There was no getting around it. Everything was hard.

Our lives had been thrown up in the air and control wrested from us. Doctor appointments trumped everything. Conversations now centered on Brad's latest treatments and how he was feeling. He didn't want to be the center of attention and definitely didn't like how he was boiled down to the role of patient first and foremost. He did his best to steer conversations in other directions, but inevitably, they always came back to his medical state, and it was maddening. Which didn't help with his slowly slipping temperament. There wasn't anything more we could do about the state of his cancer, but if there were options to improve Brad's emotional state in dealing with it, I was all in. Thankfully, so was he, even if it meant adding another doctor and more pills to the mix.

Just FYI, lifelines sometimes seem few and far between in the middle of cancer treatments. When you see one, grab it. They are a gift.

A few weeks later we got ours in the form of a small yellow pill bottle.

"I start them gradually and increase the dose until we get to my working level," Brad said as he stared at the bottle on the table.

He had just come from meeting his newest doctor and didn't look pleased to add more medication to his repertoire. These ones would work on his mental equilibrium though, so I was optimistic life would get better for him, and in turn us as a family.

"Dr. M said the interferon essentially prevented my body from producing serotonin. Serotonin is like your happy hormones. Since my body stopped producing it, my serotonin levels slowly depleted. It is directly linked to mood and cognitive functioning, hence the black moods and inability to control my temper."

"So, it's not your fault!" I exclaimed, then backpedalled. "I mean, of course, it's not your fault. It's just that now we know it's more than just a bad day or two..."

"Yes. There really wasn't anything I could have done about it."

"See!" I cried. "Aren't you glad you finally talked to Dr. J?"

Brad glared across the table at me.

"They haven't started to work yet..."

"Oh, sorry. Yes, I guess not. But these pills will help make you feel better? Help you function and feel more level-headed?"

"Yeah," he answered. "Plus, I have to meet with Dr. M to talk about how I'm feeling."

Not his strong suit, but I bit my tongue knowing this step cost him a measure of self-assurance already. Feelings had always been relegated to anger, insecurity, or awkwardness. Now though, there was a whole network of other emotions that he couldn't ignore. Fear, anxiety, confusion, and sadness were a huge part of this journey, and they couldn't be drowned with booze or passed off as irrelevant. Cancer ran the gamut of emotions, and it forced us to face every harsh reality we could dream of. In my experience, talking about it helped, but it was new territory for Brad and I knew it would be beyond hard. Embracing the pills and more importantly, the counselling, was the best news of the week.

"So how long will they take for you to start feeling the effects?" I asked.

"I have to gradually increase my dosage over the course of a week. He said I should start to see the effects within a few weeks."

A few weeks. I would take it. Especially if it meant that we could all feel like we could breathe a little easier at home, and for him, at work. Positive emotions flooded me—relief, gratitude, but mostly hope. I didn't have any problem running the gauntlet of them. I wanted to kiss Dr. M, and Dr. J for suggesting it. Of course, I would never meet Dr. M, but the timing couldn't have been better regardless. My sister was about to expand our family any day and all I wanted was to celebrate that.

I was about to get my wish…

"So, Tony and I had dinner upstairs with his parents," Kaya announced in a rare Friday-night phone call. "Tony wanted dessert, so we went to grab something. We walked into the grocery store, and then I stopped. 'We have to go home', I said to him. 'But we just got here!' he said. 'I know,' I said, 'but my water just broke…'"

"Oh my God!" I squealed.

Kaya was about to have her baby!

"What's happening? How do you feel? How far apart are the contractions? What did Tony do next?"

Too many questions to be answered at once, but I was thrilled that another bundle of joy was on the way for our family. We needed the joy in such a big way, and this was a perfect antidote to the heaviness surrounding Brad's treatments. In fact, he was happy to not own the spotlight for once.

Meanwhile, she had slipped downstairs when they returned home to change and call her midwife without being swamped by well-meaning family, then called me to share the news.

"I have some cramping, but no real contractions just yet. The midwife is going to check back with me in a bit."

"Eeeee!!! I'm going to be an auntie!!!" I shrieked.

Joy seemed so rare these days that I was overwhelmed with it, but first babies have a way of taking their time. The process was slow. That was Friday night. By Saturday morning, things hadn't progressed much further.

"The midwife told us to go to hospital," Kaya told me next morning. "She wants to examine me and get things moving along quicker. I think she wants to induce me."

"Okay," I replied over the phone as I threw random items into a bag.

The plan was to pick up my mom along the way, then head to the hospital ourselves. My Mom was going to be a grandma again for the second time in a year and didn't want to miss it. Nor did I. My problem was that I was a mum already and still nursing Taryn, but I wanted the focus to be on Kaya. Who knew how long the process would take and where we would be at God knows what hour.

"What am I supposed to do with her," Brad asked watching me from our bedroom doorway. "How am I going to feed her?"

"If I feed her before I go and express everything I can, you should be fine," I told Brad. "There is a small bottle of breast milk in the freezer too. You can give her cereal and a cube of carrots, beans, or that stew we made last week. I won't be gone that long. She'll be fine."

Honestly, I didn't even really care in that moment. I was already on my way, and nothing was going to stop me. My sister was about to have a baby and I didn't want to miss it, if she wanted me there.

"You'll be fine," I said again, as I zipped up the bag and pushed past him.

It had been all about him for months. This was about my sister—my closest friend in the world. I needed to be there, and he would have to figure it out.

"Tell her and Tony congrats from me," he said as him and Taryn waved me off with kisses at the door.

My mom and I were at the hospital by noon.

The next several hours flew by with visitors galore from Tony's side of the family. It was his mother's first grandchild and cousins aplenty came to celebrate. We filled the waiting room, taking turns going in to check on Kaya as her labour progressed. The hours ticked by and still no baby. Mom and I took turns supporting Kaya, visiting with family, going on food runs, and waiting some more. Finally, visiting hours came to a close and we were told we all had to leave. All but two.

"You and your mom stay," Tony's mother insisted. They lived a few minutes from the hospital, while our commute was a few hours. "Just let us know when anything happens."

The waiting room fell silent as they all filed out, but still we waited. Saturday slipped into Sunday. Kaya had received an epidural hours earlier to combat back labour, and while her pain was managed, the baby didn't seem an awful lot closer to presenting itself. Finally, after checking Kaya for the umpteenth time, the midwife made the announcement we had warily dreaded.

"Your water broke 29 hours ago. We are seeing signs of stress. If we don't get the baby out soon, it could put the baby at risk."

She gave us a moment to comprehend what she was saying.

"It's time to call in the OB. I know you have worked hard Kaya, but we have to think about the baby now. They are on call, so will be here as soon as possible and will check you when they arrive. But you need to be aware that we might have to perform a caesarian section. The baby is starting to show signs of distress. Once the obstetrician arrives, they will take over care and make that call. It is time though."

As much as the next few hours were intense for everyone assembled, ultimately the details are part of my sister's tale. My mother and I were blessed to be part of the journey and bear witness to a sacred event—my niece's first moments in life. For me, that was what it was all about: life. And it was something I didn't take lightly.

So many of the moments in my own life back home swirled around Brad's illness, so it was a welcome change to celebrate birth instead. We had drawn together to be a part of that. I wished all the moments in my life were as sweet and poignant, but instead they held uncertainty, procedures aplenty, and a constant vigil with threat. Cancer wasn't the journey I desired, but life was all about throwing the curve balls; our best intentions be damned. We had been blessed with marriage, buying a new home, and welcoming our own child, but our current journey was a far darker one. And I chafed at its familiarity.

With the baby now safely in her parents' arms, my home beckoned, love, fear, anxiety, and confusion notwithstanding. It was time to go home.

> ## Trauma
>
> **"Trauma is the lasting emotional response that often results from living through a distressing event. Experiencing a traumatic event can harm a person's sense of safety, sense of self, and ability to regulate emotions and navigate relationships. Long after the traumatic event occurs, people with trauma can often feel shame, helplessness, powerlessness, and intense fear." [5]**

Trauma. It was far too familiar in my young life. When I was two years old my father fell ill. He was in his late 30s. Doctors ran all kinds of tests trying to figure out what was wrong, but the one thing they didn't look for was cancer. He was too young. Or so they thought. But at the tender age of 40 years old, he died from prostate cancer; the youngest patient the hospital that treated him had seen at the time. They hadn't looked for it, so missed the signs until it was too late.

He left behind my mother, age 30, my sister a mere 2 1/2, and me, just past my 5th birthday.

At the time, children were seen and not heard. You didn't involve them in decision making and certainly didn't need to include

---

5 CAMH. (2023). Trauma. Retrieved from CAMH, https://www.camh.ca/en/health-info/mental-illness-and-addiction-index/trauma

them in events like funerals. It was inappropriate and beyond their years. But it didn't mean that children weren't affected by the events around them. It didn't mean that they were immune to trauma.

I don't remember much from when my father was dying, but poignant memories have stayed with me. Memories like me carefully bringing a glass of ginger ale to my ailing father as he sat in his favourite recliner, slowly slipping away from us. I don't recall much else of my interactions between him and my sister or me. He wouldn't have had the strength for it in the last months of his life and my memories were fallible much before then.

What I do remember is my aunt and uncle coming for a visit from South Africa. They arrived in the months leading up to my father's death and my uncle filled our home with his robust presence. He stepped in with a vitality that my father lacked, roughhousing with my sister and I to bring a spark of much-needed joy where it had lapsed.

"Who's a silly sausage?" he cried as he wrapped my sister and I in a blanket and rolled us around.

It was a simple game, but I remember us shrieking with laughter as he rolled us back and forth in our simple cocoon from the world. It was a respite we probably didn't even know we needed, but I'm sure it gave my parents solace in those dark days. The tinkle of children's joy would have been shushed from us long before.

I don't have much more to the memory than that, but it was in such stark contrast to our everyday life that it imprinted into my long-term memories. There wouldn't have been many giggles back then, so those cherished moments were monumental and incredibly poignant. And far too sad to ponder for someone of so few years.

My father died shortly after my aunt and uncle returned to South Africa. My mother surmised that my father had held on until they left, and then slipped away. The joy which was fleetingly introduced disappeared in their wake and was replaced with a pall of grief.

In that moment, I pulled into myself. Shy didn't cover it. I hid behind my mother's legs when faced with strangers. I didn't talk, unless specifically spoken to. I don't remember what my thoughts were, but it feels like I shut down. My world would have felt insecure and incredibly unstable, as my mother then faced the challenge of figuring out how to support our newly reconstructed family financially, emotionally, and socially.

My answer was to escape into the world of books. You can't control stories, but you can control what you read, and I read everything I could get my hands on; ghost stories, uplifting fiction, deep tales that left me a puddle of tears. They were my escape, my security, my friends, and my solace. And I could hold them close when other things disappeared.

Not much has changed since then. Books are still my favourite escape, my best friends, and the places where I feel seen and connected most of all. But when the world swirls into chaos, books can't fix the ills that pepper a soul. And that was a problem when cancer returned to my life.

When Brad fell ill, it brought back powerful memories of my mother's own supporting role in my father's cancer journey. She had walked the very same steps that I now begrudgingly trod. She could see my future in her past and desperately prayed the course would be different.

What would make the difference? Advanced science? A different stage at diagnosis? Brad's physical constitution? My father was only a few years older than Brad when he was diagnosed with cancer. Would that make the difference for us?

I went from a confidant young woman in the prime of my life, with a young family and the world at my fingertips, to an uncertain waif left to the medical world's mercy. I had no control over the events that stitched my life together and lived in fear of worst possible scenarios. I was prone to tears, had no time for friends and what others considered 'normal' pastimes. I was helpless in the face of Brad's next blood test results and scans.

Books couldn't save me this time. They didn't have enough power to transport me out of my reality for long enough to recharge my mental stores. As doctors took up more and more of our hours, I lost my voice once more. Gone was the joy, despite my valiant efforts to find it for my daughter's sake. The future receded and plans were marked in doctor appointments instead of baby milestones and vacation plans.

And my mother? The dark days she had walked with her own husband clouded every moment we now shared.

Making Plans

Christmas inched closer and so too did the time when I would have to return to work. I dreaded the day. I hated the idea of losing Taryn to a day care worker; a mere stranger who knew nothing of my beautiful girl's soul.

"You have to pick a place," Brad said yet again.

"I know," I snapped, uncertain whether the panic behind the words was hidden well enough to spare him.

It felt like I was losing everything. I had no control over anything once more and the thought threatened to drown me in its magnitude. And then the phone rang the week before Christmas.

"A spot has opened up for Taryn starting right after the Christmas break. She can come in to visit starting January 3rd."

"Great," I managed to reply, before cradling the phone back on the receiver.

That was less than two weeks. How? How could I even wrap my head around that? I didn't have a choice.

My mat leave wouldn't officially end until the beginning of February, but daycare spaces were a precious commodity. There were no guarantees that you would get a spot exactly when you needed one. It was dependent upon when children moved up within rooms or left the daycare entirely. You might have to wait months to get into one, languishing on waiting lists in the meanwhile. If a spot became available, your best bet was to take it when it became available.

"Good," Brad replied when I told him later that evening. "We have a spot. Now you can go back to work."

"Ya," I absently agreed as I turned away.

I didn't want to go back to work. I felt like I had lost the last six months of my life. Like I had lost all the precious moments where I was supposed to bond with my firstborn. Handing Taryn over to a daycare was tantamount to losing the last shred of control I had. How could I do that willingly? How could I make it stop hurting so damn much?

"I can go with you if you want," Brad said into the silence I left behind.

I nodded, too overwhelmed to trust myself to say anything more.

And just like that, I was wrapping my baby into her snow suit for a first visit to the daycare, just days after the new year began. To make matters worse, Brad couldn't make the first day, so I was going it alone. I plastered a polite smile to my face and slowly stepped inside, eyes darting everywhere, taking in as much as I could.

"Can I help you?" a voice called out from the office, as I inched further into the building.

This was it. I was committed now.

"Yes," I replied. "Um, my daughter has been offered a space at the daycare? We're here to visit. Uh, her name is Taryn..."

"Okay, let me see," the secretary said as she shuffled papers on her desk. "Oh, yes. Here we go. Taryn! Alright then. I'll let the supervisor know you are here."

I was left clinging to Taryn, taking in the space that would potentially be her new home for more hours than I cared to consider. Before I had a chance to flee, another woman materialized from the back office.

"Welcome to 'We Care'," the supervisor announced with a nod. "Shall we do a little tour? I'll show you the daycare and explain what you can expect from us along the way."

"Sure," I nodded, smiling down at Taryn, and adding. "Shall we go see?"

We took a quick, cursory tour of the small building.

"There is the school age room and here is the toddler room," she pointed out, as we paused in one doorway after another. "We've got a playground outside as well, and classes go for regular walks in the neighborhood."

I nodded and tried to seem engaged. Nothing jumped out at me though, from the people to the spaces. All I wanted to do was run away, but I had promised Brad to give the place a chance, so steadfastly followed along.

"And here's the infant room where Taryn will start," the supervisor announced when we got to the end of the tour. "I'll just leave you here then to get acquainted with us for a bit, shall I? Stop into the office so we can discuss a schedule when you are through."

I hoped my stiff smile wouldn't give away my fears. The infant room staff were the next to offer their charms, but I couldn't help comparing the room to infant rooms I had worked in previously. They didn't know it, but I had my own early childhood education certification and had spent most of my ECE career in the baby room. And at first glance, this room didn't compare.

Colourful pictures were at adult eye level, with nothing on or near the floor for the babies to see. Toys were missing pieces and didn't work properly. I wound up a pop-up toy to no avail and wondered how that might frustrate a young mind. But worst of all, the teachers talked to me, virtually ignoring Taryn. They didn't ask about her favourite songs, books, or food, nor what tactics worked best to soothe her when she became upset. What would they do with her once I left? Leave her to her own devices, with broken toys and little proper stimulation? Let her cry, with no idea how best to comfort her? I wanted to run from the room but forced myself to stay for Brad's sake.

Finally, it was time to go, after promising to return the next day. Not that I wanted to.

"They didn't even talk to her!" I lamented to Brad when he got home that afternoon.

I knew I had higher expectations, having worked in daycare settings before, but where were the comfy spaces to cuddle up with a book? Where were the natural elements to engage a young mind and get them interested in their surroundings? What about open-ended play? My rating of the space was critical, and I had a hard time warming up to the idea of leaving my precious baby in this less-than-ideal space.

Finally, I asked about his day.

"What did Dr. J say today?"

"He's going to start me back on interferon. My levels have come back up to a more acceptable point."

"Oh, that's great news," I exclaimed.

Although in truth, it was a mixed blessing. About a week before Christmas, Dr. J had decided to pause Brad's treatments. He wasn't happy with his blood counts, and despite constant adjustments, couldn't seem to get them to rise. The hope was that by taking a break, his body could recover a bit and they could find a better dose once he stabilized. It was excellent timing, as then Brad could enjoy Christmas and all the feasting that came with the holidays, without the grey pall and lack of appetite that went with his interferon days. But it also meant that the treatments weren't exactly going as planned, which was worrisome.

A return to treatments meant he was well enough to be bombarded with poisons once more. Back to limp appetites and waning spirits. But that was the road to a cure.

True to his word, the next day Brad came with me to see the daycare. As before, everyone was polite, but I still lacked enthusiasm about the space. Brad knew me well enough to see through my polite veneer. He could sense my reticence and forced my hand.

"Leave her with them," he murmured to me as we stood watching her in the baby room. "We can walk to the other end of the daycare. See how she does."

I bristled at the suggestion but had no choice but to relent. He was right and I had to give the daycare a chance if we wanted it to work. So, we walked, and she was fine. It didn't stop me from quickly collecting her when we returned though. I couldn't help the sigh of relief when we left.

"Go tomorrow," Brad said firmly on the drive home. "And leave her. Leave the building. Even if only for half an hour."

I hated him. I hated all of this. It didn't feel right. The space wasn't right. But it was the only space we had, so for now I relented once more.

I hadn't told Brad, but I had an errand to run anyway. My period was late. After staying a few minutes, I left Taryn and slipped down the road to a pharmacy. I picked up a pregnancy test thinking about how if I was pregnant, maybe she wouldn't have to be in any daycare for long. Maybe?

The next day, the test came back negative, but Taryn had a sniffle. I made the call to stay home. By the day after, my period started, and Taryn had the worst cold she had ever had. That was it. I put my foot down. She was NOT going back.

"Come on," Brad exclaimed.

"No," I cried. "I don't want her there! They barely talked to her and obviously their cleaning schedules leave a lot to be desired."

"She has to go somewhere though," he said. "You go back to work in a month! You said yourself that you have to take a spot when it presents itself."

I had, but I didn't care.

"I'll call Elmwood," I replied. "She's on the waitlist there. Maybe they can get her in."

Brad looked skeptical, but agreed and left me to it. I promised to call as soon as I could breathe once more. By that point, both Taryn and I were down for the count, and I just couldn't forgive We Care for that.

The following week I called and spoke with the supervisor at Elmwood.

"Hi Lori," I said. "My daughter is on the waitlist there and I was just wondering where on the list she is?"

Should I tell her that we had gone elsewhere, but I hated it? Would that sway her in my favour or send red flags that I could be a high needs pain in the butt whom they wouldn't want any part of?

I took the risk and shared some of what we had experienced at the other center. It probably came off desperate, but at that rate, I didn't have anything to lose.

"We would really love to be at Elmwood," I added after my tearful plea.

We had visited both daycares and the differences were striking. At Elmwood, there were hanging plants, comfy couches, a swing in the corner where babies could look out the window, and a wide range of appropriate toys which I witnessed getting cleaned. The caregivers had a genuine warmth and interacted with the children to build connections from the word go, putting both me and Taryn at ease. I knew what to look for, and this space was far superior. The trick was to get to the top of the waiting list.

"I'll see what I can do," was all that Lori promised, but I could tell she would give it her all.

Two days later, the phone rang.

"You are in," Lori announced. "You can start next week!"

This time, I didn't have a choice in the matter, but it felt like the right decision. And even though there were plenty of tears in the first weeks of daycare, before long we were all settling into new routines. I was still sad that my maternity leave had come to an end, but I could see the positives in returning to work too. Where I had dreamed of getting pregnant quickly to shorten Taryn's stay in care, now I relished returning to work and interacting with adults once more.

Unbeknownst to me though, the universe had heard my earlier pleas. After returning to work, I quickly realized that something was amiss. Headaches, breast tenderness, and another late period. I picked up another test and this time, it was positive. I was only a few weeks back to work, and pregnant once more. Time for a trip to the doctor—this one for me for a change.

"I think I'm pregnant," I announced when Dr. K came into the exam room.

"Alright," she said. "We'll get you to give us a urine sample to confirm, then get started on the paperwork, shall we?"

I handed her nurse my sample a few minutes later, then waited for Dr. K to return. This wasn't my first pregnancy, but things were a little different this round. I knew I was possibly up against some new complications.

"Brad is taking interferon," I said when Dr. K stepped back into the room. "What could that do to the baby?"

Unfortunately, she didn't have an answer to that question, but she did have more specialists up her sleeve. It was my turn to start stacking up doctor appointments of my own.

"I'll set up an appointment with a high-risk specialist," Dr. K said as she stared into her computer monitor. "In the interim, we'll book you for an ultrasound and the IPS. Hopefully the specialist will be able to answer any questions you may have."

How was I going to explain all these tests and absences at work? It didn't matter, as my brain raced with the possibilities of what could go wrong with the tiny new life which had just begun to grow inside me. I was pregnant, but it didn't feel anything like the celebration of my first pregnancy.

One step at a time. The first step was to be honest with my workplace. If there were complication with the pregnancy, they needed to know. I felt bad only having been back a month, but there was nothing to be done about it. Now it was about seeing if the baby was viable and if there were any health concerns due to the drugs Brad was on when I became pregnant. Leaving Dr. K's office didn't make me feel any better about what lay ahead, but at least a plan was in place.

Anyone who has been pregnant knows how crazy a time it can be. Your body is going through rapid changes and if you choose to run any tests, they need to happen at specific times. That meant that the next several weeks became very busy for me. First things first though, I needed to talk to my bosses about what was going on. I knocked on Thomas's door the next day.

"Hey," I said. "Do you have a minute?"

"Sure," Thomas replied. "What's up?"

I stepped inside his office and closed the door behind me.

"I'm pregnant," I announced abruptly. "I'm sorry. I know timing sucks, but I just found out and had to tell you. You know Brad is sick and because of the drugs he's taking, there are concerns with the baby. I have to go see a high-risk specialist next week and go for an ultrasound. I wouldn't have said anything right away, but I am not sure what is going to go on and I needed to be honest with you."

Thomas's normal joking response didn't fit in the face of my tense confession. But he understood the seriousness of what I was dealing with and nodded.

"Thank you for letting me know," he said. "We'll make it work. I'm sure it will be fine."

I hoped he was right but couldn't help worrying regardless. It seemed like that was my go-to response to life—worry, worry, worry.

Here I was pregnant, but not able to find happiness in what should have been a spark of joy. Cancer tinged everything.

The following week I parked at the north end of the hospital. The cancer clinic was on the south side of the complex, but this visit was all about me today. Me and the small fetus with an uncertain future inside me. Like so many other doctor's visits, I had to start at the beginning and explain why I was there after introductions were made.

"My husband has cancer—malignant melanoma—and is taking a drug called interferon. He took a break over the Christmas holidays, but restarted treatments again a few days after Christmas. I suspect I got pregnant the first or second week of January."

I paused, before going on.

"What I want to know is what effect does interferon have on babies?"

"I see," the doctor replied, nodding as he took notes. "Well, unfortunately, I don't have a ready answer for you. I am not immediately familiar with the drug and its contraindications, so will have to do some research to get accurate answers on how interferon impacts the fetus. What we can do is start a quick search to see what I can find while you are here and dig deeper for more information as needed."

He powered up his computer and rapidly tapped on the keyboard, his eyes darting across the flickering screen. He scrolled for a few moments, clicking through screens as I watched.

"This will take more time to investigate, but I have found a few cases. From this brief search, it looks like there are more case studies on women who were taking interferon and became pregnant. Interferon is often used for MS treatments."

He continued to talk as he scrolled.

"I am not immediately seeing any cases related to males taking the drug and its effect on pregnancy…"

"Do you think it could affect sperm?" I pushed, prodding to see if I could get some kind of definitive answer from him.

"It is hard to tell without proper case studies and findings," he replied evasively.

I deflated. I wasn't going to get any proper answers that day. He continued to scroll, but it was obvious that I would have to return later in hopes he had some answers for me.

"I'm sorry I wasn't able to procure more information for you today," he said as he turned from the computer. "With my limited research, I think the biggest risk at this point is a greater threat of miscarriage. I will get back to you once I have more time to investigate further."

Great. So maybe we wouldn't get excited about being pregnant just yet. It was back to one day at a time, just like Brad's treatments. One. Day. At. A. Time. And in the interim, a new life was swiftly growing inside of me. We were rapidly moving from embryo to fetus, and I had no idea if that was a good thing or not. Time would tell. And time had been fickle over the last year.

We moved back to wait and see. By the end of the first trimester, a fetus is fully formed, approximately 10 cm long, and has a much lower rate of miscarriage. That was what we were waiting for now. In the interim, I focused on Taryn and work, and tried not to dwell on the what ifs that surrounded us.

My follow-up appointment netted no further tangible answers. My sister was more successful in getting information by contacting the makers of interferon directly, but it ultimately didn't matter. I was still treading water. The second trimester was my goal. Until I reached it, I couldn't get excited about the pregnancy. Nobody could and the tension was rising.

"Fourteen weeks!" I said to Brad on the morning I slipped into the second trimester.

I had already had an ultrasound and done the initial bloodwork for the IPS: the Integrated Prenatal Screening checked for Down Syndrome, Trisomy 18, and other neural tube defects. They were standard prenatal tests and I thought nothing of them. In fact, the ultrasound was fun, as you got to see the tiny being that was growing inside you, plus hear the hoofbeat-like heartbeat pulsing away. I had undergone the IPS with Taryn, so hadn't thought twice about doing them with the new pregnancy. You had to do a second ultrasound and more bloodwork between 15 and 20 weeks, and I was already scheduled in for those too.

"Do you think we can get excited about being pregnant now? Maybe start to tell people?"

Brad had insisted we keep my pregnancy quiet until we knew if it was going to stick.

"Maybe wait another week," he suggested. "Just to be on the safe side."

I could understand his hesitation. Our entire universe had felt like it was in suspended animation for the last year. What was another day, another week more?

Another week, another ultrasound, and there wasn't any getting around it. My breasts and midsection had grown, and I struggled to slip into regular pants. I was pregnant and it didn't appear to be changing. In fact, although I hadn't said anything to Brad, I could feel a faint flutter deep inside of me. The baby was moving!

A week after my last round of bloodwork, the midwife called.

"The results from your IPS came in," Eve said. "You have a high screen positive result."

"What does that mean?" I asked, nervous hearing the somber tone in her voice.

"A screen positive test means you have a higher risk of having a baby with abnormalities like Down Syndrome or Trisomy 18. We recommend speaking with a genetic counsellor. They go over the risks and can order further tests to confirm the results one way or the other. If you decide to go that route, we need to schedule the appointment as soon as possible."

No wait and see any more.

"Okay," I stammered.

What choice did I have?

One of the reasons why I went with a midwife for both of my pregnancies was because I felt like I had more information and choice in what went on in the pregnancies. I learned more about the stages of development and the various tests available, plus why I should undergo

119

them or not. I was part of the team, instead of just being a patient with a condition. But this felt bigger than what I could understand. More in depth than I could wrap my head around.

Brad and I walked into the genetic counsellor's office a few days later. I needed his moral support for this appointment now. We didn't know what we were up against or how it might play out. The doctor was detailed about it all.

"Normally in this scenario we would do an amniocentesis. During the procedure, a needle is inserted through your abdomen wall and a small sample of amniotic fluid is extracted. We use ultrasound guidance throughout the procedure to ensure we do not touch the fetus. The sample is then tested to predict chromosomal abnormalities more accurately."

"In your case, because your number is so high, we can do another test while we are doing the amniocentesis. It is even more accurate, and we get results within a few days. The rest of the results come back within a week."

I looked at Brad. All these words were scary as hell to me, but what was he thinking?

"There are risks associated with amniocentesis. We are extremely careful during the procedure, but there is a small risk of miscarriage afterwards, about a 1 in 100 risk."

My stomach fluttered. Was it nerves or the baby? It had definitely made its presence known since the days when Eve had called to give me the news, making all of this even harder to process.

"We also need to discuss your options depending upon the outcome of the results. If you get positive results, there are decisions that need to be made, regarding whether you want to continue the pregnancy or terminate."

"I'm almost 20 weeks along," I stammered. "Can we do that?"

"The option is there, but we can discuss it further as needed. I just need you to understand what is entailed with the procedure and what you should consider before making your decisions. Today, you just need to decide whether you want to have the amniocentesis performed."

My breath was shallow inside me, as my brain screamed that this couldn't be happening. Didn't we have enough on our plates—new parents, Brad's cancer, and now a baby that possibly had Down Syndrome? I struggled to keep tears from slipping from my lashes, as I clenched my hands over and over in my lap.

"We need to do it Katherine," Brad said, looking at me.

I just nodded, as my hands slipped around my precious belly.

Before we knew it, we were back at the hospital for the procedure. I was the one to get a hospital band this time and it chafed against my skin. Brad and I had discussed what we would do if we found out the baby had Down Syndrome and Brad hadn't hesitated—terminate. I understood; if his own health slipped, he didn't want to sidle me with not one but two children, one of which would be extra work. Possibly a lot more And the decision was all about honesty. He didn't want to deal with it either.

The decision didn't feel as easy to me though. I had already felt movement and knew the baby was a live thing growing inside of me. For him, it was still little more than a concept. How could I live with myself ending a pregnancy? And wasn't I strong enough to be the mother this baby deserved, no matter the outcome? But could I do it alone if Brad took a turn for the worse and died?

For now, I just had to be brave enough to lie on the table and let the doctors do what they had to. True to the doctor's word, it was uncomfortable, but not overly painful. A pinch and push, but soon enough, I was redressed and getting the assurance that he would call in a few days with initial test results. All we needed to do was agonize for 48 hours or so about what the future held.

And agony was what it was. But two days later I got a phone call at work that released the air I had been holding since Eve called the week before. The results were negative! We still had to wait another four days to get the final results, but the degree of accuracy was so high, that the doctor had little issue declaring the fetus healthy.

At 20 weeks, a full halfway through my pregnancy, I could finally share and start to get excited that a new baby was on the way. We were going to have a baby!

A Pile of Stones

This is supposed to be a book about grief. So why am I talking about pregnancy, babies, and holidays? Why indeed?

The answer is simple. Grief is part of life. Grief is earned with every breath we take, with every smile, laugh, and tear we live. It is the everyday moments that make up our days that we end up missing the most. And I cannot get to the depths of grief and healing, if I don't relive the moments that come before loss. For what is loss, but the experience of losing someone who has touched us. How do you understand my healing journey if you don't know where I've been before? You don't.

Consider this my backstory. Consider this your opportunity to get to know me, so that you can better understand the journey I made. I am not just loss. No one is solely one experience. I have been molded by loss, but it is just one part of who I am. I was also a girlfriend who became a wife, a wife who became a mother, and a partner who walked beside a loved one facing a life-threatening illness. You might be some of these things too. Or you might not. The interesting thing about grief is that you can see parts of yourself in everyone's grief journey. There is confusion, shock, anger, sadness, bargaining, loneliness, denial, acceptance, and lots of reflection. Far more of it than you can ever imagine.

Why is that?

Life is like a collection of stones. Every moment we have lived is like a pebble put into a pocket. There are firsts that stick with us, that stay shiny and vibrant—first dates, first jobs, first kisses and heartaches. They hold more weight, but they are not the only stones in your pocket. There are other rocks that hold sharper edges, like arguments, disappointments, and missed opportunities. Sometimes only shards of memories remain, like the smell of freshly baked bread that Grandma made, the way the designated carver always sliced the turkey just so, or a hearty laugh that came out at just the right moments. You might not have a precise memory, but you retain the flavour of the people and places who are part of it.

All of those stones, pebbles, and shards are a part of our lives. They are all tucked away in corners of our minds, sometimes overlooked for lengthy periods, but not necessarily forgotten.

Now picture all those moments that happened with a specific someone. For some people, they might amount to a small pile—maybe a random co-worker who you only chat with occasionally during breaks. Other people might have slightly larger mounds—old high school friends whom you haven't seen in years, but still bring up memories of the good old days. And then there are the pillars in our lives—parents, children, spouses, best friends. The people you have shared innumerable moments; good, bad, ugly, and beyond beautiful. There are so many pebbles that are a part of their pile, that you can't even count them all. That pile is pretty significant.

Rocks, pebbles, shards... who cares? When someone exits your world, all you have left is their monument of stones. When you no longer have that person at hand, many people tend to look back through what is left of them. What's left is all those memories left behind. And you start to pick up the stones to re-examine the person in those memories. The more stones you have, the longer it takes to examine all those rocks. Some of them are fresh and shiny, others smooth by repeated examining, and sometimes you stumble across a pebble you forgot existed until you nudge the pile, and it shakes free.

So, why are all those stones a problem? In the immediate aftermath of loss, those stones feel like a mountain. They can feel like they weigh you down and suffocate every breath you try to take. It can be overwhelming to consider that mass and process all the moments. And it is. But the truth is, that mountain is also a gift. What you need to remember is that your loved one is in all those moments and the memories never disappear. As hard as it is when you first step into loss, at some point you recognize that while your person may no longer build new memories with you, if you know them well enough, they will still keep talking in your head and watching on as you make new memories. The rough edge of loss becomes a new stone of its own that you get to start rebuilding on top of once more.

What should you do with all those stones then? Pull them out, process the memories as they come, and be grateful for the moments you were gifted. And don't forget to keep living, even if it feels like you are walking on broken glass. Because those are new memories you will get to examine one day too.

Living in the Margins

So, I was pregnant, Brad had cancer, and life went on around us. The baby was due in October and after earlier complications, everything looked like life might be turning around. Brad continued to see Dr. J and take his interferon treatments. His antidepressants made for better moods and less swings. Taryn settled into daycare and continued to charm everyone she met. And now the focus was on preparing for the new addition to our family. Summer settled in and I began to be hopeful that we would get through all that the fates had thrown our way.

Plink…

A new pebble fell into our path.

"I'm going to trim the hedge," I announced to Brad on the Civic holiday weekend. "My belly rubs the bushes every time I get out of the van, and I can't take it anymore."

"Have at 'er," Brad announced, as he worked on the new back deck he was building with Taryn at his heels.

"Get Daddy that screwdriver baby," he said to his little adoring princess who did everything she could to please.

I dug the hedge trimmers out of the shed and began to slash away at our overgrown side. It was a beast, almost 10-feet tall and grew like mad over the course of the season. I generally pruned it twice a year, just to keep it in check. My unwieldy midsection meant that I had less room than normal to maneuver, so I trimmed with abandon in the hot summer sun, before retreating to the shade in the backyard with the rest of the family.

Long summer weekends are sweet, but always seem to fly too quickly by. Before we knew it, the work week was back, and we were hustling to get out of the house once more. Brad left first, as I finished feeding Taryn breakfast before herding her off to daycare. Before long though, I swung her onto my hip with her diaper bag, my lunch bag, and purse dangling off my other side. I stopped when I got to the van's door.

"What the..."

A huge glob of sputum clung to my driver's side window. Beyond gross. My blood started to boil.

"I'll deal with it at work," I muttered, as I shook myself out of it.

I strapped Taryn into her car seat, then climbed into the driver's seat. Splashed across the windshield were the dregs of a coffee and another huge chunk of phlegm. I wanted to scream. It wasn't a bird. It wasn't an accident. It was a deliberate act of rage directed at my family. For what reason, I couldn't even guess.

I drove Taryn to daycare, then stormed into work.

"I need a squeegee," I demanded.

Good thing I worked at an autobody shop. There was no damage, aside from to my hormonal brain. Eventually I settled into work and focused on the tasks at hand. But the end of the day had another surprise for me.

I picked Taryn up from daycare and we headed to the backyard to relax before starting dinner. As was my wont, I wandered around the garden, inspecting my growing plant babies. My garden was my sanctuary that always brought me joy. But today it brought me horror. Tall decorative grasses planted beside the fence lay flattened. On further inspection, I realized they had been chopped a few inches from the ground. I had looked at them the day before and they were thigh high. Now everything in the garden beside the fence was mangled and smashed. I raced inside to phone Brad, spluttering my rage.

"Calm down," he said. "I'll be home soon. I'm sure it's not that bad."

But it got worse. I returned to the fence and looked around some more. This time I noticed some trumpet vines that had grown through the fence from the neighbour's, now lying on the grass. I looked closer and found more.

"He came into the yard to destroy plants because I pruned the hedge!" I fumed. "What a dick!"

I picked up the plants and walked to the end of the yard. Brad's beloved 1971 Oldsmobile Cutlass Supreme sat at the front of the driveway. More vines lay beside it. I walked slowly over to the car, dreading what I might find.

"Oh no," I whispered in fear. "Please no. Brad is going to lose his mind…"

But it was too late to pray. A scratch started on the front quarter panel and dug down the length of the car. At points, the scratch ended, only to continue just below the first line. It etched every panel down the length of the car and was deep enough to be felt with your thumb. That meant it would need to be refinished. It wouldn't just buff out.

"Dear God, Brad is going to freak! Oh my God. What is wrong with him?!"

Him was our neighbour and we had had issues with him since moving into the house. He sat on his front porch heckling anyone who walked by day and night. The police often showed up in the middle of the night, their red lights eerily floating across our bedroom walls, as they tried to smooth out disputes between him and another neighbour across the road. But this time, he had attacked us, for little more than me trimming the hedge that grew on our mutual property line. And when Brad got home and saw his vandalized car, I feared he would kill him. The plants no longer mattered.

"I can't call again." I reasoned. "Like he said, he'll be home soon. I'll just show him; hopefully be able to calm him down before any rash decisions are made…"

I didn't have long to wait. Brad walked in the house a few minutes later. I led him into the back yard to show him the gardens and slashed plants, then picked up the sharp vines and walked over to his cherished Oldsmobile. He didn't say a word as he ran his hand down the marred lines of the classic car. But it was too much. I could see him trying to pull himself together, but he turned and stormed to the

128

neighbour's front door. The coward saw him coming and scrambled to escape into the house before Brad could confront him, but Brad jammed his foot into the door as it swung shut.

I went into the house so Taryn wouldn't have to hear what might be said. I will leave you to your imagination to fill in the gaps.

Over the next couple of weeks, we contacted the police, the city, and finally a hardware store. There was no proof, therefore no recourse from police.

"Without surveillance footage, there's nothing we can do. I can talk to your neighbour, but your best bet is to safeguard your property more securely."

The city had more concrete answers: they advised us how high we could build the fence.

"You can't do that," the neighbours sneered, as the fence boards were screwed into place between the yards.

But we could and we did, despite their promises to call the city themselves. Good fences make good neighbours, and the new barrier was a welcome addition to keep prying eyes and hands out.

That was not the end of the troubles though.

"Are you sure you don't want to come?" I asked again a few days later, as I finalized packing Taryn's bag.

"To sleep on a lumpy pullout couch in a basement apartment after just having surgery? No thanks. I'm good."

"You would get to see Jeff and Laura too though," I added.

"Baby showers don't sweeten the deal."

I knew he wouldn't come but felt bad leaving him a week after his latest surgery. Dr. T was away, but another surgeon had gone in to remove more lymph nodes from Brad's groin. Dr. J suggested the timing was good, as Dr. T wouldn't have wanted to mess around in an area where she had already operated, but her substitute didn't seem concerned. Brad and I agreed that infected anything needed to go, so now he was back on short-term disability recovering. His cancer didn't fill as many hours as it had the previous summer, but it refused to be forgotten. The difference was, we refused to be owned by it.

"Just go," Brad said again. "I'll be fine."

Secretly, I was happy for the break from him, but I would never admit it. There was strength in the spaces between our togetherness. Khalil Gibran[6] said as much many years earlier and I understood that all too well. Love was stronger when you were two pillars working together, but not limited to one footing. The spaces between made us better. I fretted until I turned the key in the ignition, then looked forward to my weekend ahead with a smile.

"How was your weekend?" I asked when I returned two days later.

"Interesting, to say the least."

"Interesting?"

"Ya, the neighbour officially lost his shit."

He proceeded to tell me about the aftermath of what had gone on during my absence. What should have been a quiet weekend of Brad

---

[6] Gibran, K. (1923). "But let there be spaces in your togetherness, And let the winds of the heavens dance between you." *The Prophet*. Alfred A. Knopf.

catching up on shows I didn't appreciate, turned into the farthest thing from relaxing.

"I heard the loose cannon freaking out in the backyard on Saturday afternoon and went upstairs to peek on what he was going off about from the back bedroom. He was slamming around and loudly shouting about the neighbour across the road. I figured it was same old, same old. Those two love pushing each other's buttons. But then doofus heads to the front yard, and there's the neighbour egging him on."

"Oh lord," I said.

"Ya, I figure this is going to be a good one, as it's during the middle of the day, versus their regular fights in the middle of the night."

"Anyway, the neighbour across the way starts twisting him up. Yelling shit at him and trying to get him to lose his shit. It worked. Before long they are both screaming and other neighbours are peeking out their windows too. Front row seats for everyone."

"Great," I sighed sadly.

"Oh no! It gets better!" Brad said. "Dude across the street goes in, then comes out claiming to have called the cops. In the interim, our next-door neighbour goes in and comes back out with a baseball bat. He starts shouting, 'I'm going to play baseball, but you're not going to like the way I play. I'm going to play ball with heads!' Then he starts smashing the bat into his awning calling out house numbers for all the houses around us. By this time, I had tried to calm the fucker down and gotten screamed at, so called the police myself. The older couple were now outside, as well as the two ladies across the street. It was turning into a shit show."

"Oh shit!" I exclaimed in alarm.

"So then, the fucktard goes into his house again and come out with a gun case this time—a rifle case. He starts waving that around..."

"What!" I cried. "Where the hell were the police?"

"London's finest were nowhere on the scene. I called again when the gun case came out though."

"Where were you?"

"I talked to everyone on the other side of the road to see their take on the bullshit at one point, then came home. I was on the porch until shit got serious, then dove inside to call the cops. They showed up pretty quick when I said whack job had a gun."

"Good," I hadn't realized I was holding my breath until then.

"They talked him down. Went into the house for a look around but found nothing. There wasn't a gun in the case, but after talking to all the neighbours, they decided it was best not to leave things as they were. The neighbour across the way said he wanted to press charges, so they took the nut job away."

"Oh my God," I said again. "That's crazy!"

"No shit," Brad agreed.

"Well, I'm glad they took him away. Dude is unstable."

As it turned out, he was slapped with a restraining order preventing him from being anywhere within a several block radii of the neighbour across the road for six months. I was more than happy to think that life might get a little quieter, just in time for the new baby to arrive.

It didn't last though.

By the time he came back, we had a brand-new healthy baby girl, making us a family of four. Rylie was born at the end of October after a speedy four-hour labour. I got to the hospital just before 5:00 a.m. and by 9:00 a.m. we were walking out the door with our bundle of joy. She scored perfect on her Apgar scores, had 10 fingers and toes, and latched immediately, giving me the illusion that life would be smooth sailing from there on out. We were now happy and complete. Right? Something like that.

By the time baby's first Christmas was in the rearview, we had packed away the holiday ornaments and anything else we could spare to stage our home for sale. By the end of February, the real estate deals were done, but for signing final paperwork on closing day in April. A single-level bungalow awaited us in a new neighbourhood.

As much as we had developed a bit of camaraderie with the remaining neighbours since the incident, it wasn't enough to convince us to raise our young family next door to a ticking timebomb. The first thing he did upon arriving home in March was to smash a dollar store 'No Trespassing' sign in their postage-size front yard.

No problem. We were out!

Chapter 5: Quality of Life

April Fool's

Brad was in a foul mood. He slammed around the kitchen as we got ready to go grocery shopping. He didn't say a word, but it was easy to tell he was fuming about something. By the thick tension around him, I wasn't sure I wanted to know the cause.

"I want to swing by the new house," Brad announced, after I finished clipping the girls into their car seats. "Dad went by there earlier this week and called me. Said the neighbour was up to something, so we drove by together. The guy tore out the hedge and has started building a new fence."

"Okay," I answered cautiously. "And..."

We hadn't even moved in yet, and already there were problems.

"And the question is — where is the property line? Is he building the fence on it or putting it on our property? Why is he doing it before we move in? Why not wait and share the cost? What's the deal?"

I could tell Brad and his dad had talked about it and those conversations hadn't been positive. Not only did we have a poor track record with our current neighbour, but Brad's parents hadn't had any better luck with any of theirs. Together, they had turned this new twist into something that had Brad boiling. I sensed that any of my attempts to alleviate the perceived threat would fall on mute ears, so I chose to quietly press myself into my seat and hope to point out some kind of plus side once we got there. It mattered little that the hedge was overgrown, and the rickety picket fence could barely be seen inside of it. The neighbour was obviously out to get us again. Lord help me, but I didn't have the strength to fight anew.

We didn't get out of the car, but indeed the hedge was gone, as was the previous fence. Honestly, it was an improvement, but saying that didn't help matters. Grocery shopping didn't improve Brad's mood either. It wasn't until he was ensconced on the couch with a cold beer in front of him that I could separate myself from his black cloud. I slipped into the kitchen to start pulling Sunday dinner together. I turned on the oven to preheat it for the roast chicken I had prepared, then began scrubbing potatoes to cut up for mash. I popped my head into the doorway from the kitchen and started to ask how many potatoes he wanted, but my question died on my lips. Brad was leaned over with a hand on the beer on the floor and an odd look on his face.

A chill crept over.

"What are you doing?" I asked slowly. "Are you okay?"

He was concentrating.

"Brad, what's going on?" I asked again when he didn't immediately answer.

"I... I can't move my arm," he replied with a fierce look on his face. "I went upstairs to use the bathroom, then came downstairs and sat back down again. When I reached for my beer, I couldn't sit back up."

He sat on the couch bent at the waist. At first glance, nothing looked necessarily amiss, but confusion and anger boiled in his eyes.

"What do you… what do you mean," I whispered, as my heart started to race.

"I mean, I can't move my arm! I can't feel it."

"Ummm… uhhh…"

'Think!' I mentally screamed to myself.

I looked from him to the stove and moved to shut the oven off. I didn't have the capacity to keep track of both.

"Can you move your fingers?" I asked when I stepped back into the living room.

"I'm trying," he spat.

"Okay, okay," I reasoned. "How about your toes? Your leg?"

"I haven't tried that," he admitted, as he focused anew on regaining control of his truant limbs.

"Anything?" I asked desperately, as I inched towards him. "Can you feel anything? Tingly? Numbness? Pain?"

"Just gimme a fucking second," he shot back. "Fuck!"

"Should I call someone? An ambulance? Your parents?"

"Just fucking hold on," he fumed.

With his left hand, he reached over to grab his right shirt sleeve. With gargantuan effort, he hefted the dead limb towards himself, pushing himself back into the couch with a grunt.

I shot forward, desperate to do something—anything—but held back, so as not to piss him off further. I stood trembling, undecided in front of him, my mind racing with what to do. How could

I fix this? How could I make it better? My newborn lay strapped into her swing back chair a few feet away. I clambered over to pick her up, scrambling for some kind of action in order to not look as useless as I felt. It didn't help.

I suddenly remembered a magnet I received when Taryn was born. It had a number for Telehealth on it—a resource to call when you needed advice for a sick baby. Or sick anyone. You could call and talk to a nurse to ask for advice. And that is exactly what we needed right then.

"What about Telehealth?" I asked. "If you don't want me to call an ambulance, we could call and ask them what to do?"

It had been over 10 agonizing minutes since I had poked my head into the living room. Taryn cowered in the corner, sensing the tension in the adults around her. Brad glared at his unresponsive body, too angry to let fear take over just yet. But sheer will wasn't doing enough. It wasn't doing anything.

"Fine," he grudgingly agreed.

I plunked Rylie back in her chair and scrambled for the phone. I ran to the kitchen and hastily dialed the number. It rang once, twice. Then a voice greeted me and asked how they could be of service.

"My husband can't move his right arm," I blurted. "His right leg either."

"Okay," said the kindly voice. "What happened before that?"

I explained that he had gone upstairs, then come back down, only to find himself partially paralyzed once he sat down.

"Does he have any pain?" they asked.

I spun to Brad, repeating the questions they asked. "Numbness, nausea, dizziness…"

No, no, no.

"He has cancer," I finally added. "Could that have anything to do with it?"

But they weren't doctors. Only nurses doing their best to answer questions of desperate mothers, uncertain what temperature was too high for babies or how to tell if a cough was worthy of a doctor's trip.

"We would advise you to call an ambulance," they finally stated. "We can keep you on the line and contact them for you. Would you like us to do that?"

I turned to Brad with a desperate look in my eyes. It had been approximately 20 minutes, and his right side was completely numb. Nothing he did changed that. Fear finally won.

"Okay," he quietly agreed.

They patched us through to dispatch and got our particulars, then assured us that help was on the way.

"Call my parents and tell them what's going on," Brad said when I hung up.

Time was of the essence now. I dialed Joan and explained what was happening, letting her know an ambulance was on the way.

"We'll be there as soon as we can," she replied, as they too sprang into action.

What to do until they got there? I double checked that I had turned off everything in the kitchen, then sped out the front door to scan the street for the ambulance. I ran back inside, only to check on Brad again.

"Can you feel anything? Do you have any pain? Can you move anything yet?"

No.

"Maybe I should pack a bag?" I asked.

"Just sit," Brad demanded.

But I flew out the front door once more, willing an ambulance into sight. My heart raced, as I begged the universe for this not to be happening.

"Please, please, please..." I chanted, as I stared left, right, then left again.

I returned inside, only to pace back and forth, staring out the window with my mind whirling. What was happening?

It seemed an agonizingly long wait, but they finally pulled up in front of the house. I scrambled to the front door and ushered the two uniformed men inside, stumbling over the story once more.

"Hello sir," said one of the attendants turning to Brad. "What seems to be the trouble? How can we help you?"

While my story helped, Brad took center stage. He was the patient, and I was relegated to the back of the stage once more. I felt a twinge at the by now familiar dismissal but tried to focus on their lifesaving skills. They had brought in a kit bag and now began to unpack it.

"We are going to check your vitals," the attendant squatting beside Brad stated, as they listened to his version of events.

Temperature, blood pressure, listen to his heart—all regular tests that all medical professionals started with. They also checked his reflexes, asking questions as they went.

"What's your pain level on a scale of 1 to 10, with 1 being the lowest and 10 the highest?"

"Can you feel anything when we touch you here? How about here?"

"What were you doing before this happened?"

Brad's answers didn't give any clues as to what might be going on. He was in no pain, felt nothing, and had been watching tv before his trip upstairs. Nothing strenuous. I couldn't help but remember his stress from the morning but kept quiet for fear of disturbing the EMS's work. I willed them to have everything under control.

"I think it's best that we take you to the hospital to have them assess what's going on," they finally announced after running the limited battery of tests they had available in the field.

I knew that was the last thing Brad wanted to do, but he wasn't regaining feeling or mobility. Something needed to be done and he knew it.

"Okay," Brad answered.

"I'll grab a few things," I finally blurted out.

"He'll need his health card," one of the EMS techs told me, before heading out the door to collect the stretcher.

I sprang into action, grateful to feel like I had a purpose.

"Don't go nuts grabbing stuff," Brad piped in. "We don't know how long I'll be there, and they don't have room for all kinds of junk in the ambulance."

Chastised, I nodded as I stepped out of their way. This was about Brad. I had to let the professionals do their job. I needed to stay out of the way.

As the ambulance attendants got to the porch, they lifted the legs of the stretcher and carried it up the stairs, then dropped them back down to wheel it into the house.

"Do you think you can stand for a moment, so we can get you onto the stretcher?" the first EMS asked.

"Ya," Brad gamely replied.

He hadn't moved from the couch since losing feeling in his right side, so I wasn't so sure he would be able to, but damned if Brad was willing to play invalid. As the men supported him, Brad rose and hopped onto the waiting bed on wheels. They immediately set to strapping him down to secure him for the ride, before wheeling him out onto the porch, then down to the waiting ambulance.

I followed, afraid to breathe lest tears overwhelmed me.

"Just so you know, we are taking him to University Hospital," the first EMS said.

"Okay," I replied. "Thank you."

Just as Brad was popped into the back of the ambulance, Joan and Art pulled up. They jumped out of the car and ran to where I stood.

"What's going on," Joan demanded out of breath.

"They are taking him to University Hospital," I answered. "Go with them Art!"

"You should go," Joan insisted.

"I have to feed Rylie before I can go anywhere," I reasoned.

We were all only too aware of how persnickety she was when it came to a bottle. When we were house hunting over the winter months, we left Taryn with Gram and Pup, but had to take the new baby along for the search, as she refused any bottle we tried. Plus, she wouldn't take a soother and was hard to soothe on a good day. It wasn't a fair ask to leave her with anyone for any period of time. And they knew that.

Art scrambled after the ambulance, but they swung the doors shut without admitting him. No room for other passengers. He would have to follow in his own car. As the ambulance pulled away from the curb, Art ran back to his own car and jumped back behind the wheel. Joan and I went into the house.

"Have you eaten?" I asked on auto pilot, as I reached for Rylie. "There's a chicken in the oven and potatoes on the stove. You need to finish cooking it, but everything is ready to go."

My mind raced ahead of me, as I mentally flipped through what I needed to do. Grab a toothbrush. Pack underwear (He would probably be wearing a hospital gown? Did I need anything else?). Maybe grab a magazine? I would feed Rylie, then see if I could squeeze off a little more milk to leave for her. Taryn would be fine in her Gramma's care, but I prayed Rylie would be satisfied with whatever I could leave her and hopefully go to sleep easily for her grandmother.

What other option did I have? I needed to get to the hospital myself as quickly as possible, but I also had to make sure everyone was taken care of before I left.

Go. Go. Go...

Before I knew it, I was parking the van and racing into the emergency department to get an update on what was happening with Brad. Art sat small and quiet in a row of hard, plastic chairs.

"What's going on?" I exclaimed, as I reached him.

"I don't know," he answered. "They took him in for tests but haven't told me anything other than that."

Not good enough for me, I flew to the front desk.

"My husband was brought in in an ambulance. I need to know what's going on," I demanded.

I didn't care if I was loud or brash. This was no time to be a shrinking violet. It was one thing to be respectful, but I wasn't capable of being demure as dread filled me. I needed answers.

"What's your husband's name," the nurse asked, as she checked her files.

"Brad Labravoure."

"Yes, here he is," the woman replied. "He came in about 40 minutes ago. They have admitted him and are running some tests. I don't really know much more than that. If you could take a seat...as soon as we know more someone will let you know."

Gah! Waiting!!! How could I sit in these sterile seats and stare at a tiny television set, content to silently read news bites at a time like this? I dropped into the seat beside Art to share what the desk nurse had said, but quickly got up to pace over to the doors leading into the depths of the ER. I still couldn't wrap my head around what was going on. Panic filled me, as our ordeal spread into the evening. How was the day slipping by as fast as it was? How was it that Brad had been admitted into hospital? What was going on?!

"Family of Bradley Labravoure?" a voice asked.

"Here," I called as I sprang to my feet.

A nurse stood at the door I had just vacated. Did they notice my panic and feel pity on me? Or was it more like removing someone who might make others uncomfortable with my obvious distress as I stalked around the waiting room? Whatever the reason, the nurse ushered Art and I to a room within the ER where we could wait for Brad and the doctors in privacy.

"Thank you," I offered earnestly.

"Brad is getting a CT scan done," she said before turning to leave the room. "Once he is back on the floor, someone will take you to see him."

The kindness wasn't lost on me, even if it only meant switching us from one waiting room to another. How long would we have to wait, I wondered?

It turned out it wasn't long.

The door to our small exam room opened and another nurse walked in.

"Brad has just been brought down," she said. "You are welcome to leave your things here, but I can take you to where the doctor is talking to him."

I left my coat on the chair, and Art and I followed her out into the crowded hallway. Brad lay in a hospital bed, divided from other patients by curtained partitions. As we approached, the doctor talking to Brad paused.

"You must be Brad's wife," he said with a kind smile.

"Yes, Katherine" I replied. "And this is his father, Art. What's going on? They told us you had run some tests. How long before we get results?"

"Yes, we did." the doctor answered, as he turned to Brad. "Before I get to that, Brad, how are you feeling? Have you regained any feeling on your right-hand side?"

"No," Brad answered grimly. "Nothing yet."

I wanted to reach out and fling myself around him but feared making a scene. While Brad might have appreciated the connection, neither him nor Art were comfortable with public acts of affection. Squeezing his hand would have brought me comfort, but the confines of our curtained space meant that the doctor needed all the room he could get around his patient. I would get my chance, but right now, needed to make space for the doctor's exam.

He started by listening to Brad's heart with his stethoscope, then checked his reflexes once more. I felt strangled by the questions that wanted to spill from me but forced myself to remain calm and let the man do his work. Art seemed to shrink into himself, as we watched.

After a few other cursory checks, the doctor got to the heart of the matter.

"As you came in exhibiting stroke-like symptoms, our immediate response was to run a CT scan. CT scan imagery gives us an in-depth picture of internal organs and structures to let us know what we may not be able to see from the outside. In your case, we were looking at your brain and came across some dark sections."

He paused before going on.

"Those areas exhibited what looked like a bleed. We looked at your file and under the circumstances, it led us to certain conclusions. While I am not a neurological oncology specialist, it looks like the cancer may have spread to your brain."

I grabbed Brad's hand. I didn't care any longer. Art seemed to wilt in the corner.

"We have contacted the Cancer Clinic, and they are going to send over one of their team members from the Neurological Department. In the interim, we are going to admit you to the ICU."

I had questions. So many questions. I was desperate for him to give me the answers that I wanted to hear, but he was just a doctor in the ER. He was not a specialist. He didn't know Brad's case any further than what was written on his file in the computer. He was making best guesses based on a blur on a scan. There had been a bleed in Brad's brain, which caused the sudden paralysis on his right-hand side. It wasn't a stroke. No ordinary bleed that they could jump in and stem. The cancer had spread to Brad's brain, and he didn't have pretty answers to offer us. My questions desperately battered at the truth he hung in the air around us, but there was nothing to cling to in that moment.

"Why don't you two go back to the exam room and wait while I finish up with Brad. He'll be down shortly."

Art and I mechanically shifted back to the now stifling room. The door shut behind us and Art collapsed into the chair. He couldn't hold them back any further. Sobs wracked him, as the grim news settled over us.

The cancer had spread to Brad's brain. It was news we could never have anticipated, nor dreamed of. When it comes to cancer, spread is never good. In fact, usually it is deadly.

Only a few months before, Dr. J had suggested Brad might be in remission. That beautiful hope disappeared, as Art wept in my arms. His boy was incredibly sick, and optimism was hard to find in that tiny room. We clung to each other, trying to process what it meant. What the future might hold. I held one of the strongest men I knew stripped raw and tried to offer comfort to us both in this dark hour. There was little comfort to be had though.

By the time Brad was wheeled in, Art had pulled himself back together and made to leave.

"'ll leave you two to talk," he said. "I have to let Joan know what's going on."

He clapped Brad on the shoulder and left.

Finally, I dissolved into my husband and wept for us. I crawled into bed beside him, and we clung to each other with the dawning of horror. But I couldn't stay either.

"I need you to call Don and let him know I won't be in tomorrow. He can deal with sick pay stuff and whatever needs to be done with that. We'll need to talk to Ken too about the house closing."

"I'll call Don as soon as I get home," I promised. "And I'll talk to Ken tomorrow. I'll call my mom too to see if she can come help with the kids while we figure out what's going on. While you are in hospital."

Ultimately though, after touching on those practical matters, the most pressing matter was the kids.

"You need to go," Brad said gently. "Rylie will be needing you and my Mum and Dad will need to get home. There's nothing more you can do here right now."

He was right, but my God, leaving him in hospital always stabbed at my heart. He belonged home with me and the girls, not in some stuffy hospital with no one who knew or cared about him. How could I abandon him to the thoughts that swirled around his brain? His injured brain! The cancer was there now too! Just when life was turning a corner, fate stepped back in with an evil surprise that we never saw coming.

The worst part—it was April 1st. Worst April Fool's joke ever. And it made the day the farthest thing from funny for years to come.

Hospital Stay

"Brad won't be in to work…"

"He's in hospital again…"

"The emerg doctor said it has spread to his brain…"

"We are waiting for a specialist to come in from the Cancer Clinic…"

How could I fumble my way through these conversations? I had to call Brad's work, my mom, sister, our real estate agent, and close friends to update them on this new turn of events. No, I didn't know how long he would be in hospital, if he would regain strength to his right side, or what might happen next. It all felt overwhelming and surreal and far too much to deal with, while also taking care of a 5-month-old and 2-year-old.

"I'm on my way."

That's all I needed to hear. My mom was coming to help. She would be here to help with the babies, meals, and more importantly to process what it all meant. All while I also sorted out the imminent closing of our real estate deal in a few short weeks, plus figure out what the doctors planned next in Brad's cancer journey.

There were so much better trips I had been on! I wanted to cancel this one and get a full refund on this nightmare voyage. Time to cash in our chips, hand back our cancer passport, and set sail for "normal life" again. Anyone? Anyone?!

Nope, we had to wait for the neurologist to come weigh in on what was going on in Brad's head. When he would be there was anyone's guess. Hurry up and wait, while the clock was ticking on our pending move. And I had to wait for my mom to arrive from Guelph before I could head back to the hospital to make any plans.

Of course, first step was checking to see if any of Brad's mobility had come back.

Nope.

The ICU is an interesting place. There was a nursing station in the middle of the room with hospital beds lined up like spokes around the perimeter. Machines constantly beeped and whirred, doing their part to monitor patients, keeping them stable and alive. And while some might have understood better how it all worked, my frazzled brain absorbed little more than that a fabric curtain was our wall and privacy barrier between us and the other strangers in the room. It wasn't a place you wanted to spend much time in if you had the choice.

We didn't.

I get that the layout leant itself to maximizing the effectiveness of the nursing staff, but it was scary to the lay people who found themselves there. I was certainly one of them. Until Brad got moved to a more private room, I couldn't spend long there anyway, and visitors weren't exactly encouraged. Brad was okay with that, as he wanted out more than anything. Well, maybe he wanted control of his right-hand side more, but he wasn't a fan of hospital stays by that point. Especially not emergency ones. So, my brief early visits accounted to nothing more than checking in on him and figuring out what immediate next steps should be:

- ✓ Cancel the moving van
- ✓ Talk to the mortgage broker about finalizing paperwork
- ✓ Explain what was going on to the lawyer in case I needed to sign anything on Brad's behalf as his Power of Personal Care
- ✓ Keep family members and Brad's work updated on Brad's ongoing condition

It was a lot. Oh, plus I also had to eat, sleep, feed and interact with my children, and try to wrap my head around WHAT WAS

GOING ON! Too much. I just had to keep going. Keep going and keep going. Be strong. Ask the right questions. Give the right answers. And try not to break down thinking about it all. I was the captain of this ship and damned if I wouldn't do everything I could to keep us afloat, even if we strayed way off course.

By Tuesday, physiotherapists had started working with Brad to regain strength, but we were still waiting for the famed neurologist to arrive. Needless to say, Brad's temper was getting short.

"How are you feeling today?" I asked with a cheery smile, as I walked in for my umpteenth visit.

"Fine," he answered abruptly.

Oh, okay, back to fine. That was never good.

As I handed him my newest care package of magazines and fresh underwear, I asked if he had heard word about the infamous specialist we were waiting on.

"When the on-call doctor checked me this morning, they thought the neurologist might be in tomorrow. Apparently, I'm not a priority."

What do you say to that? How could I break that sour spell he was under? Until he was home, it was a struggle.

"I'm sure he will be here as soon as he can. He probably has all kinds of patients and has to plan it all accordingly. It must be a scheduling nightmare…"

Not that Brad's world wasn't a nightmare, but he was also just a nameless number at this point. At least he was allowed visitors. It helped with the feeling of anonymity, if not the helplessness.

"Well, hopefully we'll see him tomorrow. See what he has to say."

It felt lame, but I was struggling too. I didn't have any better answers or suggestions, just updates on who I had talked to and what was going on beyond the hospital walls. In retrospect though, if I could have somehow stopped tomorrow from coming, I would have. It wasn't worth waiting for, although it did propel us out of the stasis we were stuck in. Not in the way we hoped though.

The next day, I bustled in cheery as ever. Damned if I didn't pull every strained positive mindset out of the ethers on my way up in the elevator, but the efforts faded as I stepped in the door. I could tell Brad was fuming.

"I'm leaving," he spat.

"Wha…," I stammered. "What's going on?"

"Our illustrious neurologist just left."

I looked over my shoulder, wondering if I had passed him in the hall on my way in.

"What did he say," I asked hopefully, already dreading the answer.

My world started to shrink around me as Brad reported the visit.

"Dude waltzed in here with a team of interns behind him. I told him you were on your way, but he pulled the screen around the bed and launched into his spiel regardless. Said the cancer had spread to my brain—we know that already! But with all his great expertise, there's nothing he can do about it. 'It's in a spot I can't operate on', he says."

"What can he do?" I asked desperately.

"Nothing," Brad answered. "He sat there with this team of interns staring at their shoes behind him and said I have six months to a year to live. And then he turned around and walked out. If they can't do anything about it, then I am damn well not sticking around here for shits and giggles. I am going home."

And he swung his legs off the bed to start rummaging through the bedside table to get his street clothes.

I was stunned. Six months? Maybe a year? No operations, drugs, or treatment plans? Nothing he could do? I felt dizzy with the magnitude of it but understood Brad's need to get out. We were done with waiting. But what were we heading for?

"Alright," I managed. "I'll go let the nurses know you are leaving."

This was something him and I could agree on. I wanted him home with me too.

By the time I came back, Brad was throwing things into the bag I had brought. A doctor hustled in behind me and broke Brad's angry scene.

"I heard you were wanting to leave," he said, as he approached. "We don't recommend that at this time. There are physiotherapists here who can help you regain your strength. We would still like to monitor your condition to see where things are at…"

"No offense, Doc, but I'm not interested," Brad answered point blank. "Your specialist didn't offer me anything. No surgeries or special treatments. So why stay? I am done. I am going home."

I could tell this man had done his best to wrap his head around Brad's case and find compassion for what he was going through. Brad had just been told he was going to die. Not at some indeterminate time way off in the future, but now. Not when he was old and grey—in six months to a year. You could tell he was grappling with what his medical expertise suggested and the existential crisis that the news laid bare.

"Okay," he relented with a slow nod. "I can get the release forms prepared and your prescriptions written, but will you give me a moment to let me pray for you?"

Neither Brad nor I were religious people, but that moment was a powerful one. Brad softened and we stood quietly, as this stranger poured his prayers into the ethos on our behalf. He gave us so much more than his predecessor offered, but it still felt like the first nail in a coffin. We had moved beyond pills and medicine into the realm of hopes and prayers.

I think it is safe to say that this is when I went into shock. I stayed there for the next six months.

Moving On

It was April 5th. Only five days earlier, we had been in the middle of planning our move. Now, new doctor appointments had hurriedly been added to the schedule for the day after Brad arrived home from hospital. He was slated for a full day at the Cancer Clinic, with appointments with a Radiologist, the Head of Neurological Surgery, whom I had yet to meet, and of course, Dr. J, Brad's main Oncologist. The story they shared wasn't any better though.

First stop was the famed Neurologist. Honestly, he was a waste of time. He didn't have his team of interns around him this time, but his bedside manners weren't any better. His story held doom and gloom with nothing new to report. No surgery. No chance. No point in ever seeing him again.

The radiologist wasn't much better. She at least had a plan though. In clinical terms, she outlined the plan of attack.

"I'll have you come in next week to get you fitted for a shield for radiation treatments. As soon as it is ready, we'll begin. Radiation is a powerful procedure, so we can only offer so many treatments to a given area. Our hope is to shrink the tumour, but ultimately can't make any promises."

Another ray of sunshine decidedly lacking in the warmth we could really have used right about then.

Then it was on to Dr. J. As usual, we started with his nurse, and she offered the brightest light we had felt in days. She wasn't a doctor, but she had compassion and practicality on her side, and before she shuffled us off to Dr. J, we had a temporary disability sign to stick in the windshield of our vehicle. She might not have been able to do much, but she understood that with Brad's mobility issues, having a little shorter distance to walk was handy. What might Dr. J offer?

"Brad," he said, as we walked into the office. "I am so sorry for what you have gone through this week."

"Ya," Brad mumbled. "It hasn't exactly been a party."

"No," Dr. J agreed. "And I am sorry that you have had this experience. I wish I could offer better news myself, but I have had a chance to look at the scans and talk to Dr. P as well. The mass in your head is in a difficult spot. As I'm sure he mentioned, an operation is not possible. The proximity of so many other vitals makes the procedure too difficult and risky to perform. Ultimately, it is not an option."

"What is an option then?" I asked. "What can we do?"

Dr. J sighed heavily and turned to face us squarely.

"I am not going to lie to you, but neither am I going to make any promises," he said. "Honestly, I am incredibly angry that anyone talked timelines with you at all. I do not believe they create the right mindset. If you are given a certain life expectancy, then live longer, some people get angry and want to sue. Alternately, people give up hope and fail faster than they might have otherwise. I don't feel like it helps the overall mindset to dwell on time, rather it is more beneficial to focus on what you have today."

"That leads me to my next topic," he continued. "While I do not want to talk about expectancy, I do want you to think about quality of life. You do not have to make a decision today, but I think it is time to introduce a palliative doctor."

There are so many terms in the medical vocabulary, but this was one I was familiar with. For those who don't know, a palliative doctor is essentially an end-of-life doctor. When the rest of the medical team has run their course, the palliative doctor comes in to wrap up the end game. Their mantra is "Quality of Life" over most people's

156

expectations of 'quantity'. We were now at quality over quantity. Words dried up in my throat.

The whirlwind of appointments didn't end there though. Our next stop was the lawyer. While Friday was technically a holiday, Mr. J had agreed to come in on Good Friday to discuss our predicament. My mom had finally gone home by that point, so we bundled up the kids and made our way to his office in the silent downtown core. He buzzed us up himself, as his office was only open on our account.

"Brad, Katherine," he said. "Good to see you. Sorry it isn't under better circumstances."

"We are so sorry to interrupt your Easter weekend plans," I gushed. "Thank you so much for agreeing to see us on so short of notice."

While I had spoken to his secretary earlier in the week about Brad's circumstances, it wasn't until the day before that our need had grown as dire. Today's conversation didn't revolve around Brad's illness though. This one had everything to do with the closing of our real estate deal.

"Tell me what happened," Mr. J asked directly.

"As you know, Brad was hospitalized last Sunday. I called our mortgage broker to ask him to start preparing the documents for the sale of the house, just in case there were complications. He said he would get on it, so I left him to it, but reminded him that the life insurance had to carry over. When Brad came home from hospital on Wednesday, he popped by the house with said documents, but they included a new application for life insurance. Brad can't apply though.

The doctors just told him he had months to live. We need to keep the existing life insurance policy, but he doesn't seem to understand that."

I made the exchange seem quite civilized, but it hadn't gone down exactly as I described. I had dropped Brad at home after his release from hospital, then went out to pick up his medications. While I was gone, the broker stopped by and gave Brad the forms he had prepared.

"What's this?" Brad asked when he got to the new life insurance application in amongst the other papers. "This was supposed to be a transfer. I can't apply for new insurance."

The man spluttered and stammered, which quickly made things worse.

"I was just told I am going to die," Brad stated in a measured tone, trying to keep the anger at bay. "No one is going to approve a new policy. You need to transfer the existing policy to the new house, so that my wife and children are protected. Do you understand?"

"Well, yes, but..." he might have finally understood, but figuring out how to make it happen was another thing entirely.

By the time he left with his unsigned documents in tow, Brad lost it. My mother steered the girls out of the room, as a steel bowl was smashed into a dented mess. Life had spun out of control and was just getting worse. The bowl was the least of our worries though.

"So, we hoped that perhaps you could do something to help," I beseeched Mr. J, as I wrapped up my plea. "We brought all the documents you requested."

I pulled the current mortgage life insurance policy out of the bag at my feet and placed it on his desk.

There was only so much that could be done on a holiday, but at least now I trusted that someone might be able to help. So many things were falling apart, but our house deal couldn't be one of them. With Brad's mobility issues, we couldn't stay in our current two-story house, as the only bathroom was on the second floor. But we couldn't afford to move into the bungalow and then lose the life insurance that would be so vital to me when Brad was gone. Someone had to figure it out and I no longer had the bandwidth to do so.

Life doesn't stop just because it gets hard though. The calendar dates continued to flip towards closing day and we had to figure out how that was going to play out. Would we be moving at all? If we did, how would we go about that, with Brad's strength and mobility affected and me dragging an infant and toddler behind? Could our lawyer figure it out? More importantly, could our mortgage broker? Cancer stepped into the side car to glare at us from the sidelines, as we sped towards the unknown.

"Can you figure it out between hospital visits?" it mocked.

Fuck off! Stop! Let us live our life!

But there was no time to say any of that. I drove Brad to the hospital to get sized up for radiation treatments and started pricing out moving trucks. My mother went to the bank to see if she could purchase the house for us, so that we wouldn't lose the deal altogether. And the mortgage broker, well, the mortgage broker fell apart.

"He's terminated his services," our lawyer announced a few days later. "I tried my best to get him to sort through the process, but it seems it is beyond him. Is there anyone else you know of who could help?"

159

There was, but it meant tucking tail and begging for help with a week before the deals were to close.

"Fred," I sighed. "He was the mortgage broker we used on the last house. He was alright, but our real estate agent had suggested someone new, as he played hockey with him."

"I suggest you get on the phone with Fred as soon as possible to see what he can do then."

If only we had reached out to him in the first place. I felt awful picking up the phone, like begging favours from the scrawny kid that got picked last for the team, but there was no place for pride now.

"Can you help us?" I begged, after explaining the story.

"I make no promises," Fred announced. "But I will see what I can do."

The clock ticked louder than ever, but it was out of our hands once more. Our fate was tied to the scrambled efforts of a middle-aged balding man that had been passed over in the first draft but was running for the finish line now. Would he make it?

"Where do you want this," Gene asked a week later, as he paused with a heavy box in his arms.

Books, kitchen items, rocks, living room knickknacks, linens, laundry, and more. It all filed past me, as I stood on the threshold of our new home and a stream of people unloaded the borrowed truck on the front lawn. There were friends, family, co-workers, and even our real estate agent and his wife there. Upwards of 50 people passed boxes hand to hand down the gangplank of one of Brad's work trucks. Some people wiped down kitchen cabinets and filled them with our dishes. Others put together beds, so we would have someplace to sleep that night. Brad and I spun in the middle, pointing people in one direction or another, while our daughters were safely tucked into another friend's house for the day. It was a well-oiled machine that humbled me in its magnitude.

Everyone here knew that Brad was dying. No one wanted us to go it alone. They couldn't change Brad's health, but they could make the move easier, and I was overwhelmed by the kindness.

Only days before, Fred had secured us the deal with our life insurance intact. We signed the paperwork before it was dry and wept with relief that it hadn't become even more difficult than it already was.

His parting shot, "if you had come to me from the beginning, I would have been able to get the life insurance to cover the whole home. Because I only had a few days to work with, your life insurance will only be for the amount of the previous home."

Point noted. The difference was approximately $25,000—a paltry sum that was worth his slight dig. I could never repay him for his efforts. They would keep me afloat for years to come.

But on April 21, the sun shone warm on the beehive of activity that played out at our new home. There wasn't much we could do to repay all the participants that day either, but hot pizza and cold beer had to do the trick. It was the least we could offer for the gargantuan gift of time we received.

Down We Go

I woke up the next day in our new house. The smell of cleaning products lingered in the air and the crisp sheets hugged me close begging to just stay a few minutes longer before starting the day. I could hear gentle rustling from the next room over though and people other than just me were stirring.

Day One. Things were going to be different.

I slipped from the covers, leaving Brad to ease out of consciousness in his own time. There were no doctor appointments today. No appointments with lawyers, mortgage brokers, realtors, or even work for that matter. It could have been bliss, if you forgot that time wasn't on our side. Life was though, and our babies knew nothing of their Daddy's state.

"Morning Rylie," I said to my smiling six-month-old working to roll over, as I stepped into her new bedroom. "Does someone need their diaper changed?"

By the time we made it to the kitchen, Brad was pouring Taryn a glass of milk and she had a bowl of cereal in front of her. The coffee pot gurgled, as the heady scent of French roast filled the air.

"I'm going to have a shower," Brad announced, as he put the milk back into the fridge and stepped out of the room.

It all felt so normal. Like we had been here forever, and life would always be this way. I slipped Rylie into the highchair and rummaged through cupboards looking for the mugs. I couldn't help but feel hopeful as the sun streamed warmly through the big kitchen windows. Maybe everything was going to be alright after all.

Brad walked back into the kitchen a few minutes later, a towel slung across his shoulders. I eyed him warily, as I sipped the tail end of my coffee. He rustled around in a drawer, then turned with a pair of scissors in hand.

"What are you doing?" I asked hesitantly, as I saw the somber look in his eye.

"More like what are you doing," he said. "Come on."

He walked out the back door, dragging a patio chair behind him into the middle of the lawn. He sat down and held the scissors towards me, as I paused in the doorway. Something told me not to take another step. To deny what my brain was slowly piecing together.

"My hair has started to fall out."

"But..." I stammered.

"Big clumps of it came out when I ran my hands thru it in the shower. You need to cut it."

He raised the scissors towards me again with steely eyes. Day One in the new house and the radiation had finally kicked in. There was no point clogging the drains or avoiding the inevitable, but the simple act of a haircut felt more weighted than anything I had ever done.

My heart sank, but I walked over and took the scissors from him. I carefully lifted a hunk of hair and gently snipped away at the bottom of it.

"Don't worry about making it straight," he grumbled, as I proceeded to snip and trim my way around his head. "It's all going to fall out."

There I was dreaming that life maybe wasn't so bad, but the rude awakenings just wouldn't quit. Time to steel myself to the fact that we weren't winning the game. Not today anyway. I gave up and started hacking randomly at chunks, whisps of hair escaping in the warm spring breeze. Brad couldn't see my tears as they silently fell behind his rigid back. It was all falling, falling, falling—hair, hopes, dreams, life. It was all falling apart.

The only thing that wasn't falling away was a trip to Owen Sound. This was a suggestion from Dr. J and one we took seriously. Along with suggesting massive doses of vitamin C, he had also suggested talking to a naturopath. When Brad asked if it mattered which one, Dr. J gave him this woman's contact information.

"Talk to her," was all that Dr. J offered.

So, Brad called her office and set up an appointment to see her in a week's time. We would have to take Rylie, but Brad's parents agreed to watch Taryn for the day. As we didn't know what to anticipate, it was one less thing to worry about.

"She wants me to track everything I eat and drink for a week," Brad said over dinner that night.

I sensed a cockiness in his tone, knowing his culinary skills put him in good stead on that front. It also explained the extra effort he put into that night's menu; baked salmon, fresh broccoli sauteed in garlic butter, and basmati rice seasoned with fresh thyme from the garden. Yum.

But all the delicious meals that followed did not impress the naturopath when he handed over his homework a week later. The fresh vegetables were good, but from there, she had a LOT of suggestions.

"So much of our Western diet is filled with meat that is loaded with hormones. Those hormones are meant to grow our chicken, beef, and pork bigger and faster, but they also introduce those same elements into us when we consume them. You are effectively feeding your cancer inadvertently via those growth hormones. If we have a hope of your body rallying a fight against them, you need to stop consuming all meat and dairy."

"What?" Brad replied in shock.

"What about fish?" I asked tentatively.

"If you must, you can eat small fish once a week," she replied.

"Good," Brad said.

"Sardines," she added. "Anything larger is filled with mercury. The bigger the fish, the smaller fish they eat and the higher your exposure will be. Anything larger than sardines and you are back at square one injecting toxins into your body again."

"At this point, you need to make a massive effort if you want to fight back against the cancer cells that are multiplying in your body," she continued. "I also recommend several nutrients that will help your body fight against the cancer cells and rid your body of the toxins that are built up there."

She handed over article after article about growth hormones, studies on Japanese cultures with low dairy intake and subsequent lower breast cancer rates, and further studies around the vitamins and nutrients she now suggested.

"Keep up with the vitamin C that Dr. J suggested, but I want you to add curcumin, astragalus, turmeric…" The list went on but meant nothing to either of us.

"You can get most of these supplements downstairs," she added as she handed us this last slip of paper.

I was speechless. I curled Rylie protectively into my arms to shield myself from the blow of her words. Essentially, she was handing over a vegan diet; no meat, dairy, coffee, alcohol, and several other items on the No side, with a boggling assortment of other unfamiliar items on the yes side, including adding flax seed, protein powder, and power shakes.

I stared at Brad, my meat and potatoes man who enjoyed a beer or two every night after arriving home from work, not to mention a coffee or two in the morning to get him going. How was he going to do this? How were we going to survive?

This was the only lifeline anyone had thrown our way though and we both knew that. Brad collected it all, giving it a cursory glance. It was like trying to decipher a foreign language, but one we would learn soon enough.

After booking another appointment and collecting the laundry list of items for Brad's new daily regimen, we stepped back into the car for the long drive home. The hopes we had held onto on the way there were now coloured with the gargantuan challenge set in front of us. I may have eaten a fair number of vegetarian meals in my day, but Brad's chef background didn't mesh with the new lifestyle being suggested. It was tantamount to asking him to relearn everything he knew about food; how to prepare it and pull everything together to still get all he needed from this new limited palette.

"We'll figure it out together," I assured him on the drive home.

But neither of us was so sure about that.

Over the weeks that followed, we went back to Owen Sound several times. Subsequent trips didn't hold the same sense of hope that the initial visit had, but Brad was dogged in his determination. We would be ushered into the appointment, where I would focus on Rylie in my lap, contributing as little to the conversation as possible. The naturopath would share helpful suggestions, articles about people whose health had miraculously improved after making similar lifestyle changes, and no-nonsense looks when it came to wavering on her regime.

"How is your sex life?" she asked right off the hop one visit.

"Fine," Brad gruffly answered.

I looked from him to her and back again, waiting for any kind of forthcoming explanation, but his end of the conversation was closed. In turn, so was mine, although I would have had a different answer. In truth, we had not had sex since Brad was hospitalized in April. Between radiation, the stress of our new lifestyle that we were struggling to still wrap our heads around, and raising two little girls, the presence of any intimacy between us had dried up. Sure, in the early days after delivering the girls, the onus behind that dry spell was on me, but nowadays, the lack of initiation came from the other side of the bed.

"Sexual intimacy is important to keep your relationship strong," she continued. "It releases positive endorphins, helps to keep you close, keeps blood flowing to your sexual organs, is a great form of exercise, and it improves your mood. There have been several studies done on regular sexual activity and mental health that I would be happy to share."

Of course, she had studies to share. But Brad was stoic in the face of anything that might be perceived as a slight or weakness. There was no way he was going to discuss his sex life, or lack of it in this room. And I just couldn't bring myself to cross him on that point. At least the diet he had some control over.

The diet was another sore spot regardless. Brad was used to plating a meal with a meat, veg, and starch. Without the meat to anchor it, our plates faltered. There were meatless alternatives that were an easy swap, but he hated the veggie burgers and dogs, soy milk for cereal, and rice pasta to replace the wheat. Yes, he couldn't do wheat either and we had yet to find decent pasta alternates. Every meal was a struggle and tensions ran high at every turn.

"Why don't Jeff and I come for a visit," my friend Laura offered one day after a discouraged conversation on my end. "We have cooked so many vegetarian meals. I'd be happy to go over alternates with him. I can bring some recipes too. I'll bring my Moosewood Cookbook!"

Little did we know, but that visit changed everything. Laura discussed quinoa, amaranth, pseudo grains, beans, and more. We ate peppers stuffed with amaranth and made a quinoa salad that tasted better than anything we had eaten in weeks. And changing the concept of what the plate looked like was exactly what Brad needed at a time when he was ready to throw the frying pan at the wall.

"Thank you so much," I whispered into Laura's shoulder before they made their long trek back to New York.

That improved outlook also helped us to start planning something other than just doctor appointments. By then, we had met the palliative doctor and he had talked about "quality versus quantity."

In retrospect, he was a kind man, but I hated him and his colourful bow ties, calm voice, and contemplative manner. I hated everything about what our life looked like, but we were beyond changing that. It was about making the best of what little time we had left.

What time we had left? Honestly, I don't think I ever wrapped my head around that, but time continued to march on. So, we did too.

We planned a camping trip to the nearby Pinery Provincial Park with Faye, Stu, and the kids in early June before schools let out. It felt normal, aside from having to ask for and locate the accessible beach at the dune filled area. We made light of the fact that Brad's handicap sticker got us a discount on the stay though. They never treated us different, and that was the best gift of life to be had at that point.

At the end of July, we planned another trip away; this one to Michigan with Brad's parents. We packed up the kids with promises of paddle boats, plenty of fast-food breakfasts, and a brief hiatus from Brad's diet. We lifted drinks to family and fun and found moments to just be in the little cabin by Lake Huron. The kids cuddled in with their Daddy for precious moments that seemed fleeting at home. And I did too, relishing the change of scenery and quiet moments we were able to slip away just the two of us while Gram and Pup watched the girls for a spell in the afternoons. You could almost forget that life existed beyond the campground's realm.

Too soon, home beckoned though. With vacations ticked off, home renos began in earnest, to round out our days and help balance doctor appointments. We all felt better after reconnecting, and I hoped that perhaps Brad might be able to bridge the emotional divide that stubbornly resisted breaching within his family unit. It was a tall order that they had worked a lifetime at keeping established, but I held out hope, nonetheless. And kept on hoping every day that Art came to tinker in the basement.

In retrospect, none of it was sustainable though. Brad had gone through chemo, radiation, interferon treatments, multiple surgeries, plus had a toolbox overflowing with herbal remedies and various vitamins. We no longer went out for crazy weekend getaways where we partied or drank until dawn. We didn't invite friends over for decadent dinners featuring surf and turf or extravagant bottles of wine to accompany them. Even family get-togethers seemed stilted, with conversations ultimately labouring back to updates on Brad's health. By the end of July, we were all tired.

"You know what the worst thing is," Brad said one morning as he watched our neighbours drive off to work. "I would give anything to be them; to go to work."

What could I say to that? I might have been there, but my work was our children. I got them up, changed, clothed, washed, and fed them. I put them down for naps, entertained them, read stories. Even household chores generally fell to me: grocery shopping, the bulk of the cleaning, laundry. Brad got up, took his breakfast pills, and made his morning smoothie, then waited until his dad came over to head down to the basement to work on the bathroom they were building together. At lunchtime, Art left, and we ate lunch.

"Did you talk?" I would ask, knowing the response. I always prayed the answer would be different, but they didn't know how to start, and time was running out.

"No," he would say, before heading for a nap.

Naps for all, but me. I would tackle however much I could while the rest of them slept.

"The freezer doesn't seem to be freezing so well," I said to Brad one afternoon in early August.

We pulled it out to vacuum the coils, but neither that nor a cursory inspection yielded a fix.

"We can swap it out for the one in the basement," he suggested.

As we had brought our fridge from our last house, it was an easy enough swap, but for the flight of stairs to maneuver. I temporarily emptied the contents of the fridge into a cooler, then we grappled it down two steps and out into our garage. Next step was to heave the model in the basement up into the kitchen. That proved to be a little more problematic.

"I'll pull from the front," Brad ordered. "You lift from the bottom."

"Okay," I agreed.

I was used to toting around babies. A fridge couldn't be that much worse. Except babies were easier to grip, I soon learned.

"Okay, give me a second," I puffed, as I adjusted my hands to find a decent grip on the smooth surface.

"Ready?"

"Ya."

"Okay, lift…"

And we hefted the beast up, slowly moving up the stairwell. One, two, three, four…

"Hold on," I panted, as my grip loosened, and I scrambled for purchase.

Five, six… Every step was a hard-fought purchase, but my arms were shaking dangerously.

"I'm losing my grip," I wheezed in panic.

Brad desperately tried to haul the fridge up the last two steps, realizing I wasn't going to make it, but his damaged muscles were no match for the straining 200+ pound behemoth. He grunted as he scrambled for a new purchase of his own, but the last step was beyond us. I raced backwards as fast as I could for fear of being crushed in the stairwell.

"I'm sorry!" I cried. "I'm sorry. I'm so sorry. Shit, shit, shit."

"Don't worry about it," he panted. "Are you alright?"

"Yes, but have we damaged it now?" I asked. "Damn it. We were so close."

"Catch your breath. I'm sure it's fine. We'll try again in a minute."

I cursed myself over and over and swore that I would not let it happen again. And I didn't. When we both recovered, we manhandled the fridge up the steps to the landing, then three more to the kitchen. It was just an easy push across the linoleum from there and the fridge slid easily into the slot, no worse for wear.

Brad was another story. We might have won in relocating appliances, but his reward was a headache that planted him firmly on the couch.

"You almost flattened me!" I joked from the kitchen, as I loaded our perishables into the new unit.

In retrospect, I think the fridge flattened him though. After that first headache, they came regularly and got more severe with each one he had. They went from irksome and needing a Tylenol, to instantly blinding from out of nowhere and needing to lie down. Regular Tylenol didn't touch them, but he had a supply of Tylenol 3s now. The speed and severity of them were shocking though.

"You should mention them to Dr. J," I suggested. "Or Rona when we go to see her next."

All I got back was a grunt, as he retreated to bed and shut the blinds tight against the light.

Had he broken more blood vessels in his brain when we moved the fridge? It was heavy and he fought valiantly to protect me from being crushed, but did he pay for that effort? I won't ever know, but fear that may have been the case. At that point, I was like a deer in the headlights, apologizing over every step I took, every word I spoke, and constantly shushing the children around their Daddy. I was in shock, even though I didn't comprehend that at the time. Gone were holidays, dinner parties, and any semblance of normal. Now we tiptoed around headaches at every turn. The fridge was the least of our worries.

The Advocate

I pulled up to the side entrance of the Cancer Clinic. Rona's office was in the lower level, so dropping Brad at this door meant we had a shorter distance to go to get to her. This was something we had to consider now, and I took advantage of handicapped spaces whenever I could too. I know Brad hated it, but his mobility hadn't gotten any better. The fact was, we needed those supports.

He slowly climbed out of the van and made his way towards the automatic doors.

"I'll catch up with you in a minute," I called after him.

He didn't even turn around. His painfully slow progress was an indicator that another headache was probably on the way, so I sped off to make good my promise.

By the time I found him a few minutes later, I knew my suspicions were correct. Worse than correct actually. Brad was perched on a plastic chair just inside the door with his head bowed low and his eyes squeezed shut.

"Are you alright?"

Like I didn't know. Anyone could tell he wasn't. His head barely shifted, but I was immediately in crisis mode. I paused to steel myself for this next wave, then dove in.

"Let me go find Rona," I said.

"No," he rasped. It took all his willpower, but he shakily got to his feet.

Damnit, I cried to myself. So stubborn, even when in agony.

174

"Can I at least get you a wheelchair?" I begged.

The fact that one sat unoccupied a few feet away helped. It might have felt like a slippery slope, but he was rapidly losing his ability to function. When I wheeled one up beside him, he barely had the strength to look at me before sinking into it. I didn't wait for him to change his mind, as I hurried us down the hall to Rona's open door.

"Hey Rona," I called as Brad stood up and we shuffled into her office. "Brad isn't really feeling up to paperwork today."

Rona might have just been a social worker, but she knew how to read a situation. She could see that Brad was in agony and knew him well enough to know that he never showed pain. The paperwork was the least of our worries.

"What's going on?" she asked with concern as she came around her desk.

Brad was beyond words. This was one of the worst headaches I had seen yet. His eyes were sealed shut, and his jaw was clamped tight. He wasn't capable of anything other than trying to sit upright, and it looked like he might lose that battle at any minute.

"We need to get him someplace to lie down," Rona declared, as she moved to the door. "Our paperwork can wait. I'll be back in a minute."

I followed her out the door.

"It's a headache," I explained rapidly. "He gets them every day, but they are getting worse. As soon as they hit, he has to lie down. They are excruciating and he can't function when they strike, but this is the worst I've seen."

175

"Stay with Brad. I'll be back in a minute."

And she was gone. But only for the few minutes she promised. She returned and grabbed the handles of Brad's wheelchair, then set off down the hall. She pushed open a door to an exam room and put the brake on the chair.

"You can lie down here," she said as she lowered the lights.

She had seen his wince, as the fluorescents hit him. I, on the other hand, was back to fluttering now that someone else had control. That wasn't to last though.

"Dr. J isn't here, but I am going to see if I can track down one of your other doctors to get you something for the pain Brad," Rona said as she moved to the door. "Katherine, I need to talk to you for a minute before I go."

I followed her out to the hallway, terrified of what her prognosis was. It wasn't what I was expecting at all.

"You are going to have to be Brad's advocate Katherine. He can't speak for himself. Not in that condition. If you can get him admitted, they can get an MRI done quickly, but you will probably have to fight for that. He needs you now."

It was all on me. It was finally time for me to do all the talking. I knew Brad's history, what was going on—I could be his voice—but it was hard to step into the role of fighting against a system that just wanted to dismiss you as quickly as possible. And that is exactly what Brad's radiologist tried to do.

"Hello," she exclaimed, as she breezed into the room a few minutes later. "How are we today?"

Her smile was suffocating in its complete disregard of the situation. No notice of the dimmed lights, the fact that Brad winced at the volume of her voice, or that he was lying crumpled into a ball at all.

"He has a headache," I explained lamely. "It's pretty bad."

"Oh," she said. "Well then. What is your pain level at between 1 to 10 Brad?"

Perhaps she had never seen him in pain before—I know how stoic he could be in the face of it—but every ounce of her just exuded that she didn't notice or seem to care.

"Eight, maybe nine," he mumbled.

"Okay then," she said with a cursory nod. "I can get you a shot of morphine that should get you feeling better and get you on your way."

And before I could even process what she had said, she was walking out the door. I sat for a moment blinking at the door and then looked back to Brad. Rona's voice filled my head — "You have to be Brad's advocate Katherine." No one was going to do anything unless I pushed. I followed out the door and strode up to the radiologist as she filled a report at the nearby desk.

"Excuse me," I said, trying to keep the shake out of my voice. "I don't know if you noticed, but Brad is in agony. These headaches happen every day and are getting worse. When they hit, he can't even see. He immediately has to lie down. Giving him medicine now is great and I thank you for that, but it's not enough. He needs more than that. The morphine will make him better now, but what are we supposed to do when we get home and they hit again?"

"I have two babies at home, and I cannot tend to Brad when he is in excruciating pain and to two children two and under. You need to do something more than just send him on his way."

My voice was definitely shaking now, and tears had slipped down my cheeks as I demanded something, anything more from her. She paused, finally hearing the humane behind the clinical chart number. If I wasn't so desperate, I might have felt bad that she was just trying to protect her own mental health in dealing with patients whose prognosis was poor. But my words struck the nerve I was aiming for. Perhaps she assessed whether she wanted the fight, or maybe whether she could just outrank me, but ultimately, she gave in.

"Let me see what I can do. I make no promises, but I will see if we can get him admitted."

"Thank you," I whispered, as she walked away.

It was the hardest thing I had probably ever done; standing up for someone's proper care who was unable to speak for themselves. I didn't even know what we needed, but it was something better than the band-aid she had initially cheerfully offered. My win felt hollow though, as now Brad was going to stay. They would run tests to see what was going on, but I already knew it wasn't good. I just couldn't wrap my head around what it meant though.

What did it mean?

For starters, it meant getting Brad settled, calling Brad's parents to inform them of the new turn of events, then heading to pick up the girls from Faye's house. How I ever could have done it without her help, I will never know. We were in our thirties and her best friend's husband was dangerously ill with a life-threatening disease.

What did she think about that? Did she have any idea the gift she gave or the lifeline she was on so many days, from babysitting, to playdates, to long talks about everything and nothing? I must have been exhausting, but she never once let on. She knew things were worse now though.

"Stay for dinner," she insisted. "Go home and get whatever Brad needs but have dinner here."

I was too exhausted to protest and honestly, too terrified to be alone yet. I was numb and going through the motions, one painful step at a time, with no idea what was coming next. I couldn't live in anything other than the present moment and a friend's welcome space was everything I needed right then.

By the time I visited Brad, had dinner with Faye and clan, then eventually got the kids home and settled into bed, I was numb. What would they find when they did the scans? What could they do now? My thoughts were incapable of moving beyond that.

"Hi hun'," I called out the next day, with Taryn quietly shuffling in beside me and Rylie snug in her car seat. "How are you feeling?"

"I'm alright," he replied gamely.

"And how's my big girl?" he asked Taryn, as he patted the bed beside him.

She eyed the bed warily. She had become all too familiar with hospitals in her two short years, but still didn't know about seeing her daddy in the adjustable beds. Especially with the many cords and wires strung about. Brad had an IV, which was enough to make her nervous. I picked her up to nestle her into the opposite side of the tubes. I would never get used to this, so how could she? The trick was to remember that Brad was still there behind everything and didn't have any choice in picking up and leaving when he decided he had had enough. The hospital, the machines, the medicine, nurses and doctors; they were all there to make him feel better and they were doing all they could to get him out of there as quickly as possible. It was overwhelming and scary, especially for children, but taking away the unknown made it less so.

"Just watch for the tube in Daddy's arm," I said, as I pulled Rylie out of her car seat. "That is how they give him his medicine."

It was all she needed to know, and it was enough. She handled it better than some adults who visited. Better again than those who were too uncomfortable to even visit at all. They no longer saw Brad as a person, but rather as a patient in a world so far removed from their own that they couldn't drum up any kind of suitable conversation. Brad hated the false chatter and uncomfortable silences that came with the sterile atmosphere. His choice was to have visitors steer clear to save the pain of it all. Many were relieved, but I couldn't help but think of the solitary patient left alone for hours at a time, with the reality of why they were there as their only comfort. It just didn't feel right to not visit.

The kids always meant my visits were short though. For Brad, I can only imagine it was a mixed blessing.

"Have the doctors said anything? Scheduled any tests yet?"

"Ya, Dr. P was by to see me. He's getting me moved to the fourth floor this afternoon. It's his floor. He didn't have room when I got admitted, but there's a bed now. And he figures I should get in for an MRI tomorrow morning."

"That's good news," I said tentatively. Nothing ever really felt like good news at this point, but I desperately tried to put positive spins on anything I could. "So at least another night here then that means."

"He talked about releasing me for the weekend but wants me back again next week. Tests or whatever."

"I guess we'll see once the MRI results come back."

"Ya. Something like that."

Hurry up and wait. More appointments. More tests. Never any clear answer as to when life might feel closer to normal.

"How's your head today," I added softly.

"Fine with the help of my friend here," he said pointing at the IV pole. "All them good drugs…"

I laughed but couldn't imagine him pulling one around behind him at home. Our life had split in two and it felt impossible to reconcile the clinical and human side of what our lives had whittled down to.

My thoughts were interrupted by the appearance of Brad's nurse.

"Your family came to visit. How nice. He told me about you two," the nurse said smiling at Taryn and Rylie. "I've got to check your Daddy's vitals, but I'll only keep him a minute. Promise."

He expertly strapped the cuff around Brad's arm and stuffed a thermometer into his mouth. In moments, the vitals checks were done and marked on the chart, but Taryn watched it all with wide eyes.

"Lunch will be here shortly," he added as he walked towards the door. "Would you like me to bring an extra plate for you ladies?"

"Oh no," I quickly said. "We don't want to be any trouble."

"They can eat my applesauce," Brad said with a wink to Taryn.

Before I knew it, our visit came to an end. Lunch was a fun distraction, but the drugs and headaches left him sleepy. It was nap time all around though. For everyone except me.

By Friday, Dr. P was good to his word and had Brad scheduled for release.

"I want you back Sunday night so we can start physio first thing Monday," he said. "Enjoy your weekend though. It's supposed to be a nice one."

"Will do," Brad responded dutifully, as I handed him his clothes to change into so we could leave.

And as soon as I pulled out of the parking lot, Brad took steps to ensure that happened.

"Go to the butcher on Hamilton Rd," he demanded.

"Ummm…" I started tentatively. "Are you sure? What about your diet?"

"Screw the diet," he responded firmly. "This weekend I want a steak."

He got that thick juicy steak and more. We had a big roast with his parents, with all the decadent fixings that had been taboo for the last few months. Our steaks came with baked potatoes, loads of butter and cheese, not to mention a nice bottle of wine. Faye and Stu came over with their girls Sunday afternoon to sail in the little swings Brad hung in the branches of our crab apple. And dinner before heading back to the hospital was more culinary decadence with big, fat, cheesy, gooey panzerottis with veggies and meat galore.

The weekend was about reembracing all that Brad loved most of all: food, friends, family, his wife, and children. It was perfect despite the fragility that lingered in the wings. My mother was set to arrive in the morning and the hospital awaited. But in those few precious days, we embraced living as best we could.

Those moments will forever be my fondest memories and possibly the best days of Brad's life.

Months to Years, to Weeks…

Years later, I published a short story in an online magazine entitled 'Months to Years'. In the printed publication, they noted:

'"Months To Years" is a phrase often used as a prognosis for terminally ill patients. It is a doctor's best estimate of expected lifespan. But to be clear, Months To Years (the digital magazine) is not just for the terminally ill. It is for anyone interested in exploring questions of mortality, grief, or loss.'[7]

Months to years was a phrase we were already familiar with. The infamous specialist back in April had decreed that Brad had six months to a year to live. On Monday, Dr. P edited that diagnosis.

My mom arrived early Monday morning so I could go to the hospital to meet with Brad and his doctors. She was happy for the

---

[7] Months to Years. (2018). An Unexpected Gift by Katherine Krige. *Months to Years*, Fall 2018 Issue. https://monthstoyears.org/an-unexpected-gift

excuse to spend a few hours with her grandbabies, plus already had a plan for dinner before I was even out the door.

Dr. P and Rona awaited my arrival to discuss next steps for Brad and his care. Can I share that it wasn't anything close to what we expected? Dr. P discussed the scans. Rona finished up the last of the paperwork needed for Brad's disability claim. It didn't end there though.

"So, what happens now?" I asked after the preliminary pieces were taken care of. "What's the plan?"

A look passed between the medical professionals that left me grasping in my ignorance. There had always been some kind of game plan, some course of action, but this pause was new. It felt like a sigh from someone struggling to explain a straightforward problem to a simpleton. I was the simpleton and was completely ignorant as to what was apparently plain to them.

"There isn't really a game plan," Dr. P said delicately. "There isn't anything that can be done at this point. We will do everything in our power to ensure quality of life and to eliminate as much pain as possible."

"What does that mean?" Brad asked.

"At this point, we want you to be comfortable."

"Comfortable?" I repeated. I looked from Dr. P to Rona. "Comfortable?! What kind of prognosis is that?"

"There isn't any easy way to say this. As far as prognosis goes, we are talking weeks to months. We don't want you to start counting moments though. Our aim is quality over quantity at this point."

I was speechless. Tears instantly pooled in my eyes and overflowed my lids. Weeks…

"We want you to live your best life, Brad. There's no point in you staying in hospital any longer. I am going to write you up a prescription for the headaches, then I'll release you. Go be with your children. You will be more comfortable at home and that is what is important now."

Weeks…

Maybe a month? Maybe less? Quality over quantity. I couldn't process what he was saying. My brain refused to hear the words he delicately left out. Brad was going to die, and it was going to happen very soon. Oh God. Oh no. I just couldn't.

"Take all the time you need," Rona added. "We will set up VON visits again…"

The rest of it faded into a blur. Brad was going to d…

No. I did not have the capacity to process the thought. We would pack. I would take Brad home. I would go to the pharmacy and fill the prescription that Dr. P handed us. We would have dinner, talk with my mom, play with the kids, maybe give them a bath. I lined up the tasks to give me focus and push out the thoughts Dr. P had planted there. I refused to let them in. It was the only thing left to me.

Just keep going.

"I made a curry," Mom announced as we walked in the house a little while later.

"Thanks Shirley," Brad said. "I think I'm going to have a nap."

"Okay, I'll go pick up your prescription."

Grandma was on watch once more. I was on autopilot and fraying badly at the edges, but still pushing on. Because that was the only choice available to me at that point. I couldn't fall apart. Couldn't. Babies. Husband watch. Driving. Everything was boiling down to finite basics, including me.

Telling my mom what the doctor had said was one thing, but Brad's parents were another.

"You need to tell Joan what the doctor said," my mom told me when I returned. "She needs to know. And she also needs to know that Brad needs them emotionally now more than ever."

Oh God. The thoughts ripped my throat apart, but she was right. He needed them. And they needed to show him how much they cared before it was too late. Another conversation to gut me on a day filled with disbelief. Chalk up another hardest conversation ever. Again. But it had to happen, regardless of their wish to seem strong.

"Joan," I said when she answered the phone. "The doctors have said we are talking weeks now. There is no more treatment. There are no more pills. And this is so incredibly overwhelming, but Brad needs to know you are here for him."

"We are!" she exclaimed.

"He needs to hear it," I answered. "He needs to know you care. That you are affected by this and feeling."

"We are trying to stay strong for him," she said. "We don't want to burden him with our fears. This is killing us, but Art and I try to talk about it in private, work it all out so we can stay positive for him."

"He wants to see your tears," I replied. "He doesn't think you get it. Brad doesn't have a choice and the emotions are tearing him apart. As much as he is trying to carry on, this is too hard. It is impossible and scary and overwhelming. But he needs to hear that you care. That you feel and are gutted as much as we are. He doesn't need sugarcoating. He needs real and he needs you."

Tears were streaming down my face as I pleaded for her to just show Brad how hard this was for all of us. He was losing and didn't want to go alone.

"It is so hard to keep everything in check," Joan sniffed. "But we'll try. I'll try."

I knew this was the hardest ask I could beg of them. But I begged for my husband who just wanted to hold as much love as he could in his final days. How was it that all these hard conversations were now mine to demand? Where did the strength come from to claim these emotions from others and myself?

Weeks...

There was no time left to waffle. After wringing tears from Joan, I weakly returned inside. I hadn't taken a deep breath in a lifetime, but that wasn't going to change any time soon. For now, there was Brad, my children, and my mother to hold close around me.

Brad walked out of the bedroom and joined us in the living room.

"How was your nap?" I asked. "How's your head?"

"Alright," he said. "Fine for now."

"I picked up your prescription. It's in the kitchen with your other drugs."

"Good," he answered. "Can you pass me the …"

He squinted at the table. "What's the word. Damn."

"The remote," I said, as I offered it to him.

"Ya, thanks."

"I made a nice curry for dinner," my mom added. "Would anyone like a drink before then?"

"I can get you a glass of wine, Mom," I offered, as I sprang up once more.

Keep moving. Keep on moving.

"Brad?"

He waved me off and focused on the program on the TV.

As my mom and I sipped our wine, casual conversation filled the room, but I vaguely noticed a few lapses from Brad. He didn't add much and became frustrated by a few slips when he couldn't recall the words for things. I didn't think much of it until after dinner was done.

"I'm going to have a nap," he announced as he moved back to the couch.

My mom and I cleaned up, then quietly got the girls ready for bed, so as not to disturb Brad. Grandma tucked the girls around her, as they surrounded themselves with a pile of books in Taryn's room. Such a beautiful piece of normal in an otherwise exhausting day. I relished the few moments alone, already worrying about when Brad would wake. He hadn't been to the bathroom since getting up from his afternoon nap and now it was closing in on 8:00 p.m.

As my mom returned to the living room, Brad stirred on the couch.

"Blue up, table chair?" he said.

I looked at him, then glanced at my mom.

"Glass pig borrow?" he said.

"Ummm, I don't understand," I stammered.

"Table Glass Blue," he demanded.

"Sky," he added hopefully.

What was going on? My mother tried, but she got the same gibberish in response too. Brad had gone from mild word finding problems before dinner to a complete vocabulary breakdown. The difference was even more terrifying: previously he understood his struggle, but now it seemed he had no comprehension that his words made no sense. To him, it appeared he was speaking normally, and you could see the tension rising as he struggled to make himself understood.

"Do you have to go to the bathroom?" I ventured cautiously. I couldn't help but remember the period since he had been. "I can help you to the bathroom before you go to bed?"

I was grasping at straws and trying to keep panic at bay. But it wasn't as easy as that. Brad was frustrated and getting angry.

"Just give me a minute," he said.

"Okay," I replied, relieved to hear a normal phrase come out. A breath slipped out of me.

After a few moments, he braced his arms on the couch to rock himself to his feet. I was instantly there, grasping at his arm to steady him. He leaned into me, as we slowly stepped towards the hallway before a great rush bellowed out of him.

"Mom!" I shouted, as vomit erupted down the hall.

She was there in an instant, struggling to hold up the other side of his now limp body. At 6 feet, he wasn't an easy weight to bear, especially as he had effectively lost consciousness. God love her and her 5'1" inches worth of determination, as we dragged my husband to our bedroom and manhandled him into the bed.

"What's going on," I cried in desperation, as we eased the door shut. "What just happened? What should we do?"

"You need to call the hospital," she said firmly.

"Oh my God!" I sobbed, trying to process all the jagged pieces that slammed into me.

We clung to each other for a moment, but then she pushed me on.

"I'll clean up the hall. You call."

The only problem. Brad had been released from care that afternoon, and Dr. P wasn't there. The nurses who answered the phone couldn't do anything. Next step, telehealth.

"My husband has cancer. He was having problems word finding, then violently vomited, and passed out. What do I do?"

"Where is he now," the nurse asked.

"He's asleep. I managed to get him into bed."

Every time I told the story, I had to explain everything from the beginning. Cancer, treatments, where things were at, current crisis. This time, the decision making was thrown back at me though.

After hearing everything, the woman said, "What do you want to do? If he's sleeping, you can leave him and see how he is when he wakes up."

"I have two children I have to take care of too though. I don't know what to do."

Hysteria threatened to take over, but my mother squeezed my arm beside me.

"I can't tell you what to do. It is your decision. It is up to you."

"But I'm not a doctor!" I cried. "What happens if he throws up again in the middle of the night? Or worse? I don't know what to do."

Tears were streaming down my face, as I shook. How was I qualified to make this decision? Where were the doctors to tell me what to do? I couldn't do this. I. Could. Not. Do. This. Oh God, oh God, oh God.

"If you want, I can call an ambulance. You can stay on the line, and I will connect you."

Should I leave him to sleep? Would he wake up fine and be pissed that I had made a scene? What if he peed the bed? He would be livid if I let that happen. When was his last medication? What should I DO?!

"Mom," I croaked. "What should I do?"

Tears streaked her face as much as mine.

"Tell her to call," she answered. "You can't deal with the babies and him if he has a crisis."

A sob erupted from me. What was happening?! It didn't matter at this point. I couldn't deal with it. I could no longer cope.

"Call," I whispered. "Please call."

"You made the right decision," she said kindly. "Stay on the line while I call. They will be there soon."

True to her promise, an ambulance pulled up in front of the house no more than 10 minutes later. While one of the attendants moved to collect a stretcher, the other quickly strode to the door.

"How can we help you this evening?" he said, as he placed his bag on the floor.

"It's my husband," I said.

The familiar story of his cancer spilled out of me—malignant melanoma, various treatments, headaches—but the new spin tonight was his lack of word finding and violent vomiting.

"We managed to get him to bed," I added. "He's sleeping now."

"What would you like us to do," he asked, as his partner walked in the front door.

I looked to my mother for support. Was I making the right decision? Should I just leave him, and hope things would be better in the morning? She saw my hesitation and stepped in.

"He needs to go to hospital," she offered. "There are babies, and we won't be able to help him, if they wake up. You can't take care of all of them alone Katherine."

I nodded, unable to trust my voice for the moment.

"We'll have to wake him then," he replied.

"That's fine," I agreed. "Let me show you where he is."

"Just give us a minute to bring in the stretcher."

I jumped up as soon as they went outside to see if Brad was still asleep. I could hear the faint sound of his breathing, but no movement shifted under the blankets. I flicked on the overhead hall light and glanced around to see if there was anything else I should move, pick up, put away, pull out. Anything at all I could do to give myself a semblance of control, when all my brain wanted to do was scream that all of this was just wrong, wrong, wrong.

"Ma'am," he said, as they walked up behind me.

"Oh, yes," I exclaimed, as I stepped aside so they could bring the stretcher closer.

"Sir," they said, as their focus turned to Brad. He gently tapped Brad's arm. "Sir, can you hear me?"

Brad turned his head and opened his eyes, obviously confused at the sight of the strange men in his bedroom.

"We're EMS personnel. Your wife called and is concerned about you. How are you feeling?"

"Gimme a minute," Brad answered groggily, as he struggled to keep his eyes open.

As they drifted closed, the EMS attendant paused, then shook his shoulder once more.

Now that they were here, I just wanted them to take charge and make things better, but it wasn't as easy as that. Brad was still the patient and appeared to be cognizant. Without his permission, the attendants could do nothing. It now became a waiting game.

"Can't you just take him?" I asked the second attendant in the hallway. "I don't think he actually knows what he's saying."

Every second was excruciating now that the power had left my hands once more.

"Glen is good with people," he answered. "He'll make sure your husband is comfortable and ready to come with us, but we need him to consent before we do anything."

"Just gimme a minute," Brad said again, as the attendant encouraged him to sit up in bed.

This verbatim repeated phrase was more worrisome than if he had told them to fuck off and get out of his house. It was worse than anger or silence, as it spoke far more of the divide that was cleaving his brain. The fact that it appeared to be a cohesive sentence made things worse though. My fear was that this delay would cause harm, but there was nothing that could be done, until either they agreed Brad was in danger or he agreed to go with them. As the minutes ticked by, it became increasingly obvious that his words were more than just stalling tactics though.

"Brad," Glen tried again.

Brad's eyes slid open once more as he struggled to focus on the man standing beside him.

His unfocused gaze and tentative grip on consciousness helped to convince the men that something more was going on than what appeared on the surface. With persistence, they finally managed to convince Brad to let them take his blood pressure and temperature. Once his vitals were noted, the last step was getting him on the stretcher, then out to the waiting ambulance. And every moment they patiently worked with him to agree that they could care for him was an agony on me. He obviously was no better, and I had no idea what worse might look like. Had no interest in finding out either.

Patience finally paid off.

I had moved to the living room to sit with my mother, when the men emerged pushing Brad on the stretcher. While they had managed to keep him awake long enough to agree to go, he was now asleep once more. I sprang up as they reached the doorway.

"We are taking him to Victoria Hospital," the second attendant said, as they worked towards the door. "We have to turn the sirens on, just to warn you."

I nodded, unable to offer more. My mother clutched my hand, as the men opened the door and carried Brad down the few steps, then dropped the wheels once more. I knew I couldn't go with them but would follow as soon as they left. Now more than ever, I was the voice Brad needed.

Final Voices

It is one thing to be the voice someone needs, but it is quite another to sit vigil during trauma. For months after, the sound of sirens brough me to tears. Some days, it still does. Those sirens, the hours spent in emerg, they gutted me. I relived them over and over again—in dreams, in therapy, and in every waking moment in the weeks to come. It was suggested once that I probably had post-traumatic stress from the next few hours.

Post-traumatic Stress Disorder

"Post-traumatic stress disorder (PTSD) is a mental health condition that's triggered by a terrifying event — either experiencing it or witnessing it. Symptoms may include flashbacks, nightmares, and severe anxiety, as well as uncontrollable thoughts about the event." [8]

By that definition, I guess I did.

I arrived at the hospital and asked about Brad at the admitting desk. After alternately sitting in the empty waiting room and pacing, the nurse finally allowed me to join him. I found Brad asleep on the gurney, with the two ambulance attendants idle beside him.

"What's going on?" I asked, taking in the scene.

"He hasn't been admitted yet," Glen said. "We have to wait until they have a bed."

"We won't go anywhere until he does though," the second attendant assured me. "He's in our care until then."

---

[8] Mayo Clinic Staff. (2018). Definition of Post-traumatic stress disorder (PTSD). Retrieved from the Mayo Clinic, https://www.mayoclinic.org/diseases-conditions/post-traumatic-stress-disorder/symptoms-causes/syc-20355967

"Oh."

Hallway medicine. The ambulance parked out front with two attendants tied up until a bed became free. That wait became hours.

As the minutes ticked by, I frantically thought of everything that could go wrong. Brad hadn't gone to the bathroom since early afternoon, and it was now past midnight. He was past due for his meds and without them his headaches were bound to make things worse. What would my mother do if Rylie woke up and couldn't be soothed back at home? What could I do to advocate for my husband, who apparently had lost the capacity to coherently speak for himself?

All I could do was wait.

When the clock pushed closer to 1:00 a.m., I tried again to see what could be done.

"He gets vicious headaches," I beseeched the EMTs. "Can we give him his pills?"

They didn't know Brad at all, only saw a sleeping man, but had heard some of his story as we sat beside his stretcher in the hallway.

"Normally, we don't like to administer anything. We prefer to leave that to doctors. But as you can tell, we have no idea when your husband will even be seen. If you can wake him, you can give him something though."

I'm sure they thought, "let a sleeping man lie," but their compassion and patience were the only things I had to hold onto as the hours stretched out before us. Even in my distressed state, I understood what they were getting at though. What would the doctor want to do? What tests or medicines of their own would they want to administer and note on a chart? So, I dug my nails into my palms and tried to leave the doctoring to the doctors who lay just behind the emergency room doors.

My frayed patience was finally lifted when a nurse came out to collect Brad from the EMTs.

"Just wait here while we get your husband settled," the woman said, as the lot of them wheeled Brad beyond the imposing double doors.

A few minutes later, the two ambulance attendants returned with their empty stretcher.

"It shouldn't be long now," they assured me, as they returned to their waiting ambulance and the rest of the wee hours left of the night.

They were right. Fifteen minutes later, another nurse came out to the sterile waiting room.

"Mrs. Labravoure?" she asked.

Now was not the time to correct anyone yet again on my surname. I was in a panic to know what was going on and cooperation was key.

"Yes," I cried, already on my feet and rushing to her.

"You can follow me. I'll take you to your husband. You can sit with him while you wait for the on-call doctor to see you."

We walked past a line of beds, separated by cloth curtains. Every bed was filled: some with people moaning, some sleeping, many with visitors sitting quietly beside them. It was late and aside from hushed murmurs, the only sound was the hiss of machines and squeak of nurses' shoes on the floor. Near the end of the line, Brad was tucked into another bed, asleep once more.

"Did he say anything? Wake up at all?" I asked, desperate for some sign things were getting better.

"No, I'm sorry," she replied before walking away to tend to other patients and duties.

So, I stood, staring down at my husband, wondering what in God's name was going on.

"Brad," I whispered to him, as I leaned in closer to his waxy face.

But he lay motionless as before. Vitals acceptable. Asleep by the look of him, with staff probably wondering why he was taking up precious bed space. I knew something far more insidious was at work but was too terrified to piece together what it might be.

After standing vigil for close to an hour, a woman walked by collecting garbage and straightening areas.

"Would you like a chair?" she asked.

Did she see the panic in my stance? Feel for the trauma behind my glassy eyes? Wonder why no one had offered me a seat already?

"No, no," I stammered. "I don't want to be a bother…"

But she was already returning with a chair scared up from somewhere.

"Can I get you a juice? Tea? Maybe a biscuit?"

I sank into the chair, trying not to be overwhelmed by the simple kindness.

"Ummm, sure?"

"Just give me a minute. I have to finish this up, but I'll be back shortly."

True to her word, she had a juice box and plastic package of cookies in my hand within five minutes. Before I could open either though, a man in a white coat appeared. The doctor had finally arrived.

"Good evening, sorry for the wait."

It was closing in on 4 hours since I arrived and over 12 since Brad had taken his last pain meds. But first, to repeat Brad's story; the history of his cancer journey boiled down into a two-minute summary, finishing up with tonight's vomiting episode, word-finding loss, and ensuing confusion.

"I'm going to have to speak with him," he said kindly.

"Mr. Labravoure?"

Nothing.

"Brad? Can you hear me?"

Brad's eyes inched open, then immediately fluttered closed again.

"Brad," the doctor tried again. "I need to ask you a few questions."

"Gimme a minute," he slurred.

The only phrase he had managed all night.

"Alright, there's no rush."

But the ER doctor had a line of patients waiting for his attention and didn't have a minute to spare.

"He says that, but I don't think he is really conscious," I said, as the doctor glanced at his watch.

If he left again, how long would it take for him to come back again?

"I understand what you are saying, but I have to give him the benefit of the doubt," the doctor said to me.

I think he could sense there was more going on but was also bound by Brad's appearance of cognitive understanding. If Brad was requesting time, he had to honour that.

"Brad," he tried again.

His eyes fluttered once more, then slipped shut.

"I'll come back again in a few minutes," he said to me, as I desperately fought to figure out a way to make him stay. To make him make Brad better. To make this all go away. But the only thing that was going away was him.

I was alone beside Brad's prone form once more. Watching the clock inch mercilessly forward. Tears pooled in my lashes, but I was helpless to do anything. My voice had failed me. Failed Brad.

"How are you feeling, Mrs. S?" a nurse asked the patient in the next bed.

Even though a twilight had settled over the long room, the nurses still flitted back and forth. I couldn't help but hear the exchange and learn the neighbour's story. A dinner party. Heartburn. Perhaps a heart attack? Maybe just a little old lady in need of attention? I had no idea but couldn't help but feel anger at the seeming irreverence behind the woman's presence there. She didn't need to be there. Probably needed nothing more than a Pepcid. But she was getting more attention than my husband, who was fighting a mysterious new symptom that terrified me. It wasn't right, but in that moment, nothing was.

The nurse walked away, but a few minutes later a buzzer went off from the woman's bed. She had pulled the call cord.

"Turn it off," Brad murmured.

"It's okay," I tried to reassure him. "It's just..."

"Turn it off," he said louder.

"Turn it off," he screamed, as he sat bolt upright in bed and vomited across the sheets and onto the floor beside him.

He screamed. Howled. Screamed and kept vomiting, as nurses came running in a panic. I heard one of them switch off the call button that had set Brad off, as another grabbed my arm and pulled me to my feet.

"You need to go to the waiting room, while we tend to him," she insisted as she pulled me down the hall. "Someone will come speak with you when we can."

Brad's screams followed me down the hallway, through the double doors, and into the hallway where I had waited for hours with the ambulance attendants. The doors swung shut behind me, and I was alone, but for the screams that continued to echo in my head.

That was agony. That was pure torture and the sound of Brad being ripped apart was too much. He was beyond pain into oblivion on a scale that no longer marked 10. It was absolute torment and I had been slammed out of the way so they could save him. His screams kept echoing off my insides, as I sobbed and sobbed, and doubled over in my own private agony and fear.

What was going on? What had just happened? What were they doing for Brad right now?

My wails tapered to sniffs, whispered to hiccups and catches of my breath. But still I sat alone. How could no one come to fetch me? What should I do? I rocked and whimpered and suffered in the dread that engulfed me. Finally, a nurse came out to the waiting room where panic was my only companion.

"We got him stabilized," she said, as she led me to a private room at the end of the ER. "He had a couple of attacks before we were able to sedate him fully. He is heavily medicated now, so won't wake up at this point."

I stared down at him. In a clean, fresh gown. Breathing shallowly. A machine humming quietly beside him, checking his vitals.

"There's really no point in staying at this point," she added. "You might as well go home."

How could I leave him like this? How? I stared glassily at the woman, with no clue as to how I was supposed to process everything that had just transpired. Brad was alive, but far from good. She was right in that there was nothing that I could do for him physically but leaving felt monstrously wrong.

And yet that is exactly what I did. I sat there staring down at the shell of my husband for 10 minutes, then got up and walked to my car in shock. I looked neither left nor right. I saw nothing on the drive home. It was 4:30 a.m., so almost no other travelers were out. It was just me and my nightmare memories of Brad screaming and screaming, nurses running, and then being shoved aside into the void.

The void was where I stayed.

My mom came out of the bedroom when she heard me walk in the door. I brokenly explained what had happened, as we held each other trying to understand what was going on.

"You need to get some sleep," she said when I finished. "The girls will be up soon and tomorrow will be a busy day."

I was too weak to protest. Too shattered to do anything more than follow directions from those who seemed to know better than me how to function. So, I fell into bed and slept for a precious few hours. Morning would hold more than I could wrap my head around.

Phone calls. There was a list of people to call, starting with Joan and Art. Yesterday I had called to say Brad needed them. Today I was calling to say conversations were too late. The hospital had no updates, other than to suggest that Brad would be moved upstairs to Dr. P's floor as soon as there was a bed. This wasn't what I wanted to share, but I was beyond compassion now. I was hollow.

While I was on the phone with them, my mom called my stepfather to let him know what was happening. The next call was harder.

"Kaya, you have to come. Now."

I didn't make it through the why before I was sobbing.

She was in the middle of work and ran to get off the floor as tears streamed down her own face. She told me later that she had immediately tracked down her boss to tell him what was going on and explain that she had to leave. Ajax was two hours away, but she also had to pack a bag with a few clothes, tell her partner, and make sure people were in place to take care of her daughter. While she could manage all of that, the drive was too much for the torrent of tears that clouded her vision though. A call to my stepbrother pulled him into the mix and soon they both were on the way to London to hold vigil for whatever was to come.

With my sister, brother, and father on the way, it was time to turn my attention to the girls. They needed to get dressed, eat, and get some explanation as to what the day might hold.

"Daddy had to go back to the hospital last night," I explained, trying to keep the tears from spilling all over again. "I'm not sure how long he is going to be there, but we will go see him later. Grandpa is coming for a visit too, so we can go see him once Grandpa gets here."

It was enough. I didn't know what more I could say, as I didn't know what was happening. Couldn't understand anything more than the echoes that still replayed in my head from mere hours before. There were still more phone calls to make though: Faye, Cassie, Brad's work. Mom and I tried to focus on the mechanics of the morning until people arrived.

"Brad's parents plan to go straight to the hospital," I said. "They will tell Tracy, so I don't have to worry about calling her. And they can let us know what is happening until we can get there."

"Try to eat a little," Mom said, noting that I had done little more than push food around my plate. "You have to keep your energy up."

I wasn't hungry. I couldn't focus on anything more than immediate tasks. My brain kept running trying to make sense of what was happening when nothing made sense. Food was irrelevant and seemed the least of my worries. But I swallowed a few bites to appease her concern, despite tasting nothing more than dust in my mouth. The waiting killed me.

"Joe's here," my mom cried, as she stepped up from the table.

"I'll go help him bring in his bags," I responded on autopilot.

Do, move, pretend to function, even as my brain was melting with the exertion of staying still. The hug I received triggered a fresh onslaught of tears, but I was nothing more than raw nerves by then. My mom needed just as many hugs as me though. She was a rock for me, but the events that had ensued from the moment she arrived had shaken her to the core too. We all loved Brad, and this wasn't where any of us wanted to be.

The difference was my mom had been here before. She saw between the lines; understood better what was unravelling, even if I couldn't see. Was incapable of seeing what was right in front of me. It was beyond my capacity, despite the dreams of Brad's funeral I had suppressed the week previous. If I just moved fast enough and functioned well enough, the doctors would fix the chaos that swirled around us.

The phone rang as Joe went in search of his grandbabies to greet next.

"We are here with him now," Joan said. "He's still in emerg, but they will be moving him in the next hour they said. Tracy is on the way too."

"Has he woken up? Said anything? Have the doctors said anything?"

"No, but we are talking to him. Telling him that we are here and that we love him."

The conversation we had yesterday. She heard. He couldn't say anything in return, but he could still hear the words he craved.

"Good."

So good. This was their time. And as much as I wanted to run to the hospital to be there every waking minute, I also recognized that Brad's family needed their moments too.

"Joe just got here, and Kaya and Dany are on their way. Maybe I will wait until they get here, and then we'll come over. Let me know if anything happens. If they move him or anything changes. But you stay with him for now."

It was their time. I would be there soon enough.

"They are here," I shouted a few hours later.

I ran out to the car and collapsed into my sister's arms.

"Oh Kaya," I cried.

There were so many words, but none of them needed to be said.

"Thank you for coming, Dany," I said as I turned to hug him too.

"There is no way I could have driven," Kaya laughed. "I can't see for all the tears I've shed. I cried all the way here."

"Come in," I said. "Let's get your stuff inside. I haven't been to the hospital yet today, but Joan, Art, and Tracy are with him now. I told them we would be over after you got here."

I wasn't capable of driving anymore either. Thankfully, Joe took over.

After Kaya and Dany dumped their bags, we got everyone up to speed. The story wasn't good, but nothing could be done about that now. Everyone knew that. This was about gathering around our loved one. I couldn't bring my brain to understand the unspoken next steps. My blinders were solid.

With seating for seven, we all squeezed into my van and headed to the hospital. Joan had let me know that a space had opened on Dr. P's floor, so they were planning to move Brad as soon as possible. It hadn't happened yet, but the timing was imminent. The fourth floor was therefore our destination. I prayed we wouldn't have to return to the emergency department.

As the elevator opened, I saw Joan walking down the hall.

"Joan," I called. "Have they moved Brad yet?"

"He's getting moved now actually. We'll have to wait for them to get him settled in, but he is on his way upstairs as we speak."

"Oh, that's fantastic news," I cried. "How is he doing now? Has he woken up? Has he spoken at all?"

"No," she replied. "Art and Tracy are coming up with him. I had to make a call, so came up ahead of them. He hasn't said a word, but we have been with him all morning."

I hugged her. Nothing more needed to be said. I could see how hellish the hours had been. She was ragged. All I could hope was that they had found comfort in being by his side. That Brad had somehow known they were there and felt comfort in their presence. It was all he had wanted for so long. It wasn't too late, but I hope they knew that. Hoped they all had gained a measure of peace in this grim time.

The double doors at the end of the hall swung open and Brad's bed emerged, flanked by Art and Tracy. My mom stepped up to hug Joan too, but I lost sight of my family as I laser focused on my prone husband being wheeled into a sterile room down the hall.

"Give them a minute to get him settled in," Art said with a catch in his voice.

I nodded and turned to Tracy.

"Thank you for being here."

I didn't trust myself to say anything more, so opted for a hug for her too.

"I couldn't be anywhere else," she answered with a catch, as she pulled away. "I'll leave now though so you can visit."

I nodded and she was gone.

For a family who didn't do emotions, this was more than they could handle. Tracy looked awful. Art's face was drawn, and Joan couldn't hide the pain that overwhelmed us all.

"We should leave too," she said. "Give you some time..."

It didn't have to be either or, but public pain was more than they could bear. We weren't public, but they were too conscious of the nurses, doctors, interns, PSWs, cleaners, and other visitors who made up the background noise around us.

They were gone as soon as everyone had a chance to say hello and goodbye. With seven of us in tow, we couldn't stay long ourselves, but somehow my family all knew this was the end. I didn't: only thrashed upstream in the pantheon of panic I struggled to breathe in.

There had been so many moments of turmoil, chaos, and crises over the years where I had adeptly asked questions, planned for next steps, handled whatever needed to be handled. Now though, I was lost. Brad wasn't waking up. There were no next steps. No answers would change the outcome of what was going on. But I didn't know that. I couldn't comprehend the magnitude of the moment and stared like a deer in the headlights at every soul that filled my eyes.

What was going on?

My mother knew. The doctors knew. I just couldn't... I had dreamt about Brad's funeral the week before, but that was just doom mongering. This wasn't real. Couldn't be...

"We should go," my mother said after about an hour. "We need to pull dinner together."

"Okay," I said reluctantly.

We all came together, so had to leave together. She was right of course, but food was the last thing on my mind. How could I eat when Brad lay prone in a hospital bed? How could I leave him like this, with no one to stay with him?

"Visiting hours end at 8:00 p.m.," a nurse mentioned kindly, as I left my number at the desk. "You are welcome to come back and stay as long as you like."

"Thank you."

It was all I could muster.

I have no idea what dinner that night was, but it was made, eaten, and I was back out the door as soon as possible. There were enough people to tend to my babies and right in that moment, all that filled my mind was images of Brad alone.

"I'll drive you," Kaya said.

Still not allowed behind the wheel and that was a good call. The distance was negligible, but my nerves were beyond frayed. True to their word, when we arrived on Brad's floor, no one looked at us twice.

"Hey hun'," I called gently when we walked through the door. "How was dinner? Is the hospital food as bad as your last visit?"

I knew he wouldn't respond. Wires snaked from him with beeps punctuating his heartbeat, but his eyes didn't flutter open as we entered. I kissed his cheek regardless and Kaya and I pulled chairs close to either side of his bed.

For the next several hours we sat beside Brad's sleeping form. He didn't squeeze my hand as I stroked his, didn't sigh or roll over to escape our chatter, but I like to believe that he heard our stories and was comforted by our presence. We laughed, we cried, and we did our best to process what was going on—Brad was in a coma. There were no signs he was going to snap out of it. As much as I never wanted to leave his side, eventually the stories slowed.

"I guess we should let you sleep," I sniffled after the last teary memory settled. "You are probably cursing us and begging us to just leave already."

"Yup, bunch of bitches," Kaya chimed in. "Don't know enough to go to bed. What else is new."

Jagged laughs weren't enough to truly buoy my spirits over faded stories though. I rose and planted a kiss on his forehead. The only thing that helped me walk out of that room and away from Brad was my sister's arm around mine, as tears streamed down my face anew. It was time though. Long past visiting hours, which didn't matter any longer. What did matter was that my babies needed me at home as much as my husband needed me at his side. I could hear him saying as much in my head, and reluctantly turned away into the night.

Early the next morning I rose and slipped into Rylie's room. I changed her soiled nighttime diaper, then slipped into the rocker to feed her. As much as she had started eating solids, I still breastfed her. It helped us both start our day. I needed the cuddles more than anything but was hollow behind my glassy eyes. Thank God for grandparents and the presence of more relatives to spread more love around.

I took Rylie to the kitchen where Grandma and Grandpa had already started fussing over Taryn.

"I'm going to have a shower," I announced.

"Coffee is on when you get out," Joe announced.

I nodded, then walked down the hall. I stepped into the bathroom and gently pushed the door shut behind me. These precious few moments would probably be the only alone time I would be able to carve out from my day.

I turned on the water and waited for it to warm up, before slipping off my robe and stepping under the steaming water. All I wanted was to wash the breast milk from my belly, the smell of hospital

212

that clung to me from my hair, and to indulge in a brief respite before stepping back into the nightmare that my world had become.

The water sluiced through my thoughts and ran rivulets of memories down the drain. How long would I have to stand there to reset the months that had crashed into each other, straining the bounds of normal until all hands had emerged on deck to stem the shock waves that trembled through me? If I inched the temperature to scalding, could I burn the images from my brain of my husband screaming in the emergency room. or worse, lying motionless with a machine beeping softly beside him, the only proof he lived?

Come on water. Work your magic.

I heard the doorknob turn and waited to see the tiny head of my toddler peak through the shower curtain, wondering where I had escaped to. Not today though.

"Katherine, the hospital is on the phone," my sister said.

Her eyes were dark, as she held the phone out to me. My mother emerged beside her.

No. Not this.

I slammed the water off and snatched the phone from her, my heart already hammering in my chest.

"Mrs. Labravoure?" a voice said. "We're sorry to inform you, but …"

I dropped to the floor naked and shaking, as the rest of her announcement split my life in two. They had warned me this was coming, but with those few words, my surreal bubble burst and I stepped into 'after'.

"Brad passed away a few minutes ago…"

Nothing would ever be the same again.

PART TWO...
YEAR ONE

"There is a sacredness in tears. They are
not the mark of weakness, but of power.
They speak more eloquently than ten
thousand tongues. They are the messengers
of overwhelming grief, of deep contrition,
and of unspeakable love."

Washington Irving

Chapter 6: Unravelling

Shock and Denial

This is where the story changes. We leave behind reality and enter magical realism, horror, and a brutal fiction that I didn't understand. Brad was dead.

Reality had begged me to consider that plausible outcome for months. Screamed the obvious in the weeks and days leading up to this moment. But dead? Really? Really?! What did that mean?

People talk about the 'Dearly Departed' like they have just stepped out to the store to grab a carton of milk. 'Gone, but not forgotten' was more accurate, but still not exactly right. The dead are certainly not forgotten, but they aren't truly gone either. Deceased hit closer to the mark, although it felt more like a verb rubbed in my face - "no longer living."

Deceased

"deceased, adjective: no longer living

deceased, noun: a dead person." [9]

In that moment, those seconds when reality finally crashed around me; I was a howl of pain. It felt animalistic. Raw. Surreal. How

---

[9] Merriam Webster. (2022). Definition for Deceased. Retrieved from Merriam Webster, https://www.merriam-webster.com/dictionary/deceased

could someone be living and breathing one moment and no longer in the vessel of their body the next? A hollow shell that doesn't even look like the person anymore without blood flowing through their veins and plumping up their skin. How did that remotely make sense? It never does and never will.

The bigger problem in that moment though was that it didn't matter how the world defined it. I had to explain death to my children. They were 2 ½ years old and 10 months. What words could I use to explain that their father had died and was never coming back? Every phrase I contemplated felt like vicious lies that were too hurtful to give voice to. What could I say that wouldn't kill me and irreparably harm them in the process?

Thankfully, I had help.

"I need to get to the hospital," I shrieked. "I have to go!"

"You need to get dressed," my mother reasoned. "You should eat…"

"I can't eat!" I cried. "I have to go! Now!"

I was already scrambling to my room and flinging clothes out of drawers. I didn't care a goddamned about decorum or what I should or shouldn't do. I needed to be with my husband. I should have been there already. I had to go.

Knowing she was powerless to stop me, my mother stepped away. By the time I emerged from my room, she held a piece of toast out to me.

"You need to get something into your stomach," she urged. "You can take it with you."

She had been there too. Lost, shattered, unmoored. Knew that routines were gone, but those left behind still had to perform their basic tasks: eat, drink, sleep.

I took the toast as Dany, Kaya, and I hurried out to the car. It tasted of dust in my mouth: my saliva evaporated into tears that refused to stop.

I willed the car to go faster. To somehow spin back in time and prevent the reality that had already been presented to me. If I got there quick enough, I could change things…

But nothing could now.

"I'll drop you at the door," Dany stated as we pulled into the parking lot.

All I could do was nod. I was laser focused. Couldn't see anything other than Brad breathing in the hospital bed I had left him in mere hours before.

It wasn't true. It wasn't true. It wasn't true…

The elevator inched painfully to the fourth floor. The doors seemed reluctant to let me pass. But nothing could stop me. My heart raced, as I ran to Brad's room.

"Mrs. Labravoure," a nurse jumped in front of me inches from the open portal. "He slept through the night, but when we checked on him at morning rounds, he had quietly slipped away…"

I pushed past her. She was slowing me down. I didn't want to hear what she said. Needed to see my husband. Had to hold Brad.

Joan and Art stared back at me as I burst into the room. I paused for half a beat—taking in her holding his hand, Art standing beside her—then flung myself on top of Brad.

"Nooooo…!"

Sobs wracked me, as I clung to him. Oh my God! How could this be true? He was exactly where I left him, but no beeps filled the room, no breath escaped his lips.

I smashed my face into his chest and fell apart. There was nothing left to do. No more running. No more begging. No more breath, heartbeat, or voice. Brad was gone and I was left in the void flailing against the reality of that. Everything else faded, as I clung to him. Fuck decorum. Screw manners and niceties. My husband, my life, was gone.

If I could have crawled inside of him and stayed there forever, I would have done so. Death is irrational and, in those moments, nothing made sense any longer. Not the fact that Joan and Art had arrived moments after the nurse found Brad dead. They too had missed saying goodbye. Not the fact that my sister and brother quietly entered the room moments later and joined the grieving mass that filled every shred of space. Not the fact that I was still there and had to pull myself together at some point to process everything.

Nothing made sense until Rona and Dr. P quietly entered the room behind us.

"Katherine?" Dr. P said. "We are so sorry for your loss."

I struggled to lift my head from Brad's chest to look at them.

"I know this is incredibly hard, but Dr. P and I need to speak with you," Rona said.

I looked from one to the other. Rona approached and put her hand on my shoulder.

"Perhaps we can give Joan and Art a few minutes alone with their son while we speak."

I stared at her in confusion.

"There's a private room down the hall."

I had sobbed shreds of my life into Brad's cooling form, but it wouldn't bring him back. No matter how much I wanted it to. And now, with careful tones and gentle words, I was being guided towards the after. They weren't going to let me go. I wasn't being abandoned. But there were things we needed to decide, steps needed to be taken. I couldn't stay in that space forevermore and it was their job to delicately help.

I allowed myself to be led away, disbelief streaming from me as the others in the room closed around our lost one. It wasn't the end of my tears, but it was the beginning of forward movement.

Once my breath hitched to a slower gait, Rona began.

"Do you have a funeral home picked out?"

"No," I mumbled, as fresh tears slid down my chin.

"I can make a list of places to consider," she said. "Do you know if Brad wished to be cremated or buried?"

"Cremated," I whimpered.

How could this be real? This was a nightmare I had weeks ago. A horror story the dark had terrified me with. It couldn't actually be happening. But Dr. P and Rona sat on either side of me, peppering me with questions, until we got to the hardest stumbling block—my girls.

"Your mother and father just got here with the girls. You need to explain to them what has happened to Brad."

"Nooo," I whimpered once more. "Oh my God, my babies. How can I explain this to them when it makes no sense at all?"

But this was what Rona was trained to do. She might not have liked this aspect of her job but coaching me on explaining death was the most important role she had ever had. That day anyway. I listened and tried to process the words she was giving me.

"Don't worry so much about Rylie. She is too young to understand. With Taryn, you want to explain as simply as possible. Remind her that you love her and that her Daddy loves her very much. Explain that the doctors worked extremely hard to do everything they could, but that the medicines they were giving her Daddy no longer worked. That his body was very sick and couldn't fight off the illness anymore. You don't need to go into detailed explanations. Keep it simple and tell her that Brad didn't want to go anywhere, but his body stopped working.

Give her the basics to explain death. He can no longer breathe, talk, or walk. We'll remove all the wires before you take her in, so as not to scare her, but you need to be gentle. Hug her. Tell her you are still here for her and aren't going anywhere. That even though her Daddy can't eat or drink, that he will still be with her in memory and that it is okay to be sad. Check in to see if she has any questions, but don't force anything. It is a lot to take in and she might have questions later, but for now she just needs to know that Daddy won't be coming home anymore. That his body stopped working and there is nothing more the doctors could do."

Simple right? Now if only I could breathe. Could understand and process all of that myself. I didn't want to say any of that. I didn't want any of it to be true. It couldn't be true! I didn't care what the doctors had said or done. Brad was 34 years old! He had two babies to raise. I couldn't do it on my own.

But I had no choice. This horror story was all too real.

"You can do this, Katherine. Take your time. You don't have to rush."

She handed me another tissue. Her words might have said 'no rush,' but the reality was otherwise. We couldn't stay in this moment forever. I had to work through it; process first steps, begin to make a plan, and move. It was time.

I wanted to throw up. I wished I could just close my own eyes and stop this reality forever. But Rona was right, and my babies needed me. Grandma and Grandpa were incredible supports, but right now, the girls needed their mother to step up to hold them and show them that she was still there. Would always be there. Shakily, I pushed myself out of the chair and took a deep breath, exhaling all the fears that threatened to overwhelm me once more.

Taryn and Rylie were waiting.

My Mom and Joe lingered in the hallway near the nurse's station. Dany murmured to his dad, as Kaya picked Taryn up to give her a hug. They were all ready to envelop me and were there to catch my fall, but right now I had to stand taller and pick up my own babies. They needed me more.

"Hey baby," I said to Rylie, as I reached to pull her out of her stroller. "Mommy loves you."

I stifled the hitch in my voice by squeezing my baby into my chest. This was supposed to be the easy moment. I kissed her cheek, then handed her off to my sister. Now it was about the words. I had to explain love, loss, and the power of eternity in memory—to a 2-year-old.

I dropped down to a knee in front of my beautiful blonde little girl, who stared at me wide-eyed in fear. Everyone around her was sad and crying, and nothing made sense anymore.

"You know Mommy loves you very much," I started. "Daddy loves you too. But Daddy has been very sick. You know that. His head hurt and we had to be quiet lots. It wasn't much fun for anyone.

"Lots of doctors have tried to help. They did operations and gave him medicine, but the medicine stopped working. Daddy tried so hard to fight and stay with us, but his body couldn't fight anymore."

Taryn stared at me with unblinking eyes, taking in every word I said, but saying nothing in return.

"Oh baby, Daddy died," I said.

I wanted to weep, cut out my tongue to stop the vile words spilling out of my mouth, but I had to continue.

"Daddy's body doesn't work anymore. He still loves you so, so much, but he can't talk, or eat, or breathe anymore."

What else could I say to a little girl who was killing every part of me with that silent gaze.

"Do you want to go in and say goodbye to him? We can go in together."

I pulled her into a hug and held her tight, then stood and took her hand. We slowly walked into the room where Brad lay, the rest of the family quietly following behind us. Brad's parents had already left the room, disagreeing with my decision to give this moment to Taryn. Everyone's emotions were running high though, and in this moment, I had to do what I felt was right for my family.

Brad lay motionless in the hospital bed he had lain in for two days. As promised, the tubes and machines had been removed from the room, to lessen any potential fear they might cause.

"You can touch him if you want," I encouraged. "Talk to him. Say goodbye, or anything you want."

She stood there staring. I picked her up and walked closer.

"See," I said, as I touched Brad's still arm. "It doesn't hurt to touch him."

She tentatively reached out a hand, her eyes glued to her Daddy. But she was two and her processing would take a long time to figure out what death actually meant. No more Daddy at the breakfast table. No more Daddy hammering away in the basement at another project. No pushing her or her sister in the swing or making dinner for us all. No having to be quiet because of his headaches or crawling into his lap to watch TV. He wouldn't be anywhere except memory now and she only had two and a half years of moments to draw on. It was not enough.

The moments from there sped up. Too soon Rona was back with suggestions for funeral homes to use. I needed to decide, so they could come to collect Brad's body. She also asked about whether we had a preacher, or some other member of the clergy to contact to lead the funeral. Other details would be attended to once we went to the funeral home that afternoon. Obituary, date of funeral, visitations, flowers, food, music: the decisions would require my attention. But not yet. Until the funeral home attendants arrived, we could cry, share stories, hold each other, and touch Brad one last time.

His body cooled as our grief filled the room.

By the time Rona gently advised me that the attendants had arrived, we were all raw. Others might have seen this moment coming, but I was in shock and denial. For me, none of it seemed real.

The Funeral

When someone dies, there is a lot of work to do. You would think the moments after death should be filled with uncontrollable sobbing, gnashing of teeth, ripping out of hair—but that is just in the movies. In real life, there is a list of tasks to accomplish and typically, the timeline is tight. You have days to pull it all together, plus invite everyone and anyone who may have known the deceased and their immediate loved ones. You might face differences in opinion, apathy brought on by your grief, or complete bewilderment when it comes to finalizing choices.

For example, did you know that when someone is cremated, they need some kind of vessel to be burned in? They don't just slide the body into a big cavity in a blazing furnace. You need a coffin, or combustible box of some sort; wood, plywood, or carboard will do, as long as it burns.

After picking dates for the funeral, visitations, arranging food, and a minister, we wrote Brad's obituary. This was shortly after lunch, just hours since Brad took his last breath. Everyone was present, and the funeral home director did his best to ensure everyone's voices were heard in the decisions. Ultimately though, the final decisions were all mine. And the next one was overwhelming.

"I'll take you to go look at the coffins now," the funeral director said after the other business matters were resolved.

We all filed downstairs into the basement where a staggering number of coffins were displayed. There were oak ones and pine, fancy detailed ones and plain. All I could think about was the fact that Brad was a woodworker and it seemed wrong to just shove one of these fine works of art into a blast oven to incinerate.

"Take your time," he said, as he showed me box after box.

Time didn't help though. In no time flat, I was overwhelmed and fighting back tears. They all cost so much money and it felt like a waste to burn them.

"They just seem too beautiful to burn," I mumbled.

After watching me walk in circles, he returned to my side once more.

"Another option is to go with a cardboard container for the cremation but use a rented casket for the service."

A cardboard box. It sounded so cheap, but still held a significant price tag. More importantly though, I felt like Brad would approve. No one else dared make the decision for me and most had left me to wander aimlessly in the sterile space.

I picked a tissue from one of the many boxes scattered around the room and nodded.

"I think that would work," I finally agreed.

After choosing between the rental units, there was one last detail to finalize before we could go home.

"Can you bring an outfit for Brad tomorrow?"

"Yes, of course," I agreed.

"Again, I am so sorry for your loss, Katherine," he said. "Please call us if there is anything more we can help you with, or if you have any questions."

I nodded before rejoining the family, so we could fall into the rest of our day.

The next day passed in a blur. We had an appointment at the florist to pick out casket sprays first thing. Joe drove me to meet Joan to pour over flower and colour options. Kaya stayed back to start the process of contacting friends and co-workers. My mom oversaw the kids.

Before dealing with flowers, Joe and I stopped at the funeral home to drop off an outfit for Brad. We planned to stop again on the way home, so I could say my final goodbye.

"Hello Katherine," the funeral director said as I walked in on our second visit. "Wayne will be calling you this afternoon. We have Brad ready for you when you are ready."

I looked to Joe at my side.

"Do you want to come with me?" I asked hopefully.

He shook his head.

"This is your time. I'll be here when you come out."

The tears threatened as soon as we walked into the visitation room. A screen stood at the front of the room. Brad lay behind it.

"As we arranged, Brad has been embalmed. We dressed him in the clothes you brought earlier. You are free to stay as long as you want. Once you are done, he will be taken to the crematorium. Is anyone else planning on visiting before that happens?"

"No," I said. "Just me. Everyone else has said their goodbyes."

"Very good," he answered with a nod.

He gently directed me forward to the curtained area and led me behind. Brad lay in the coffin in the outfit I had picked the day before: the outfit we were married in.

"Oh…"

Oh God. The tears were instant. Everything else disappeared.

"Oh Brad," I sighed. "Oh sweetheart."

I leaned in to kiss the man who had been by my side for a decade. There was no returning that touch anymore though. His skin was waxy, face lined with makeup to hide the sallow colour left behind when blood stopped pumping through him. This was no longer my husband, but all that I had left, and it gutted me. These were the only moments we had left.

I spilled tears, asked his advice, shared the excruciating steps I had taken in the hours since I had seen him last.

"Guess who is going to lead the funeral?" I said with a crumpled laugh. "Wayne; the man who married us. I have to speak with him this afternoon. Isn't that perfect?"

It was, but all Brad's answers were now in my head. His voice might be disembodied, but his thoughts echoed strong in my mind. They always will.

At some point, I heard him pause and look towards the clock.

"I know." I said mournfully. "I know it's time. Joe is waiting for me. It's time to go. I just…"

…hate to leave you again…

I didn't need to speak the words out loud anymore. But they were words I choked on, nonetheless. This time—this leave-taking—would be the last. I wanted to stretch it out forever.

Brad said nothing.

As much as everyone had said 'take your time' repeatedly, this moment was finite. And I knew I would never have another opportunity to say what needed saying, to touch, to hold, or see him How do you cross that line when you can't ever walk back?

You force yourself.

I reached for my purse on the floor. My internal voices began screaming and throwing themselves at me, trying to get me to sit back down. To stay five more minutes. Or…

I had to go. The Angel and Devil on my shoulders made my thoughts spin, but I steadied my resolve. I reached over and planted my lips on his, then slowly pulled away. This wasn't Brad anymore. Only his shell was left. I rested my hand on his, then turned.

That was the last time I ever saw him again.

You know, that's not exactly true. Anyone who has ever lost a loved one knows that you never truly lose them. They live on in your head. They visit your dreams. You breathe life into them in stories around the dinner table or with others who also knew them. Every moment and memory you had with them lives on in you. All you need to do is pull those memories out and they spring to life once more.

I didn't get that then though. It would take months, if not years to fully appreciate the gift of all our days together and the moments accumulated between us. They are different for everyone, even from one person who knows the departed to the next. I started to learn that immediately, as my family and friends worked to pull together a celebration of Brad that week.

My God, the tears. But there was laughter too. We cried for our loss and that no new memories would be built, but collective stories started the catharsis. Don't ever underestimate the power of time spent together. Those moments are the pearls of life.

Over the next few days that is what we did. We pulled out pictures to put on posterboards. A smiling picture of Brad was found in order to be blown up and placed on the closed casket during the funeral. Stories were shared between us and with Wayne, the minister, to create a fuller picture of the man we had lost.

Because this was not just my loss. Brad was a husband, yes, but he was also a father, son, son-in-law, brother, brother-in-law, uncle, nephew, grandson, cousin, and co-worker. In every role though, he was also a friend. The aim was to capture it all to touch everyone whom Brad left a mark on. For every soul who stepped into the funeral home

232

to pay their respects, many more nursed their sorrow their own way and in their own time. For me, I was just desperate to get it all right.

"Do we have pictures of him from high school?"

"Are there any pictures of him as a child?"

"Should we include any of him in his work uniform?"

How do you capture everything that makes someone human? My desperation pushed me to look for more and more and more. Like my time with Brad's physical form, the planning of a funeral only had so many moments to spare. We picked a passage from Khalil Gibran's *The Prophet* to read at the funeral and arranged for sandwiches and fruit trays through a local church group. We finalized pictures, chose our own outfits to wear at the visitation and funeral, and fielded phone calls from well-wishers devastated to hear of Brad's passing.

It didn't feel like enough.

But Friday loomed and time ran out once more. Shock kept me moving, if not functioning on all gears. I still wasn't driving. Food was an afterthought that my mother kept reminding me to eat. And slipping into bed at night was a nightmare.

Every morning I woke up and the story began anew. The place beside me in bed was cold and untouched. When I stepped into the shower, the phone rang over and over again with news of Brad's loss. He wasn't there to touch, to ask questions of, to laugh with, or even to be pissed off at. All I had was a loop in my head screaming "Oh my God! Oh my God!" over and over.

This couldn't be real. But it was. I shouldn't be planning a funeral, but I was picking out shoes to wear and deciding if putting contact lenses in was worth the tears that might wash them right back out again. It was all WRONG. So wrong. And yet, every day this new reality smacked me in the face again. All I had to do was to get through the funeral.

The lines of people who snaked out with sad eyes and limp hugs.

"I'm sorry for your loss." on repeat.

The faceless well-wishers sharing platitudes that I somehow needed to respond to ad nauseum.

What do I remember from it all?

"Katherine, I am getting you a plate of food and a drink. Would you rather coffee, tea, coke, ginger ale, juice?"

That was Ruth. She knew I was incapable of thought and immediately noticed I had lost 10 pounds that week. I needed to replenish liquid from all the tears I shed and would never get a break to get near the food table as long as I was the belle of the funeral ball. She was on it.

"I want you to meet a few of my co-workers who came."

This was just as hard on Joan, as the mother of the deceased. I needed to recognize that. Tearing myself away from others to focus on her and the different incarnation of Brad was important. Even though she was the reason I was there, they wanted to pay their respects.

Brad's aunts and uncles came from across Ontario. My sister's in-laws came *en masse* to pay their respects from the other side of Toronto. His coworkers and high school friends jammed pews and spilled out the back. Our investment broker and his wife shook my hand, as did Dr. T, the plastic surgeon who started Brad's cancer journey with us.

It was a blur and endless, until my mom came up to me with my baby.

"Rylie needs you," she said.

And that was it. It was all over.

I was no longer the grieving widow. I was Mom. That hat usurped everything.

I hid away to breastfeed my baby and then gathered up everything we had filled the funeral home with. Ken had brought the cabinet that Brad had worked so hard to craft, and he carefully packed it back into his truck to bring home for me. A cabinet Brad had made while he and Cassie took woodworking classes together. Now just another box full of memories, that Ken and Cassie lovingly wrapped for transport. How many real estate agents help out at client's funerals? A friend does. That care wasn't lost on me or her. It was another link to the man we had lost.

While there were more pieces to collect, they didn't come close to capturing all of Brad. Cassie grabbed pictures. My sister gathered Taryn. Someone else packed the casket spray and other flowers into waiting vehicles. It seemed a paltry amount for a life cut short too soon. Nothing could have been enough though. When the parking lot emptied out, a few remaining friends trailed us back to my house to hold a small mass of our own, complete with remaining food and drinks stronger than tea. More tears, more lopsided smiles, more disbelief, and then it all trickled away.

Kaya and Tony left to take possession of their very first home. My friends Scott, Cam and Ruth drove back to Brantford to step back into their own lives. Faye and Stu took their babies home to put to bed. The only ones left were Mom and Joe, Taryn, Rylie, and I. Joe left the next morning, leaving Mom to help me out for a day or two more, but before I knew it, it was just the girls and myself left.

This was our new normal.

Chapter 7: Finding My Way

The New Normal

"Wed, Sep 5, 2007
Brad passed away a week ago today. I am just about
to hit the exact time of his passing. At so many
points the thought has made me feel sick to my
stomach. Every step of the way, from his diagnosis,
to hospitalizations, to treatments has been surreal. I
keep on wondering when I am going to wake up. But
I just wake up to another day alone."

The New Normal.

I know some of you have heard that phrase. I'm not sure if it is meant to help heal, but it sticks in the throats of most newly grieving people. Your loved one is gone, and this is what life looks like now. You count the minutes, hours, then days since you saw them last. Since you spoke. This is the 'new' normal. You are no longer a 'we' or an 'us' if you were part of a couple before. You are now an 'I' and 'me'. And that reality takes a long time to process and accept.

Here is just one example: I am going to the grocery store. I need to buy potatoes. How many do we need?

Oh…

That was one of my firsts in the "new normal" that was now my life.

Yours might have looked slightly different. Maybe you paused before buying your wife's favourite pickles: the ones you can't stand. Possibly you bought the hand cream they use because it was on the list before they died, and you didn't think about the fact no one will use it anymore. Or maybe you got stuck on how much toilet paper to buy, now that one less person will be using it moving forward.

For me it was potatoes.

Before my mom left to return to her 'normal' life, she and I went to the grocery store to pick up a few things to restock my house with. We needed veggies for dinner, milk, and bread. And I was out of potatoes. I walked over to where they lay. There were 10-lb bags of white and yellow potatoes. A pile of loose potatoes sat in a mound on the other side of the display. And small bags of new round potatoes lay nearby. Which ones should I choose? This is what my mind did.

I need to buy potatoes. Oh... potatoes. How many should I buy? Brad was the big potato guy. Taryn likes them well enough, but she is only 2. How many will she eat? Rylie is only 10 months. She doesn't even like potatoes. Should I buy a bag and have half of them rot? Should I only buy a couple? What am I going to make with them? Is it worth it to even buy any at all?

I stood there staring at potatoes and a tear slid down my cheek. I don't know what my mother's moment was, but she quietly steered the cart and my babies away to give me pause in this grief moment. I'm sure people thought I had lost my mind standing there crying over stupid spuds. I guess I had.

This was the first shockwave of life post-Brad. The decisions were now all mine. Whether they were right or wrong, they were my choices to make. I could waffle and refer to other people's thoughts and opinions, but eventually I would have to own that I was no longer part of a 'we'.

After falling apart over tubers, I finally walked away with nothing.

"Thur, Sep 13, 2007
Brad passed away two weeks ago yesterday. I still
can't believe it..."

It happened again a month later. After my mom left, I fled to my sister's new house in Ajax. Before I left, I made arrangements for Brad's parents to feed the cats. Honestly, I don't know how they survived, as I had nothing left for them with everything else that drowned me, but I knew enough to ask someone to help with my poor struggling kitties too.

"Do you want me to finish the laundry room?" Art asked before I left.

Currently, it was framed in, and insulation lined the 2x4s.

"No," I answered deliberately. "The laundry room is functional. It's fine. What I can't look at anymore though is the bathroom."

Every morning, the fateful phone call rang through my mind, and I sobbed my way through shower after shower. I couldn't stand it anymore.

When we got home a week later, the toilet and floor were all that remained. The old tub, glass slider, vanity, mirror, cabinets: they were all gone. I was never so happy to see a deconstruction. The reconstruction was harder though.

"We'll go pick out a tub and toilet. Think about what kind of vanity you want to replace it with."

No problem. Until I was standing staring at bathtubs hung up on a wall, and a line of toilets that all looked similar enough to make them indistinguishable.

I hadn't grown up in a household of handy people. My mom could change a washer on a faucet, but that was about it. She hired neighbourhood kids to mow our lawn and I don't ever remember any major construction projects undertaken at any of the houses we lived in. Paint was the height of our transformations. But now I had to choose a toilet.

"Which one would you pick?" I asked Art. "What's the difference between them?"

This was supposed to be Brad's job. I could pick paint or tile colours but wasn't savvy enough to fathom that bathtubs were either right- or left-handed. Sure, it made sense in hindsight—where the drain lay was important—but I had never thought about it before. It felt so far out of my wheelhouse as to be overwhelming, but there was no way that Art was going to step on my toes to take over this little project I had started.

"I don't know," I said staring at the porcelain thrones and baths. "That one?"

What if I picked the wrong one? What if he thought I was stupid for my choices? What if, what if, what if?

What if Brad were here? He would know which one to choose and wouldn't make a big deal about it. He would laugh at my indecision, with an "Okay princess."

Why wasn't he here?!

Because he was dead. This was my new normal. If I wanted to make big decisions like ripping out a bathroom, I had to make the big decisions of what I wanted to replace it with.

My new normal.

With a toilet chosen, the vanity came easier. I may not have understood the logistics behind different plumbing pieces, but I had measurements to guide choices here. And colour preferences. I could do this.

That was until it got delivered.

Art and I slid the vanity into place and… I didn't like it. It was the wrong height. It was kitchen counter height, which was higher than traditional bathroom counter height. I had a baby just learning to crawl and a toddler who would never reach the water without a stepladder.

I looked at the vanity. I looked at Art. I looked at the vanity and talked through what to do with Brad in my head.

"Taryn won't be able to reach that. It's too tall. But we brought it home. Will they take it back? Will store policy prevent me from getting what I want and what's right for my family? What should I do?"

"Can we take it back?" I asked Art tentatively, hoping this time he would share his expertise in the matter with me.

"We can try," he said.

And despite initial grumbling, the big box store allowed me to return it. In its place, I got a new vanity that fit the space and my family far better. It took a few months, but I was learning. The hard way, but I was learning.

One of the things I vaguely understood but couldn't fully comprehend was how this relatively simple bathroom renovation affected more than just me though. Art had been there day in and day out in Brad's last days working on our other bathroom. Every day I checked in with Brad to see whether they had taken the opportunity to talk while gazes were averted and hands busy with tools and supplies. They never did, instead seeking solace in their proximity and the mutually understood reality that their very presence spelt love. Art, and a whole generation of men, hadn't been brought up to share feelings verbally. It just wasn't his way. Emotions were the realm of women (even though fear, anger, sadness, enjoyment, and a whole host of other emotions were experienced by all).

I was about words though. And emotions aplenty. At that point, I didn't yet understand that grief looked and felt different for others than from my experience of it. For me, Art's presence was a godsend for his handiness and an opportunity for the two of use to connect over our mutual love of Brad. Talking about him pushed Art's boundaries though. That wasn't in his comfort zone, and I certainly wasn't the one whom he felt comfortable enough to unpack the heaviness around his grief. Ultimately, my emotions were too much for him.

I didn't see it. I asked too much; my persistence to talk wearing the very air we shared thin. The renovations couldn't be done soon enough. Too many awkward pauses marked the vast divide of who we were fundamentally as people. I couldn't see the damage wrought by my push to bond, but it was there. This was just a painful renovation, nothing more. The damage caused by our mutual loss wasn't a loss we could carry together. Eventually, the renovation came to an end.

Tackling a bathroom renovation is one thing, but making major life decisions is another matter entirely. One that experts generally don't recommend in the first year of grief. There are too many firsts to stumble through, too many hiccups to smooth over, too little straight thinking to make decision making reliable at this point in your life. In the grand scheme of things, choosing floor tiles was a reversible decision. Selling a home and moving to another city to start fresh only changes the scenery, not the thoughts in your head.

My brother-in-law encouraged me to do just that.

"You should move to Ajax," he said when we stayed with him after the funeral. "We're here, my parents and family are here, and they've already claimed you as part of our family. The cousins will be closer together, and you'll have your sister and I for support."

I loved him for the offer, but knew it wasn't the right decision at the time. Sure, I might be closer to my sister, but then I would have to find a new job, lawyer, doctor, mechanic; the list went on. I didn't want to be dependent on them for everything from my entertainment to helping me find new friends, and that new life I was supposed to be embracing. I didn't want to be a burden but that was what I felt like for everyone. I was the poor grieving widow who people tiptoed around asking "Are you alright? Are things getting better? Is there anything you need?"

No! I needed my husband back! No, it wasn't getting better. The shock was only wearing off after a month. I was still raw all the way through. Felt like I always would be. And I had no idea what I needed to make any of it better. Would a cookie help? A hug?

I was drowning.

"Sun, Sep 30, 2007
Brad has been gone for just over a month.
Wednesday it was four weeks. Cassie had me over
for dinner. Mom called. Kaya called. The phone call
that affected me the most was the two hours I was on
the phone with Kelly. It is so sad to have other
people know so well the depth of your sorrow. Too
many have been in similar circumstances. Those
people help the most.
Not a day goes by that I don't cry..."

I counted life in weeks. Then months. It anchored my days and kept me moving, if not feeling better. Tasks accomplished felt hollow. Steps forward only spelt betrayal to my person lost. And despite not knowing what else to suggest to people at that point, in my heart I knew one thing. I was the loneliest I had ever been.

"Oct 3, 2007
I got a letter today that Brad's credit card has been
paid off. On Friday I heard tell and got note that the
van loan has been paid off. I also heard that the
mortgage protection has been approved, just
figuring numbers with the financial institution.
Monday, I got two cheques from Brad's life
insurance.
None of this makes me happy. I would give it all
back in a heartbeat. I don't want it. I want Brad. The
money just makes me sad. Brad would feel good that

244

What should people have done or said? How could they make it better? At that point I had no idea. Today, I know that time is the biggest healer, but the people along your journey are key too. The ones who mean the most are those who aren't afraid to just be there and who keep talking and asking, regardless of what the conversation or outcome is.

If that sounds daunting, I get it. I am asking you to step inside someone's fire to sit with them while they burn, to tread water with them while their waves smash over them again and again. You can feel their heat, see their tsunami, despite it not hitting you in the same way. Your job is to just be there. When they are ready, you might be the one to point the way towards the shore. Or you might not. You don't have to be their everything but be someone. All those someone's add up. Just please don't leave them alone. Alone feels like the worst thing ever.

Being courageous enough to sit with someone who is grieving is a gift that shouldn't be undervalued. You are offering a colossal service, even if it doesn't feel like it in the moment. The many people who let me talk or shared their stories of Brad with me were hugely appreciated. I promise you, I appreciated every one.

So, my recommendation? Don't be shy talking about the person who is gone. The widow/widower is already thinking about them. Constantly. I can guarantee you of that. Talking about them helps people process what is going on in their head. They might need to tell their grief story over and over again in the early days. Or they might not want to talk at all. Where I needed to talk and have since listened to many friends who just lost spouses and needed to share their stories, I know there are plenty of others who can't or choose not to.

There is no right way to grieve.

I know that truth firsthand. Not only did various grief counsellors remind me of that, but I saw others grappling with different losses in their own ways. Some people embrace counselling, some throw themselves into work, others journal, and plenty more work through their grief internally in their own time frame. No path is wrong.

There is no right way to grieve.

There is a right way to help someone suffering through loss though. Don't let them feel more alone than they already are. Losing a spouse feels like losing a part of yourself. The adage 'the better half' speaks to that. You don't need to be two halves of a whole, but when you enter a significant relationship, so much of your day-to-day is tied into the other person. When you lose them, you need to relearn almost everything all over again. That might be cooking, driving, tending finances, doing or organizing someone else to complete household chores, repairs, and tasks, and even entertaining oneself. Couples learn to compromise in every step of their relationship and losing the other person in that dance is hard. There isn't any other way to say it.

And that first year after loss? Every. Day. Is. Agony.

Dramatic? Maybe, but it doesn't feel like it most days. Don't get me wrong. You will still laugh, love, and smile. But know that it all happens through a fresh lens. Grief changes you. In what feels like every way. And it all starts on the day you learn your person is gone.

Little secret? It never ends.

But all the person needs to do in the early days is get through one day, one moment at a time. People kept reminding me to breathe, which sounds funny, until you realize that you aren't taking more than shallow breaths to keep moving.

"Breathe."

As I worked so hard to keep from crying every moment of the day. I lived clenched, physically battling to stay upright. The sight of bills with Brad's name on them, the empty housecoat on the back of the closet door, the death certificate—all things I steeled myself for, little realizing that it kept me in a state of fight or flight.

"Breathe."

But every time I tried to relax, it turned into trickles, if not sobs. I couldn't chance breathing for fear of losing it even more when I was trying to solo-parent two babies, run a household alone, and wind down another person's life.

Did you think it all ended with the funeral?

Not at all. In some ways, the busyness after the funeral was good. Where doctor appointments filled the days before, now it was lawyers, mortgage specialists, financial advisors, and the funeral home. I had to cancel Brad's health card, SIN card, passport, as well as notify life insurance, mortgage insurance, loan insurance, and credit card insurance. Once final cheques came in and bill payments were switched to my account, bank accounts had to be closed. There was also car insurance, house insurance, and city taxes that all needed to have his name taken off And everyone needed a copy of the death certificate, so that meant trips back to the funeral home.

I was lucky that Rona and I had already started the process of getting daycare in place. By the time I got back from my sister's home, I needed those precious daycare hours to get all the new running around done. Rona was another slot in my schedule too: now as grief counsellor. She always had lots of tissues and heaps of patience, but after a few visits into my 'new normal' she brought up something I hadn't seen coming.

"Katherine, I think it is time you think about finding someone new to speak with. This is my only office. I don't think it is good for you to keep coming back to the Cancer Clinic to see me. If I had another location, it might be different, but my location makes it difficult for you to move forward in your grieving."

To be fair, by that time it was several months after Brad's death, but still. For me it was another loss and it hurt. I didn't care that she was probably right: I had already struggled walking through the gauntlet of patients and memories from the outer doors to Rona's office. Having her gently suggest I shouldn't come to see her any longer felt like another colossal tear in the fiber of my life that I didn't want to process.

But yes, that was where Brad reclined in a chair for interferon treatments. And Taryn and I escaped to the little waterfall just down the hall, while her Daddy was pumped full of 'medicine'. The people I walked by to make my way to her office all had old faces, no matter their biological years. They were a reminder of the disease that stole my husband, but also a burr in my psyche. I couldn't help but begrudge them the years they had on my Bradley. Old people suddenly became my nemeses, and they were everywhere at the Cancer Clinic.

Rona knew.

But how could I find someone new when I was this fragile? Where should I even start to look? The phone book seemed far too impersonal, as did clerical descriptions on dry websites. It was more than I could wrap my head around, but I knew I needed to talk to someone.

I tried my GP, but one visit was enough to let me know she couldn't help.

"Do you want me to write you a prescription for antidepressants?"

No. I needed to talk. I needed to process what had just happened. Who I was and where I was going. I needed someone to tell me I was functioning well, because I was damn sure I wasn't. I lived under constant fear that CAS would knock on my door to question the level of my parenting skills and debate whether or not they should step in. I cried every day after all. And when I wasn't crying, I felt like I replaced it with yelling. How was that for good parenting? It wasn't. It didn't feel like it anyway.

What I didn't see though was that I was making breakfast, lunch, and dinner, plus providing snacks for the girls. I bathed them regularly and read stories every night. They had clean clothes and they fit. And despite the tears, there were so many hugs. I didn't recognize it, but I was grocery shopping, paying bills, and accomplishing all the tasks required in laying a life to rest. I was doing more than alright, but all I could feel was the massive pain in my chest that blinded me to everything else. I felt like I was failing because I couldn't breathe.

My breaths might have been shallow, but they were there. Life existed in the moment. Only this moment today, as I had lost faith in tomorrows the day that Brad died. For now, I just needed to learn how to live again. It felt like an illness in its own right and time was the only cure.

Learning to Breathe

"Nov 1, 2007
It has been two months since Brad died. I am
numb..."

I couldn't breathe. I was crying and couldn't stop. It was too much. I couldn't handle it all. The new normal. Every step away from Brad. I didn't want to take any more steps. I wanted to stop. To lie down and stay there. I didn't want to keep going. I needed help.

But every day, I woke up to a cold pillow beside me and two babies who needed me to clothe and feed them and start us into this new day that somehow began all over again. Every day I cried. Every day I struggled. But every night I crawled into bed and miraculously woke with the dawn once more.

"Nov 6, 2007
I want so badly to wake up. This is a horrible
nightmare. I don't want to be alone anymore. I want
Brad back to talk to, to help with the kids, to love.
Why is this happening?"

All the entries asked why. All the entries screamed pain. But what I didn't see were the movements too. They were tiny against the gargantuan mound of grief I had to process, but today I see it. I see the in between of what I didn't say.

By three months, I had added reiki sessions into my life in hopes it would help my healing. Then therapeutic touch. Then debated meeting with an energy healer. I deciphered dreams of Brad and poured my aches into a journal. None of it lessened my pain and I felt desperate, but despite myself, I was also moving through all those firsts.

First week, first month, first birthdays, holidays, and seasons. They all hurt because you don't know what they are going to look like or how they are going to feel.

Just FYI—they suck.

Which ones sucked worst? Going to my sister's house and wanting to call home to tell Brad about what we were doing.

"We went to the zoo!"

"Rylie started to climb the stairs. Nothing is going to stop her now."

"I miss you and can't wait to get home to see you…"

Oh ya, that one won't happen. Actually, the phone call couldn't happen either. And wanting to race home to see him wouldn't help, because, well, he wasn't there. He wasn't anywhere other than my mind.

Walking into the house for the first time knowing he wasn't there to greet us—crazy awful sucky moment too.

Writing thank you cards was pretty hard as well. The worst one was the first. To Dr. J. He told me the day that Brad died that he planned to leave melanoma care. That it was too hard. But his presence in our life during those awful few years were a lifeline we clung to that I somehow needed to convey.

"Thank you for the hope. Thank you for trying.
Thank you for caring. Thank you for your hours
spent with us in body and in spirit. Thank you for the
people you brought to us that helped in the fight.
Thank you for your smiles. Thank you for your fears.
Thank you for your tears.
There is so much we have experienced over the last
two and a half years. You have been there for most
of our journey. You listened to our concerns, offered
help, support, solutions, and hope. While there has
been so much pain, we have been blessed with an
amazing amount of people who stepped up to try to
balance the load. You were a cornerstone in our
struggle. I don't know if you can ever realize the
depth that you touched us. Where words fail, all I
can say is,
Thank you."

It could never be enough to express my gratitude. The tears that sealed the page weren't enough either. How could I share that his positive attitude helped Brad live every day, despite everything? He never stopped living. Brad knew better than almost everyone what was going on, but he never stopped pushing and breathing in every day. Did he steal all our breath when he left?

No. I lost the ability to inhale on that first phone call in 2005. When the ambulance took him away on April 1st, I lost my ability to see. By the time he died, I couldn't think any longer. I was a shell, walking but incapable of little more than numb actions.

God, so many awful days. But there were also days that helped to peel back my inner cage. Days that cleared my vision and breathed a little clarity into my soul.

Like on the one-month anniversary of Brad's death. I talked to my mom. I talked to my sister. I had dinner with Cassie. But a phone call from Kelly reminded me that Brad existed in more places than just my heart and that all of us experience trauma at some point or another. They are all relative to our own experience, but our own worst days are our own, and the lessons learned in them can help prop another up during their darkest hours. Her son had a serious accident when he was a few years old, and they feared he would die. He spent months in hospital, with many surgeries to repair the damages done during the accident. They feared he would be forever scarred. But in their grief and fears, their family rallied. Yes, there were bad days and setbacks, but not only did he survive, he learned to re-walk, and today, he is a thriving young man with a job and living on his own. In that moment though, Kelly's gift was sharing that she had been there too. I was not alone.

Breathe…

I saw someone other than me and the world got bigger.

Most days, I couldn't look at myself in the mirror. I couldn't look in my eyes. There was too much pain there and seeing it made me want to cry even more. I felt so bad for the poor woman looking back at me who was so broken. It didn't feel like there was anything I could do for her, so I just averted my gaze. I couldn't look at her.

But Kelly effectively touched my hand and sat with me for a moment. Not family. Not even my closest friend at the time. Just someone who saw me and offered what she could to help. Recognizing that she saw me—a first. Somehow, she knew. It was a revelation.

Others saw me too. Hunched over a rake, shuddering through another grief moment—first fall season raking leaves alone. I was broken, shattered anew at the injustice of having to do it all alone. Having to figure out firsts and new roles and everything I just didn't want to do.

Alone.

"Hey Kathy," a kind voice broke in. "How are you doing today?"

I looked up from the rake that supported me. There stood Barry, my 80ish-year-old neighbour with a rake of his own in hand. Barry, who looked like he weighed 100 pounds with all his clothes on and maybe some boots too. He had seen me. He had lost his own spouse a few years previous and recognized my struggle. The struggle made us kin.

"Do you need a hand?"

I could see his own history in that watery gaze. He knew the path I was on and obviously remembered how hard it was. His rake wouldn't make a dent in the pile, but that wasn't the point. The point was in solidarity in grief. In knowing that I was not alone, despite how lonely everything felt.

And then Cody was there with another rake. He worked from home and had seen Barry slowly make his way over to me. He knew Barry might have meant well but wouldn't make a dent in the physical labour. The hunch of my shoulders spoke to the fact that I wasn't alright and that I needed a hand, regardless of whether I asked for it or not. Cody knew that while Barry's offer was kind, it wasn't enough.

"Hey Katherine. Hey Barry. Need a hand? Can I join the party?"

We were now a quiet work gang of three. No one spoke of my loss, but I felt their love in their unspoken support. I couldn't have asked but needed it desperately. In grief I felt alone—so many feel alone in early days of grief—but in helping tackle a concrete task, they reminded me there were others around me that cared and were there when I needed them.

Together we swept the yard of the first of the season's debris. We readied my yard for hibernation in anticipation of the coming winter and rebirth of spring. I might have wondered how they could see me when I couldn't see beyond myself, but it was a good lesson. Barry saw himself in my sorrows. Cody knew compassion and his sturdy muscles would make more of a difference than words. They gave because it was the right thing to do. It was something they could do when nothing would make my world whole again, when nothing would bring Brad back. And it was enough in that moment.

Bless the souls who know. They are the ones who taught me I wasn't invisible. Their presence alone helped me pause and give room for my breath to return. They were neighbours, friends, staff at the daycare, family, and sometimes strangers. I had no idea what I needed beyond the impossible task of stepping back in time, but slowly, slowly, the kindnesses which people shared out in the world gave me pause to focus again.

If you have someone whom you would like to help, what you need to do is to go about this vigil in the right way. Don't say, "Call me if you need anything" because a grieving person is struggling to make sense of the world and their place in it. They probably don't have any idea what they need, beyond their next meal. What that meal might be, could be just as big a mystery. Calling might be too far beyond their strength on their worst days too. Instead, be specific. There are so many ways to help, many of them costing nothing more than a moment of time or the gift of listening.

This is by no means a complete list, but it gives you an idea of where to start. I urge you to use your best judgement around what you know of the grieving person. These ideas are also helpful for those in crisis, as they are often so focused on the pressing events at hand that menial everyday tasks (like eating some days!) can be more than someone can handle.

As to my suggestions, you might have others of your own. If you are grieving, feel free to share this list with well-wishers who aren't sure how to help. If you are trying to support someone, be creative and keep trying, even if you get turned down the first, second, or tenth time. Be patient. Be kind and compassionate. This is an incredibly hard road to walk and there will be so many stumbles and falls along the way. Know that those stumbles are alright: really, they are expected.

NOTE: I am not a grief counsellor, nor specialist in the grief industry. I'm just someone who experienced their own grief journey firsthand and note what worked for me. That doesn't mean any or all of them will work for others. Use your best judgement. For those who you are struggling, I encourage you to seek out a professional you can trust.

How to Help

- "Can I mow your lawn?"
- "I shovelled your driveway."
- Rake someone's leaves with them or offer to do it for them if you sense the task is too much.
- Cut a bouquet from your own garden (sometimes even more thoughtful than bought flowers from the store).
- "Would you like to join me for a walk? I would love the company."
- Offer to walk their dog, or if you also have a dog, go together for the exercise (exercise is good for mind and body for all).
- "I made a second lasagna for you while I was making one for me, because I know you love it. Feel free to eat it tonight or freeze it for later."
- Deliver a meal during a crisis, baked goods just because to let them know you are thinking of them or offer to share a meal, so they have company and conversation for a few hours.
- "Let my daughter babysit, so you and I can go to the movies, or you can run errands without dragging children along with you."
- "I am going to help you paint the living room. Is there a day that works best for you?"
- "I'm running to the grocery store. Do you need me to pick you up anything or would you like to come with me?"
- "When you are ready to go through your loved one's clothes, I will help you sort and pack them up."
- "I just popped by to say hi. If you don't feel like talking don't feel you need to, but know I am here whenever you do."
- Ask if they would like to go for a coffee to give them a chance to talk about their loved one, or something completely unrelated, anything to give an opportunity for an activity outside of day-to-day routines.
- "Do you want to talk about your loved one? I remember when they did... (share a touching/funny/whatever story)"
- Invite them to join you for holiday celebrations (holidays and celebrations, especially firsts, are difficult for those trying to establish new normals.

257

Ultimately, you want to recognize that someone who is grieving is still human. They are hurting and uncertain how to behave or who they really are anymore from one moment to the next; sometimes just wanting to be 'normal' and not treated like a delicate creature of unknown origin and other times recognized for the trauma and loss that fills their souls. We are messy and hard and contrary, and craving love. Even in the moments when we don't think we will ever see that or deserve it again. Especially then.

Breathe...

Day one, day two, day three, day four... week one, week two... month one... Where would it end? When would it get better? It felt like never.

Wellspring

A few weeks before Brad died, a VON nurse was at the house. They came regularly at that point (not that it felt like they made much difference in the grand scheme of things). While their focus was Brad, it was hard to miss myself and the girls. This particular visit stepped beyond his medical needs.

The woman must have sensed my frayed ends, as she asked about our emotional supports.

"They assigned a social worker at the hospital," I replied. "She's alright, helps with forms and the like..."

"Have you been to Wellspring?" she asked.

I looked at her blankly.

"Wellspring is a cancer support center," she continued. "They offer counselling, art programs, yoga, and other supports for those dealing with cancer."

"Oh?"

"It is a free service open to anyone," she continued as she saw my face brighten, then immediately fall. "You can access their services whether you are facing a cancer diagnosis, are a family member, or a friend helping support someone going through a cancer journey. They have a little something for everyone."

"Really?" I answered a little more hopefully.

"They have locations across Ontario, but the London location is right downtown."

Open to anyone. Anyone touched by cancer. That was certainly us. And God knows, I was desperate for someone to make my world feel more manageable.

She finished up her wellness visit with Brad but made a point to mention Wellspring again before she left.

"They really are a great organization," she reiterated. "You should check them out just to see if they have anything that might help you."

The wheels were turning already.

The next afternoon, I packed up Rylie after putting Taryn down for a nap.

"I am going to go see what Wellspring is all about," I said to Brad. His headaches generally precluded any trips most afternoons.

I made my way downtown and found a parking spot down the road from the old yellow brick house which had been converted into Wellspring's London, Ontario headquarters. A large front porch beckoned passersby, with a ramp to ensure anyone could visit, regardless of mobility. I was grateful for the accessibility, as I pushed Rylie's stroller up to the front door. That is where I stopped though.

"You can do this," I told myself, as I paused on the threshold.

Instead, I read the sign and their hours, then glanced around at the planters and gardens. My heart raced, as I stared back at the street and slowly pushed Rylie's stroller back and forth to calm my nerves.

No lie. I was losing the battle.

My chest constricted and I cursed the world, as I pointed the stroller back towards the ramp. I couldn't. I didn't know what to say. I didn't know what I wanted. I just couldn't put myself out there when I just didn't have anything left in the tank. There were no pleasantries in my bag of tricks. No bubbly "hi"s or the lie of "I'm fine," which was supposed to be your pat answer when anyone asked how you were. I was stretched too thin and didn't have what it took to cross the threshold that day. Tears already prickled the corners of my eyes, as we started down the ramp.

"Hi, can I help you?" a voice called out. "Would you like to come in?"

I was a deer in the headlights. Someone had seen me and called me out, regardless of whether I was ready to actually speak to anyone or not. I hadn't even had the nerve to cross the threshold to anonymously poke around, but now someone was talking to me.

The woman smiled warmly and took another step onto the porch.

"Please come in and take a look around. My name's Barbara. I would be happy to show you around and tell you about some of the programs we have available."

I was trapped, but in the best way possible in that moment. It was the most hopeful scenario I could have asked for. Barbara swung the door wide and shone me the most welcoming smile I had felt in as long as I could remember.

I squeezed past her and stood awkwardly in the hallway looking around. While I might have wanted to only quietly wander around and not cause anyone any trouble, that wasn't an option with Barbara. She might have just been the volunteer on the front desk that day—she had seen her fair share of damaged souls in her time there, plus during her previous medical career—but she was so much more for me. She recognized my fear, could sense the reticence which the medical field had formed around me, and somehow knew that all I needed was someone in my corner. Katherine's corner—not Brad's wife, nor Taryn and Rylie's mother. I couldn't shrink from her gaze and that was a gift I didn't know I needed. Barbara was bigger than the cancer that owned everything in my world, just because she wasn't afraid of it, no matter what it looked like or what the potential outcome. She was beautiful.

Stepping through the door was a brave first step, but Brad's time ran out before I ever got a chance to visit again. I spent half an hour learning about the many programs Wellspring offered, along with getting a brief tour of the rooms where some of the programs were held.

"We offer reiki and therapeutic touch in these rooms," she said as we walked down the hall. "You are welcome to take out any of the books from our library. Peer support counselling appointments are available by appointment or for drop-in whenever needed. Plus, there are art therapy classes, nutrition classes, look good feel better programs, and so much more."

I nodded, as I followed along behind her, trying to take it all in.

"Do you have cancer?" she asked delicately as we paused at one of the doorways.

"No," I exclaimed quickly.

"All are welcome here," she added gently. "You are welcome to sign up for any classes, talk to peer support counselling, or just come in for tea and a cookie. We are here to help support you as you support whomever in your life is facing their cancer journey."

I started to tear up and furiously tried to blink the familiar tears away before they spilled and derailed my plan to learn more.

"My husband," I stuttered. "It's my husband who has cancer."

"He must be young," Barbara said. "And you with a baby. She looks very sweet."

I smiled, through moist lashes. "She's 10 months old. He's 34."

"I'm sorry to hear that," she said. "That's a lot on your plate."

"I have another daughter at home," I added. "She's two and a half."

I was rambling now. She didn't need to know that, but I had lost my filter.

Barbara wasn't embarrassed though. Far from it.

"Do you have any supports? Family? Friends? Co-workers?"

"I'm on maternity leave right now and haven't seen many co-workers. My mom and sister live out of town but come visit as often as they can. And I have a friend who helps with the kids pretty regularly."

I don't know if that was the right answer or not and I didn't feel very convincing. It felt like making excuses and that I had no one. How many people did I have though? And how many had drifted away since we moved to London? Or since Brad was diagnosed?

But Barbara's kind look that afternoon made me feel more connected than I had felt in ages. She seemed to see my struggles, feel for me, but not judge me due to my perceived failings or ability to cope. I wasn't the first person to walk in the door with a hard story. She had met plenty of people and heard more stories during that time than I could fathom. And while she couldn't physically fix me or anyone in my world, she made the journey better just by listening and reminding me that I was not alone.

The tissue she handed me wasn't offered in shame, fear, or embarrassment. And it felt like the most humane act I had personally experienced in forever. She didn't look away. She held my gaze. And she was present.

"Can I offer you a hug?" she asked tenderly, as I wiped my eyes furiously.

All I could do was nod, as I stifled outright sobs. I lost the battle at composure, but Barbara won in shaving a measure of stress out of my soul that day.

"Let's get you a cookie, shall we?" she said as she patted my back.

It took several months to gather enough courage to go back again.

The next time I walked through the door, both girls were at daycare, but I had just as warm a welcome. There were still cookies, tea, coffee, conversation, and compassion on offer. They were there every single time I walked through the door after that too.

On my next visit, I signed up for a therapeutic touch session and enrolled in a gentle yoga class.

Over the time I frequented Wellspring, I met other beautiful souls volunteering at the front desk and spoke with a wide range of peer support counsellors who shared an endless supply of tissues and understanding. I met people who were battling cancer, and those who were supporting spouses, siblings, parents, and friends. I met survivors and grief support counsellors. I melted under the powerful hands of reiki and therapeutic touch practitioners. I stretched through the knots and tensions embedded deep into my body through multiple yoga sessions. And I pounded my pain into skins during many an uplifting drum circle.

There was so much healing needed and Wellspring was a fount of recovery for me. Not all of it was easy. God, was any of it? For every knot I released, a torrent of tears spilled out. But there were so many people who were there to walk with me along the way.

During one of my early yoga classes, I arrived feeling fragile. There were a lot of those days, but as soon as I laid on the mat that day I started to break.

Savasana: the art of relaxing and letting go of tension. That tension was the only thing that held me together in those days though. I couldn't relax. I didn't trust myself to be able to pull myself back together again if I started to breathe. If I allowed any space in my thoughts.

Tears immediately started to roll down my cheeks as soon as I closed my eyes. I desperately tried to tense up and force the waves of emotion away but knew there was no winning the war that day. Emma welcomed us to practice with her signature warmth, but I couldn't. Was breaking. No breathing. No coping...

"I'm sorry," I mumbled, as I rolled over and pulled myself to standing.

"Are you alright?" Emma asked.

I didn't trust myself to speak, so just shook my head as I hurried to the door. I heard her call out again, but I was fighting with my shoes and my tears, and the world, as I raced for the stairs.

"I'm sorry," I called out behind me as I thundered down the creaky stairwell.

I pushed through the front door, past the startled volunteer at the front desk, when a voice called out.

"Can I speak to you for a minute?" a man called out, as he hurried towards me.

I had made it to the sidewalk but hadn't escaped. Could never escape the horror that was my life. There were no words. Only oceans of tears that I couldn't hold back. And I just didn't have what it took to pass in that moment; to convince others that I was fine.

While all I wanted to do was flee, I paused. Tears streamed down my face, but there was nothing I could do about them. By leaning into savasana, I had sprung a leak. The leak held sorrow, frustration, dismay, an infinite level of overwhelming angst that I didn't know how to manage. It had been months since Brad died, but the grief seemed to only grow inside my torn chest.

"I spoke to Emma, and she said you were having a tough day," the man offered gently as excuse for his presence. "I don't believe we have met yet. My name is Daniel. I'm the Program Director at Wellspring."

Oh God. Pleasantries? I swiped at my eyes, as I tried to stem the wave of grief that was swamping me.

"Um, my name is Katherine," I mumbled. "Sorry, I'm having a rough day…"

What could I offer? I had no positive thoughts, sparkly conversation, or even a semblance of niceties I could dig into. Grief is cruel like that. It feels like it pushes you into a hole where you question everything and don't know or trust anything any longer. What was wrong? Nothing and everything. How could I explain that?

"That's alright," Daniel replied. "You are allowed tough days. Did you get bad news today?"

He thought I had cancer. That maybe I had just received a new diagnosis or something along those lines. Shit, it was a cancer wellness center after all. I didn't have cancer though. I didn't even have a friend or loved one who was dealing with cancer. Anymore. I shouldn't be there. I didn't belong.

"No," I snuffled, unsuccessfully trying to pull myself together. "I don't have cancer. You don't have to worry about me."

I turned to go.

"You're obviously struggling right now though," he persisted. "Do you want to talk about it?"

He wasn't giving up.

"My husband died from cancer in August," I offered as explanation. Like that would give me a pass. "Some days are just harder than others."

"I am sorry to hear that," he said. "He must have been young."

"Just shy of his 35th birthday," I answered with a nod. "We have two children, 2 ½ and my youngest just turned a year."

"That's a lot to handle on your own. Do you have any support? Family? Friends?"

The same questions that Barbara had asked me the first day I walked through the door at Wellspring. They knew only too well that supports are key to how well people cope.

Somehow, Daniel kept me talking. He wasn't afraid of my story or my tears. He asked questions, offered kindness, and listened. We ended up walking around and around the block, him without a coat, but so present it was stunning to me. He didn't pity me. There was no fear about me getting too maudlin. Somehow, he just knew that I needed to release the barb that had ripped me open that day. He couldn't fix my reality, but that wasn't his purpose. His role was to walk with me as I grieved. Literally, but it was so much more profound than the physical steps. Daniel's concern let me know I belonged. That this was an incredibly hard journey, but that I didn't have to struggle through it alone. He was a gift not only in the moment, but as a reminder that echoed forward through my grief journey for many days to come. I learned so much about grief, just in that simple act of giving.

After walking for the better part of an hour, the pain eased back to a more manageable level. Daniel had abandoned whatever work was on his desk and I had taken up enough of his time. Plus, the chilly fall day must have been tough to ignore without the protection of even an extra sweater.

We paused on the sidewalk in front of Wellspring, and he asked, "Can I offer a hug?"

That hug spilled a few more tears, but those ones held more gratitude than sorrow this time. Human touch had been lacking since Brad's death. Connection too. Daniel brought me back to the present and steadied my steps. There were still plenty of stumbles ahead of me, but in that moment, I had a glimmer that perhaps I would survive.

"I'll let Emma know you will be back for the next yoga session," Daniel said as he turned to go.

What he meant was that I belonged.

Today, Wellspring is found across Canada. You can access many of their programs online, or step through the doors at one of their many centers in Ontario and Alberta. All programs are free of charge and are accessible without a referral. Whether you are someone newly diagnosed, in the midst of treatment, actively dying, or in remission, there is a range of excellent programs to help you cope, from nutrition, health and wellness, financial, workplace, and other counselling services. The services are also available to friends, co-workers, and family of those touched by cancer. If you are touched in any way by cancer, you belong.

Wellspring

"Wellspring Cancer Support devotes itself exclusively to the unique non-medical needs cancer presents. At Wellspring, we provide a caring community in-person and online, so anyone living with cancer, their caregiver and family members can access vital information, meaningful support, and effective coping strategies." [10]

Holidays

Dec 8, 2007

"It is closing in on Christmas. Last weekend, I went to the Insurance Association Christmas dinner with Bodgood. Tonight, I am going out for dinner with some of the Bodgood boys from the back. Next weekend is the O-Line Christmas party. I go because I feel that people are being nice, and it shows I am coping well. Honestly, I usually don't feel like going out when it comes right down to it. I am sad. I am

---

[10] Wellspring. (2023). Helping people live better with cancer. Retrieved from Wellspring Cancer Support, https://wellspring.ca/

sad a lot. Celebrations continue though, despite my grief. Who knew grief could be so profound?"

There is no getting around holidays. They are hard. First ones being the worst. It is the first time you experience whichever holiday is happening without your person at your side. There are lots of ways this can bring up painful memories.

My first holiday was Thanksgiving. My family gathered at my aunt's home for a big feast. A chair was noticeably missing beside me. Worse though, was the moment that struck harder. When the turkey came out of the oven, it was left to rest. While it was doing so, Dylan gathered up the tools to carve the bird. Normally Brad had jumped into the role, but Dylan was the man of the house, and he took on the job this day. I stepped into the kitchen to watch him wielding an electric knife on the unsuspecting bird and was gutted.

Brad would never have used an electric knife. I could hear him mocking the high-pitched whir of the ridiculous machine. I couldn't watch the meal get massacred by the inane device. Whether right or wrong, I was galled through my grief lens.

Christmas was a bigger deal though. For those who celebrate, the lead up lasts for weeks, with decorating, gift shopping, holiday parties, and the culmination of it all on Christmas Day. There was so much involved, and it required more time and effort—qualities I had been lacking for months at that point. Not to mention a decided lack of caring about it at all.

I may not have been interested, but my kids were. So, Christmas had to go on.

In the past, I had decorated the house the month before the big day, both inside and out. There were lights outside, wreaths on doors, decorations spread on every surface. That didn't even include the Christmas tree. Finding it was a whole adventure in itself; trekking into the bush to find the perfect real tree to decorate our home with. Once the tree was in place, presents slowly crept into place underneath it in the days leading up to Christmas Eve. Plus, cookies too. There were always cookies to bake.

As jack-o'-lanterns got tossed to the curb in 2007, my heart contracted with what the familiar next steps were supposed to be. Once Remembrance Day passed, the exterior lights hit the to-do list. But the idea of sparkle and celebration made me sick. What did I have to celebrate? The still cold space in the bed beside me, constant colds for my children, and the knowledge that as the year inched towards its end, Brad would not be there to help celebrate any of it.

The first year is hard. The first of anything is hard, but celebrations seem especially difficult for most. That goes for any celebrations, whether you are Christian, Jewish, Muslim, Hindu, or anything at all. We all have days or weeks that mean a little more, and those days often center around the gathering of people. When one of those people is absent for the first time due to death, your loss rears itself up again anew. How can it not?

For me, I envisioned how things would have looked with Brad there—and keenly felt his loss. I remembered years past and felt his absence. And invariably, the rest of the people whom I normally gathered with would still get together, which meant many more delicate conversations about how I was doing. All I was, was loss. I didn't want to be a part of any of it. But I did my best to rally.

When Frank called from O-Line to invite me to their Holiday party, I hesitated.

"I'm not much company, Frank," I said.

"Oh, come on," he cajoled. "Don said he would get you a taxi, so you don't have to worry about driving. The spread will be fantastic, and you can have a few drinks to let your hair down. It will be fun!"

"I don't know…"

"Gene asked about you too. We would love to see you."

I just wanted to hide from it all, but it didn't look like Frank would take no for an answer.

"Okay, I'll try my best," I said.

"No trying," Frank chided. "You deserve a night out. We will see you on the 15th. Okay?"

"Okay," I limply agreed.

It wasn't quite as easy as that though. I had two little girls at home and needed to arrange a babysitter next. As I used Joan and Art for my Bodgood Christmas dinner, I decided on a different route for this one. I called up my cousin Angela.

"How would you like to babysit Taryn and Rylie so I can go to Brad's Christmas dinner?" I asked her.

"I can come get you earlier in the day and maybe you can help us get a Christmas tree?" I added hopefully.

"That would be fun!" she answered enthusiastically.

"Great," I answered. "We can make a weekend of it. Thanks Angela."

When the day arrived though, I didn't have it in me to drag the children out to a field and wander around joyfully finding the perfect centerpiece for an event that still felt uncomfortably painful. My compromise was a lot full of trees at the nearby Home Hardware.

While that sounds fine and festive for most, for me, it felt like a failure. It was the first time I had missed out on the cherished tradition of tramping through the snow to seek the perfect tree. Not too short or tall. No skinny trees or ones too fat to fit through the door. How could you judge merit from a tree that was trussed up and leaning forlornly into a stand? While my children didn't know any difference at a year old and 2 ½, Angela did, but she didn't show it. Her radiant smile filled the spaces that mine couldn't reach into.

"What do you think?" I asked her. "It's not exactly a tree farm."

My disappointment in myself was rubbed in by the icy temperatures.

"It's freezing too," I added. "I guess it's good we didn't go any further than a block away. Hot chocolate at home is way closer."

"It's all good," Angela answered. "This one looks nice, don't you think Taryn?"

She held her mittened hand tightly in her own, as we wandered back and forth amongst the trees.

Taryn nodded enthusiastically. She didn't care where we were. The biggest treat was that her oldest cousin was there for the excursion and would help to decorate once we got the perfect tree home. Any tree was perfect in her eyes.

I saw her excitement and tried to match it. Rylie couldn't offer up much of an opinion, wrapped as she was in her snowsuit, scarf, and blanket, but I included her regardless.

"What do you think baby? Is this the one?"

As all of our breaths puffed in front of us, I answered my own question just to get us out of the cold.

"Yup. I think you are right, Angela. This is the one. Let's go tell the man and see if he can wrangle it onto the van for us."

It felt forced and painful, but it got done. So did the decorating. And cookie baking. And singing Christmas carols throughout. I couldn't have done it alone, but I was graced with an angel to help me get through this painful first and for that I will forever owe my beautiful cousin so much.

The next step was celebrating with Brad's coworkers. Not what I wanted to do at all, but the pizza had been ordered for Angela and the girls, and somehow, I had found something to wear. All I wanted to do was snuggle onto the couch with them to watch Toy Story, but festivities awaited.

"I won't be late," I said as I stepped out the door.

"Take as long as you want," she called back. "Have fun!"

I wasn't sure how much fun it would be, but I put my game face on and set out.

"Okay Katherine, you can do this," I told myself as I sat in the parking lot of the restaurant.

I don't want to.

"It will be fun. Frank will be there. And Gene. Everyone. And you know they will all be nice to you."

They are going to ask me how I'm doing. I suck! I cry all the time, and no one wants to hear that.

"You will be fine. Just go."

I gripped the steering wheel and tried to call up a smile and polite banter.

"Go in. You don't have to stay all night. Eat dinner and then make your excuses. Just breathe. It will be alright."

This felt like what my life was now. Convincing myself to leave the house. Talking myself into chatting others, as necessary. Breathing. And pretending that I was fine. Over and over again.

I walked in the door and glanced around, still deciding if I could escape or not.

"Hi, can I help you?" said a server who materialized in front of me.

"Uh, yes. I am here for the O-Line Christmas party?"

"Excellent! If you would like to follow me, I will show you where they are."

That's it. I was trapped now. I took a deep breath and prepared myself for an evening of dreaded socializing. The woman led me to a back banquet room and excused herself with a smile. I was now on my own.

"Katherine!" Frank said, as he stepped away from the person he was speaking with. "You made it. Can I get you a drink? There's an open bar before dinner. I hope you didn't drive."

"I did," I said. "But I can have one for now. Maybe a rye and ginger?"

"What?! You should have taken a taxi. Oh well, we can get you a 'keys thanks' [11] You deserve a night out. I'll get you that drink now though."

God love Frank and his uncomplicated ways. I thanked Brad again for the gift of this man into my life. Not only had Frank shown up at my house many times just to chat casually and check in with how I was doing, but he brought his son that fall and finished the laundry room Brad had started. No wishy-washy hand wringing uncomfortableness. Just straight talk and taking care of business. He showed me how to winterize the riding lawn mower the O-Line crew had bought us just before Brad died. He told stories about work, Brad, his family, and how he met his wife, Shelley. And fast-forward to the following spring, he would be the one organizing a new fence to be built for me. While I felt broken most of the time, he had a way of making me feel stronger than I felt. This night was no different.

Before I knew it, I was chatting with Shelley, then Gene and his wife Patty, and then Don was there saying hello too. There were smiles everywhere I turned and none of the lopsided smiles I got from others who treated me like I was fragile. To be fair, I was, but the concern just seemed to make it worse. There were moments, but on the whole, I fared better than I expected.

---

[11] Driving service that drives you and your vehicle home.

Dinner gave us all a whole other thing to focus on and I gladly dug into the salad, then main course, grateful to not have to cook for a night. Don had slid a glass of wine in front of me when the meal began and somehow, I felt like breathing wasn't something I had to think about.

A clink on a wine glass drew me out of my conversation with Shelley and I turned to the front of the room.

"I want to thank everyone for coming this evening," Don announced. "Happy Holidays!"

He raised his glass in a toast, then moved into the speech section of the night. There was someone from head office, one of the women in the office was retiring, and others who received awards. I clapped politely through it all. And then Don looked at me.

"Katherine, can you come up here for a minute?"

I looked around startled, then paled. What was this about? I rose slowly, looking at Frank beside me.

"Go on," he encouraged with a laugh. "Get up there."

When I stood beside Don, he began.

"You all remember Brad. He was an incredible employee who was hardworking and always willing to lend a hand wherever he could. He was with PGO, then O-Line for six years, until he lost his battle with cancer this fall. I think I can safely speak for all of us, when I say that it gutted us. So, after talking about it, we decided that we wanted to do something for his family."

Heads nodded in the audience that had now become a blurry, faceless mass in the room.

"We started a pass the hat, which quickly morphed into something bigger. There were 50/50 tickets, raffles, and more fundraisers all in the name of one of our own. The love and generosity ended up stretching across the entire country. We know this is an incredibly challenging time for you and your family Katherine. This was the best way we could think of to help you out.

Here is our gift to you," Don finished as he handed me an envelope. Inside was a cheque equalling the amount they had raised.

I stood there shocked at the turn of events. I was speechless. I literally had no words to offer thanks or praise for their generosity in thinking of me and my family. Tears instantly sprang to my eyes, as I stood rooted to the spot.

I would love to say I pulled myself together and made Brad proud by sharing how much working with these incredible humans had meant to him. Brad had fought to return to work, even when his body failed him. They were a family that took care of their own, and he went to work every day, happy to be a part of it. If he could do more, he did so willingly and never complained about a day's work. He enjoyed being a part of their work environment and loved the people he worked with.

And this act of generosity showed how wide his influence spanned. People across the country had opened their hearts and pockets to help take care of the family of one of their fallen. I was gutted. Thank you didn't feel like it sufficed, but that was all I could squeak out without becoming overcome by tears.

Today my words are stronger, and I would add so much more.

"Thank you, to those here in this room and the others who are here in spirit. Your generosity is beautiful and oh so touching. It will never be forgotten. While words cannot truly express what your gift means, know that your kindness will echo forward for years to come. You won't see it, but your gift will give me a roof over my head, it will heat that home, and will provide a place for growth there and beyond its walls. For both me and my children, both literally and figuratively.

Everyone here in this room is family. Brad cared so much about you all. When you included him in your barbeques, you gave him the community he always wanted. When you pulled together to help us move, he felt your love and reached deep to give back with the strength he still possessed—by cooking. His first love was always food, and carefully preparing a feast for you after you gave him the gift of a lawnmower—a gift he knew represented seeing his disability but rallying around it to lessen its reach—that decadent spread was his heart. All he wanted was to belong and you gave him that every day. It was beautiful in the way of unspoken understanding. Every act was love and he knew that. I do too.

So, this gift today? It is just another example of how incredible you all are. You see I don't even know it yet, but this gift that might have cost a few dollars and moments of your time, will equal home repairs, vacations, and the bonuses Brad might have received had he lived. Your thoughtfulness will remind me over and over again that there is good in this world, even when bad things happen. And on days when I feel more alone than I ever thought possible, I will remember that I was seen at my weakest hour, and someone cared. You cared. How incredible is that?

I am not going to lie though. For every generous and kind act given to my girls and I, I ache a little more in my loss knowing that

Brad's amazing spirit brightened so many lives. My loss is deepened by the love that flows and by the amazing pictures of Brad which are given back to me by others via this generosity. I wish I had more time to learn, love and grow beside him, but his legacy lives on through us all."

I didn't say that then or know how the gift would ultimately be used. I had no idea what to do with the money or how I could ever repay the kindness of so many faceless people. I didn't need to though. Sometimes we repay gifts of this magnitude in other ways.

Over time, my acts reflected what their giving meant to me. I volunteered at my children's school. I gardened for someone who loved their garden but was dying from cancer and could no longer tend it. And I listened to many people's own struggles with grief and loss, offering empathy and insight to those I could. These are but a few of the gifts I have given back. I'm sure there are others I don't even know I have bestowed, but which have touched others none the less. And I guess that's how it should be. For we should give, without expecting anything in return and receive from the depths of our soul, in recognition of other's love.

Honestly though, that day my offerings felt paltry—tears. Pure emotion. The truth of the depth of it though was that it renewed my faith in life and people. This moment continues to be a touchstone for me today and always will be.

Because I couldn't say it then, I repeat it again now. Thank you.

I wish that feeling of love could have sustained me throughout the rest of the holidays, but firsts are hard, and this was my first holiday season without my husband at my side. It got harder as the days went by.

My family did their best to ease the worst of it. My aunt and uncle flew out from the west coast to add extra merriment as we all gathered at my mom's house on Christmas day. We went to see the lights in the park, Santa managed to find the girls in their makeshift beds farther from home, and the turkey tasted better for having more people to share it with.

New Year's Eve was a different story though. New Year's is when we say goodbye to a year past and welcome in a fresh new year with new promise. "Next year has to be better!" people said. I wanted none of it though. I didn't want to say goodbye to 2007. That was the last year I had had with Brad. Once the calendar switched over, we would be yet another step further away from when he was in my life. It felt ridiculously monstrous in size and meaning, and all I wanted to do was stop time to keep him with me a little longer.

Time doesn't work like that though. And while you never lose the memories or feelings the person leaves behind, their physical presence remains rooted in the past. I could no more stop 2008 from arriving than I could turn back time to when the ball dropped on New Year's 2007. There was no hiding. No stopping. No reprieves.

There were a lot of tears. Despite those tears though, there was also a lot of love. I might have literally run from the room just before midnight, but my mom was right behind me, and we both sobbed our way into 2008. We mourned the loss of Brad, the loss of innocence, the loss of hope. But in doing so together, we also had each other in the moment, and I would do a disservice if I didn't note that now. We all loved Brad, and his absence was a hole in everyone's lives.

So even though holidays—especially first ones—are hard, remember that there are still people around you. And the place missing at the table is not vacant. It might not feel like it in the moment, but the empty spot is actually full, overflowing even, with memories. And those memories are a gift you can turn to over and over again in the years ahead. Your person isn't really gone. They just fill their shoes a little differently.

Fresh Loss

With the holidays behind me, it was time to settle in for winter. Wintertime tends to feel long and dark in Southwestern Ontario. Christmas decorations come down, holiday parties and get togethers fade into memory, and frigid winds typically amount to more time spent indoors. Alone.

Not ideal for someone feeling isolated and alone already. I was learning to live with it though. Somehow, I found myself not crying all day, or even every day any longer. With 2007 behind me, I was beginning to accept that this was my new life. It didn't mean I liked it though. And there were certainly days that set me back.

Jan 21, 2008
"I went through Brad's dresser last Tuesday. It was devastating. I don't know how it started, but once I did, I had to continue.
I had previously offered bits and pieces to friends, but now the dresser is empty. There are a few things I am not ready to part with yet, but it is done…
282

Brad's clothes weren't important though. He wore what people gave him. Clothes aren't representative of who he was. But his housecoat still holds some of his scent. It is amazing how important that is. I can't touch him or hold him but smelling him brings him back. I wish there was more…"

For every day that was hard, I finally began to notice progress. I celebrated painting the kitchen, completing two bathroom renovations, updating my fireplace, and finishing the laundry room that Brad had started months before. There were many projects still on my to-do list, but I felt like he would be proud of what I had accomplished thus far. Not one to make lists before, now I lived by them.

The next items on my list were finding a new financial advisor and me. Yup, me. How could that many tears be normal? I needed to talk to someone about my grief, before I got sucked into giving away all my money to clairvoyants or energy healers in the hope they could heal my broken heart. I still had no clue that grief was a journey you travelled for life. It was still early days, despite me feeling like I had been morose for too long already.

The financial advisor was a comparatively easier fix. It started due to another loss though

Chase had been Brad and my financial advisor for a few years. I had met him through work, and we had sat down with him when practical Brad decided we should plan for our future. After Brad died, Chase and I had worked through a plan on what to do with the funds I received from Brad's life insurance settlement. Just when we had everything worked out, I called to make the last appointment to finalize the paperwork.

"Can I speak with Chase please?"

"I'm sorry," Chase's assistant said. "Chase doesn't work here anymore."

"But I talked to him last week," I said incredulously.

"Yes, it was a sudden departure," she acknowledged. "We have assigned someone new to take over your care though. Marsha is quite nice and very competent. She will be reaching out to you shortly to set up a date to sit down to meet you."

I was in shock. How could he not work there any longer? He had not said a word about leaving the company the last we spoke. I hung up the phone and bawled.

"Shit," I moaned. "I don't want to meet someone new!"

This was fresh loss all over again. It might not have been of the same magnitude, but it represented a loss of trust and security from someone who could help me make big financial decisions in Brad's absence. With Chase, I didn't have to get to know anyone new. I had known him for years and was confident in his abilities and direction. Even more important, I had a personal connection to him. He and his wife had come to Brad's funeral and offered touching words at my weakest. You cannot replace that overnight. How could I build another relationship of that scope once more when I was so compromised?

What I did know was that if I had to meet someone new, I had to do my research to find someone whom I felt a connection with and that could help me through my present financial journey in a competent manner. Yes, I would meet this Marsha woman, but I also made a plan to interview other financial advisors as well. I might have been emotionally scarred, but I was savvy enough to not just take the first advisor that came along.

In the interim, a grief counsellor became a higher priority again too. If I could find someone who could help me work through my mountain of grief, perhaps that might help me pick someone who could assist me on the financial front too. Scale down the big things, so the little things didn't feel so gargantuan.

Ah, grief counsellors. Anyone I had talked to thus far had been nice enough, but no one had the solutions I sought. No one was dynamic enough to reach through the wall of pain I struggled to hold back, and they certainly didn't show enough promise to get me through to the other side. The trick was, where could I find that person? Where could I find all the someones I needed, including a new financial advisor too?

It felt like every step I took was a lesson in learning new skills. I had to learn how to handle home renovations myself, balance cooking, cleaning, bill payments, and child minding myself, and how to heal the mental rift that had torn my soul asunder on my own too. It felt like too much, but nothing could really change that. No one else could step in to take on any of those responsibilities. Well, no one that was close enough or whom I trusted. And my trust was in low reserves. I didn't feel like I could ask anyone for anything, as the fear of rejection was crippling. If I asked and got a no, it split me wide open again, so I just didn't ask. Ever.

Ultimately though, I was tapped out. The weight of everything was more than I could physically and emotionally bear. I might have lost a financial advisor, but if I had to meet someone new, it made sense to interview a few candidates. The same went for grief counsellors. Which meant pushing myself even further out of my comfort zone.

Amazingly though, every task I completed and step I took did lighten my load. The proof was in the knots that eased from my back and few less tears that fell at night. I still might have operated on autopilot with my children, but somehow, I was making progress. Somehow, those tears were releasing the pain that owned every waking minute of my days. Breathing came easier and my search for champions to add into my toolbox of support began to net some hope.

February is a challenge for many though with its long, dark, cold days. By the time the middle of the month rolled around, the walls were closing in. I could feel them close, trying to suffocate me anew. The progress I had made—mostly through the help of journalling and the many days I had spent at Wellspring already—was enough to help me recognize that I needed to push back. Maybe a change in scenery would do, even if just for a few hours.

"What do you think about going to the mall ladies?" I said to the girls one Saturday. "We need to get out of the house. Go for a walk."

"Okay, Mummy!" Taryn said excitedly.

"Can you grab the coats baby?" I asked, as I began to throw a few snacks into the diaper bag.

My intrepid girl pulled them off hangers and dragged their outerwear into the kitchen where I filled juice bottles for them.

"Okay, Rylie, let's get you zipped in," I said, as I tickled her and placed her on the kitchen floor atop her gear.

I stuffed her legs into the pants, then speared her arms into the waiting jacket. The cutest little starfish gazed up at me with a smile, as we all anticipated a much-needed escape.

With a ring, the phone broke the magic. I debated ignoring the phone, instead putting our mini adventure first, but responsibility was deeply imbedded in all I did at that point. I could no more ignore the ringing than I could my baby's cry in the middle of the night.

"Just a minute, Boo," I said with a sigh.

"Hello?"

"Hello?" said an unfamiliar voice. "Is this Katherine?"

"Yes," I replied cautiously.

"This is Donna, Cassie's neighbour. I'm sorry to bother you, but it's just that we heard some disturbing news on the radio and thought you might be able to help. I've been trying to get a hold of Cassie or Dylan, but neither of them is answering their phones."

Alarm bells began to jangle in my brain.

"Okay..."

"Have you heard from them? I figured you would know if anything had happened."

"Um, no," I replied nervously. "I haven't heard from them."

What was going on?

"She would call you, if something happened, wouldn't she?"

"I haven't heard anything, but I can try to call her if you like. I can call my mother too, as she might know more than me. What did you hear?"

"There was an accident. A skiing accident up in Blue Mountain. That's where they are this weekend. The story said a girl was injured and it sounded the right age for Cassie's girls."

No. No, this couldn't be happening. All thoughts of the mall disappeared.

"Give me your number and let me see if I can find anything out," I said, as panic started to inch in. "I'll call you back in a few minutes."

"Okay," Donna answered, but the fear in her voice had my hackles raised.

No answer on Cassie's phone. No answer on Dylan's phone. My mother was next. Her home line rang through to the answering machine. Her cell phone was next. She answered on the third ring.

"Mom," I said with a shaky voice. "Cassie's neighbour called me in a panic. She was trying to get a hold of Cassie, because she heard there had been an accident up in Blue Mountain. Where are you? Have you heard from her?"

"Joe and I are in the car," she answered slowly. There was a quaking in her voice that made me start to tremble.

"What's going on?" I demanded.

"We are on our way to see you. We are just outside Woodstock. There has been an accident."

"What are you talking about?" I asked, my own voice starting to wobble. "What happened?"

"Angela was skiing and went off the trail. No one saw and they couldn't find her. By the time the ski patrol found her, it was too late. We were coming to tell you in person."

"No!!!" I cried. "No, no, no."

"Oh Katherine. I am so sorry. Cassie wanted me to be there with you."

My teeth started to chatter. I was shaking and tears streamed down my face. It couldn't be true. This couldn't be real. Angela was just here helping me through Christmas. She was 15 years old. She couldn't be dead. Dead?

I fell to the floor and lost it. Taryn cautiously inched towards me, fearful of what was going on, as Rylie still lay prone at my side.

This couldn't be real. There was no way my cousin—a member of the ski team for years and more than competent on the hills—there was no way she could have died in a ski accident. But my mother's tears, the neighbour's fears, my gut instinct, it all told me the worst was true.

"We will be there soon," she said, as I collapsed into this fresh horror.

How do you deal with fresh loss after a major loss? Two deaths in my close family unit within five months of each other. How?

Hold on tight. Roll with it. It is going to be tough. Especially if you still have residual issues you are working through like I did. And, as people kept reminding me — Breathe.

Loss is hard enough to process. Loss of spouse/partner, child, parent, sibling; they are all devastating. Couple that with loss of other important figures in your life and the ground seems to crumble. Nothing makes sense and any progress you have made from your first loss disappears in the wake of the new loss.

We were starting to tread water after the loss of Brad, but an accident involving a young teenager pulled the rug out from under all our feet. My aunt had geographically been my closest family member and a source of support, but this changed everything. She was now buried in this tragedy. Angela was her first-born; smart, beautiful, giving, talented, a friend to all, and an amazing big sister to her two younger sisters. This loss meant they were no longer part of my bigger support team. We could support each other, but their journey was far different now and their new grief took them on a different path.

In the immediate aftermath, my mother now flew to her younger sister's side to support her as she began her own grief journey. We all put our own lives down to support our own, as we reeled in shock at this turn of events. My sister and I took our young cousins under our wings to shop for funeral garb. When we weren't spending time with them, we were compiling photos for a slide show that would play at the funeral. My stepfather joined the ranks of support for my uncle. We all dropped everything to mobilize and rally, even as we tried to wrap our heads around the unbearable hole that had ripped open in our universe.

What did that hole look like for me, who had barely stopped crying daily? In the days that followed, my hands shook. Shock stepped back in and left me feeling physically sick to my stomach. My teeth chattered, my brain stuttered, and minutes stretched into hours, as we worked through the steps to pull together another funeral. I leaned into the daycare for extra care for my girls, and my friend Faye stepped in when they weren't open.

The chasm wasn't done yawning open yet though. Angela's death brought another unexpected loss which would reverberate painfully through the years—Brad's parents. After initially getting off the phone with my mother the day I heard about Angela, I called them to help. They immediately dropped everything to do what they could. I had no idea what was going on, but immediately reached out for help with Taryn and Rylie.

After hearing the story from my mom and discussing what the next days would hold, I turned to them.

"Can you take Taryn and Rylie tomorrow, so we can be there for Cassie and the family when they come home? I have a key to their house so can let everyone in before they arrive."

It would be a difficult day, receiving casseroles, cookies, and questions, but our presence would help make the transition easier for Cassie. If that was at all possible.

"Of course," Joan said.

What I hadn't seen coming though was how this fresh loss would affect my in-laws. They had lost a child only months before. They were private people, not comfortable sharing the emotions that loss generated. And being that close to fresh loss all over again was too much for them. They couldn't handle my grief. They fought back against the onset of another wave of their own grief over Brad. Ultimately, the proximity to that much sorrow was more than they could bear. They needed space, even while I was reaching out for more. And our relationship broke.

Grief is different for everyone and that is okay. For me, I cried, talked, and journalled my way through it to process what it all meant. Not everyone takes that path though. While no way to grieve is wrong, some coping mechanisms grate against each other. That was the case with my in-laws.

The emotions I outwardly expressed threatened the carefully constructed coping strategies they had in place. They built a fortress around their feelings and were stoic in the face of them, refusing to share with anyone. In my case, it meant pushing away from me. In doing so, I was left reeling anew.

What did that look like? At the height of my own family's loss, I couldn't find the extra compassion to support and accept them the way they needed. Both of us ruptured and fell away from each other. Sadly, that rift fissured into a lifelong break we couldn't reconcile, one that I struggled with for years. Again, I learned that grief is a powerful emotion, and you can't always control how it affects yourself or others. You just have to make peace with the path you choose. It was an incredibly difficult lesson I would rather not have been dealt with at that point. But I was.

Life wasn't done with me yet though. Just when I thought I couldn't take any more, one more loss loomed on the horizon. Within weeks of the funeral my best friend Faye called.

"Stu lost his job," Faye said. "The company is downsizing. They let a bunch of employees go."

"Oh no!" I replied. "What is he going to do?"

"He has done a lot of thinking and feels like he might want to go back to school. He is debating teacher's college."

"That sounds like a good idea."

"In Thunder Bay."

"Oh."

That didn't sound as good.

Thunder Bay is over 1,300 kilometers away. It is a 14- to 16-hour drive from London, depending upon the route you take. It is not somewhere to which you can commute.

"It would mean selling the house and moving into his parent's basement to save money while he's in school. But it's not permanent."

"Oh."

The trick was, I knew it would be. They had two small children. They would establish a life there while Stu got an education and started a new career path: friends, school, routines, life. And even if by some miracle they decided to relocate after he finished school two years down the road, there were no guarantees they would move back to London again.

Oh…

Faye was my best friend and one of my most important supports both mentally and physically while Brad was sick and after he died. We talked about everything. She took the kids when Brad had doctor's appointments, plus for occasional sleepovers when I needed a break. I couldn't imagine my life without her either. The losses kept piling up and I was at a loss as to when they would stop.

My answer—walls. Build them thick. Build them tall. Don't let people in and you can't get hurt. The trick is, you don't feel joy that way either. But losing my husband, a trusted advisor, a family member to death, and other family members due to differences in grieving, then my best friend—it was too much. I was drowning and it felt like I had nothing left to hold on to.

Chapter 8: Learning to Live

Grief Counselling

"Hello, how can we help you today?"

Tears, so many tears. I can't breathe and don't even know what words to say to express the numbness that owns me now.

Finally, through shuddering breaths, I manage, "I'm hoping to talk to someone. I am looking for a grief counsellor."

All the people I met before, the random strangers with 'messages from Brad', the well-meaning counsellors, doctors, and friends, they weren't enough any longer. I was tired. I wasn't coping. I felt like I was at the end of my rope.

"Are you having thoughts of harming yourself?"

"No."

"Harming others?"

"No."

But I was sobbing into the phone. All I knew was that I needed help. Someone must be able to make it better.

"I want you to take a deep breath. Hold it in with me; one, two, three. Now let it out slowly. Again. One, two, three, and release. I'm here. I'm listening. I've got you. Let's breathe in again…"

It always came back to breathing. I sat on the phone for probably 20 minutes with the intake counsellor, as she eased me through my meltdown. I got off the phone with the promise of an appointment and more to come. It didn't change my reality, but it was a start.

Grief counselling isn't for everyone. Some don't find a good fit. Others aren't comfortable talking about their feelings and emotions. Timing can make it problematic too. For me though, grief counselling saved me.

Mar 1, 2008
"I am so confused. I feel… what? Stagnated, numb,
withdrawn. I don't have the energy to step forward
for almost anyone. I can't muster the strength to
care for friends, who have been my closest
supporters. I feel stretched too thin. Too much grief.
Too raw. All mixed in together and not sure what to
think or do. Don't want this reality. It can't be real.
What is it supposed to mean? What could we
possibly be meant to learn from all this tragedy? I
just don't want to know today. I just want it all to go
away. I don't want to do this anymore."

I met Cynthia through Family Services Thames Valley. They offered a sliding scale for cost and a limited window of counselling, but from the first moment I met her, things shifted. She made me own my grief and pointed out the weight of it.

"But other people have worse experiences than mine. Losing a spouse of 50 years. Refugees fleeing war-torn countries…"

"No, your grief is your grief," Cynthia said. "Do not compare yours with others. If this is your worst, then it is *your* worst. Don't take away from that or belittle your struggle. You lost your husband after a two-and-a-half-year battle with cancer and are now raising two young children alone. That is plenty heavy enough."

She paused to stare at me to see if what she said sunk in.

"I suspect you have some residual post-traumatic stress. You need to own your experiences and make peace with them. I'm here to help."

While Cynthia asked the occasional questions, more importantly, she listened. And she told me that what I was feeling and experiencing was normal. She thought I was doing better than I gave myself credit for and applauded me for how far I had already come.

It was eye-opening.

Many people reach for antidepressants to help them cope after loss. Alcohol and other drugs help numb the pain but are a temporary and slippery slope of survival. There are plenty of therapies you can use to help manage your loss too. For me though, I needed to talk Beyond just retelling stories to friends and family and feeling like I was burdening them by my weight. I needed a professional who could help me look at what had happened and give me steps I could take to move me forward. Grief counselling was a game changer.

I saw it in the slowing down of tears, the change in tone in my journals, and the conversations I had with others. I finally felt like I was moving beyond straight sorrow.

"There is a stress scale," Cynthia said during one appointment. "The Holmes and Rahe Stress Scale[12] measures stressful

---

[12] The Holmes Rahe Stress Scale is a self-assessment tool developed in 1967 that measures stress based on 43 life change units. Your score is used to assess the risk of illness based on level of stress: the higher your score the

live events and weighs how those events affect you. Some events, like death of a spouse, rate incredibly high on the scale, while others rank lower, like trouble with in-laws. If you have several life events that occur during a relatively brief period, your ability to cope becomes compromised."

That gave me pause. Looking back over a relatively short period, I had lost a spouse, dealt with a major illness, lost close family, had trouble with in-laws, lost business connections, my spouse stopped working, I had gotten pregnant and subsequently added new family members, bought and sold houses, gotten engaged and married, changed careers, plus moved to a new city. I had also had changes to my sleep, social activities, eating habits, and family get-togethers. Sure, there were plenty of boxes on the scale that were left unticked, but looking at the whole picture like that was sobering. My numbers were through the roof! Apparently, I had really good reason to feel stressed. Not all events were bad, but they still caused wrinkles in the day to day that you had to wrap your head around. Like home renovations. And having too much on one's plate was more than anyone could handle.

Cynthia helped me see that. And in seeing, I was able to step back and start to be a little kinder to myself.

In the nine months after Brad had died, I had wrapped up all the paperwork surrounding his death: the will, life insurance, closing of accounts, and anything else requiring a copy of his death certificate. I tackled several home renovations, including gutting and completely redoing the main bath, finishing the laundry room renovation Brad had

higher your risk for a breakdown of health. You can download a copy of the Holmes Rahe Stress Scale for free from
https://www.dartmouth.edu/eap/library/lifechangestresstest.pdf

started, installing a new fence on the property, and painting several rooms in the house. I went through his personal belongings, purged household goods I would never use, and reestablished new routines for my family. While I struggled to reach out to ask for help, I had leaned into daycare, found a new financial advisor, and finally found a grief counsellor who I clicked with to help me work through the major life traumas that threatened to wash me away. There might have been far too many days cloistered away at home alone, but I also had friends step up to help with many of those projects, plus I began to establish new friendships on my own. I attended yoga, reiki, and therapeutic touch at Wellspring. Most importantly, I felt like the short temper I had with my girls was finally abating and I could see their growth with love. We were all growing.

And somehow, time was healing me. Everyone said time worked its magic. It was true. I cannot stress this last point enough. Grief counselling was a major help too.

Whether you are having a bad day, hard week, or are staring down longer periods of stress and emotional turmoil, counselling is a great source of help and support. Don't be afraid to keep looking for the right fit, as a counsellor is an important part in your healing journey. And don't ever give up on yourself. You are worth it. Reaching out for help is one of the hardest things to do but is also one of the biggest signs of strength, so when you recognize you need it, ASK.

Reconstruction

Healing is a long journey. For me, I battled with anger that cancer had stolen the life I should have had with Brad. I was angry at myself for not being able to cope and make all the decisions, as readily as I felt like he would have been able to. And I was extremely disappointed about the rift that had formed between his family and mine. Too many days I sat sad and depressed, reflecting on what should be or could have been. I was lonely and adrift, unsure what direction to point my life in. But I was also determined to make him proud of my accomplishments and fierce in my will to do right by our girls. It was time to turn a corner.

7 Stages of Grief

1. Denial/Shock
2. Pain/Guilt
3. Anger/Bargaining
4. Depression
5. Upward Turn
6. Reconstruction/Working Through
7. Acceptance/Hope [13]

What did reconstruction look like? All of the steps I didn't even realize I was taking. Every time I got out of bed in the morning. The decisions I made around renovations. My conversations with friends, family, and my grief counsellor. Recognizing that it was hard but doing it anyway. Going through denial, shock, pain, anger, reflection, and more. These were the stages of grief. It was almost textbook in my own unique and individual way.

Famed Swiss American Psychiatrist, Elisabeth Kübler-Ross described the five stages of grief in her book, *On Death and Dying*.[14] She outlined them as denial, anger, bargaining, depression, and

---

[13] Holland, K. (2023). The Stages of Grief and What to Expect. Retrieved from Healthline, https://www.healthline.com/health/stages-of-grief

[14] Kübler-Ross, E. (1969). *On Death and Dying*. Macmillan.

acceptance. Over time, others adjusted those stages to add two more. I feel like they better capture the whole grieving process, but remind people that grief isn't linear, straightforward, or a process you go through in neat steps. Some people go through all the stages. Others skip stages. And sometimes you jump around or dive back into other stages all over again. Grief isn't easy. Healing is demanding work.

You might have noticed that some of my chapter headings pay homage to these stages. The reason why is because they might be defined as clinical stages, but they are rooted in universal truths. And many people experience them during any period of loss.

For example, you discover your spouse has been cheating. You don't believe it, you blame yourself, then lose your mind in anger. Once the dust settles, you might get depressed at the direction your life has taken and spiral, before hopefully seeing the light and rebuilding to a better place.

Loss comes in other forms too: loss of a pet, a friend, relationships, your job, or your security. Any time we face loss, it shakes up our world and causes stress. While your reaction is exclusive to you, the emotions around loss really do transcend individual autonomy. We all grieve when we face loss. In healing from that loss, we need to accept the changes that have occurred in order to rebuild one's life on the new path.

You might not like it, but we all experience the New Normal through a grief journey.

What did mine look like so far?

Apr 9, 2008

"Today is the start of a new life, a new reality, a new me. Every day we are reborn and must find our destiny. Some days it is the little things. Painting the laundry room. Moving Taryn's new bed into her room (girl power!).

Today I made a list of tasks and got many of them done. I make many lists nowadays. They serve to give me purpose and give me a sense of accomplishment. They remind me of the myriad tasks that present themselves and help me to prioritize. I never used to make lists. My life revolves around them now. They help me put one foot in front of the other. No stagnating. Things to do. Keep busy!"

But those buoyant moments were counterbalanced regularly.

Apr 11, 2008
"No warnings for the meltdowns this week held. Many tears that have come out of nowhere, but from everything. So raw. Beating myself up over things that are difficult, if not impossible to control. Single mother with all the decision-making resting squarely on my shoulders. My shoulders alone. Anger at being alone. Not only Brad, but other people too. Feeling ugly, undesirable, unworthy..."

Have I mentioned that grief wasn't easy? I battled waves of emotions every single day. It was cyclical. I felt sad and depressed, so stayed away from others, then got angry and lonely because of it. When

I accomplished something, I felt like things were turning around, only to be faced with the reality that I couldn't always accomplish tasks on my own. I had to rethink the way I did things, the way I thought, and my expectations for the future.

Who am I kidding? I wasn't there yet. I still wanted to live in the past and had yet to accept my present. I kept waiting for new catastrophes to befall me. Trust was in miniscule supply. But I was moving forward, cried a little less every day, and marked plenty more better days in the calendar.

That first year is all about the calendar. I didn't realize it then, but Year One is all about working through the firsts. Suffering and surviving Mother's Day, Father's Day, birthdays, anniversaries, holidays, special celebrations, and moments you must relearn and restructure without your person there. It doesn't matter your faith either: loss feels the same whether you are marking Ramadan, Hanukkah, Diwali, or some other celebration. Where your loved one once was, they are no longer, and you have to learn what that feels like and how you want to move forward without them physically by your side.

Working through the firsts. I didn't get how hard it would be. At eight, nine, ten months, I felt like I had grieved for a lifetime.

"When does this get easier?" I asked peer support volunteers at Wellspring when I dropped by there and invariably used up boxes of tissues.

"When did your husband die?" they would ask.

Followed by the remark, "Oh, it's still early days" when they heard anything less than a year.

"How long would this take?" I wondered. "When would I be done?"

Other people wondered too. People who hadn't been there or lost someone close to them. More than once, people assumed that I should just pick up where I left off and get on with things.

What things? My life before was shattered the day Brad died. In fact, it changed the day he got diagnosed. There was no going back to normal. I was learning what my new normal was and reinventing me every step of the way.

I went from a married woman—a family of four with two income earners—to a single parent who left her career for an uncertain future. These were new roles, and I didn't know how to wear them nor what the expectations of them even were.

Did I even mention the career thing before? That I told the body shop I wasn't returning to work after my maternity leave ended? That I couldn't face the idea of listening to people complain about their broken cars when my whole life felt broken? But that in leaving my full-time job, I threw another upheaval, another complete stressor and change into my life. Yup, I did that too. And I don't regret that decision one bit, either then or now. It did mean I had another restructuring to figure out, but I was working on it.

Who am I? What do I want to be when I grow up? I was in a Freudian nightmare everywhere I turned. It might have felt like a nightmare, but dawn was on the horizon.

I was working through it.

Acceptance

As that first hard year of mourning rolled out in front of me, I knew that something had to change. Aside from the obvious—that I was a widow. I also needed to start looking forward, to plan for the future. The future started with a job. I needed to return to work.

What did I want to be when I grew up? I had asked myself that question umpteen number of times over the years. Society always seemed to be there pushing and prodding me along, insisting that I should have it all worked out. But somehow that lightning bolt moment never seemed to arrive. I couldn't avoid it much longer though.

And then the universe nudged me.

"I'm coming into town for a baby shower for Ellee next week. It is going to be at her friend's house, who just moved to London a few months ago. I think she has kids around your age. You should come."

"Okay," I agreed half-heartedly. Social excursions were still difficult, but I knew the expectant mother and it was always a good excuse to spend time with my girlfriend.

A week later, we walked into an old home across town and joined the party in progress. There were name games, guess the mess in the diaper, cut a length of string to measure the mama's middle—all lighthearted activities meant to elicit laughter and good cheer. There were presents, nibblies, and conversations all around. And I was feeling okay.

As I went to sample some cookies, the hostess walked over to say hello.

"Hi, my name is Denise. Ellee tells me you live in London."

"Yes," I replied. "I am actually only a five-minute drive away."

"I hear you have children?" I continued.

"One, yes," Denise answered. "Sophie is three and a half."

"My oldest is the same age!" I said. "Her name is Taryn. Rylie is just about two."

While the party swirled on around us, we started a fledgling conversation that would take us so much further. They had moved to London only a few months before. She worked for Acme Animal: the same company that Ellee would shortly be going on maternity leave from.

"I hope you don't mind, but Ellee mentioned you might be looking for work. Would you like to go for lunch one day next week? Maybe we could discuss it and get to know each other a little better. I could use a few new friends in town."

And with that, I tentatively stuck my toe back into the world of responsibility. Where so many have fulfilling careers to return to, I had been at a loss. Grief had been my career, but it was more than time to move on. I just needed to see if I could successfully balance raising two children, running a household, and working outside of the home once more. On my own. Could I do it? I was going to find out.

Around the same time, my mother's birthday approached. She was turning 60 and my family decided that a surprise party was in order. Guests were invited from all over the place, and I was to be the distraction. While they decorated the community center at my parent's trailer, I would take my mom into town with the girls to get her out of the way. That way she wouldn't see the guests arrive either.

"My brain is still so mushy!" I planned to say. "I forgot Rylie's diapers!"

The ideal excuse—we couldn't live without those—and town was 20 minutes away. I would let the kids dawdle, hum and haw over random things, and do my best to keep her occupied for a few hours, checking in to see how preparations were going and whether they needed more time or not. It was perfect.

A few days before that, I started to pull together final preparations at home. One stop was the liquor store. I went in for a bottle of wine, then wandered over to the wall of beer and stood debating what to get.

"Can I help you find anything?" an employee asked me.

"Yes," I said turning to him. "I need something to go with roast pork. A pig roast, actually. Is there anything you would recommend?"

I spent the next 15 minutes or so chatting with the clerk over wine, beer, and places to enjoy them.

"Chaucer's is a great place to peruse beer menus," he said. "They've got a huge selection of beers on tap. I hope this doesn't come across too forward, but I'd love to take you there some time for a drink."

Holy crap! A cute guy, who smelled oh so good, was asking me on a date! Oh my God, what to do?!

Fluster and laugh it off, even as I was melting inside. No one had looked at me like that in I couldn't remember how long. I had been in a good mood, having gotten encouragement and positive comments on a new haircut earlier in the day, so possibly I flirted? Did I even remember how to do that? Apparently, as a guy was looking at me like I was an attractive woman. I hadn't seen that looking in the mirror in over a year. Heck, probably longer than that. I hadn't been on a date in over 10 years.

"I'm going away for the weekend, but I'll keep that in mind," I promised.

That was the start of something else new.

Before I got too far into that possibility though, there was another milestone to pass. A year of grieving only passes when you mark the year since your loved one died. While the anniversary of Brad's death wasn't something to celebrate, it wasn't anything I could ignore either. And the days marched steadily closer to the date.

Something I learned as time passed was the best way to deal with difficult known anniversaries is to plan for them. My mom knew that and planned to be with me on that day. She had experienced plenty of firsts and the subsequent waves that came with grief. The first death day was a difficult one, so her presence would help to mitigate the pain of it. She had been there in the days before Brad died and knew how difficult those days were. In reality, we could both lean into each other as the memories washed over us. Distraction helped.

A week earlier, we had been at her trailer celebrating my mom's 60th birthday. My present to her was a day at the spa and the perfect time to schedule that was the following weekend: instead of dwelling on the minute details of the last days of August 2007, we would get pampered with massages, steam rooms, hot tubs, and hairstyles, followed by dinner out. Tears were not invited to the sushi table, as Grandma kept the kids chatting and colouring at the table. The lead-up had been building, but when the actual day arrived, the worst of the memories didn't have space at the table. Even when we finally made it home, grief wasn't given much purchase. There were bedtime stories to be read and kisses meted out for the babies before being tucked into their beds. By the time they were asleep, we were almost ready ourselves.

"Would you like a nightcap?" I offered.

"Maybe just one."

And one was all I got before she was ready for bed. Not before we shed a tear mind you, but Mom didn't let the night get away from us. Instead, she shared the wisdom from her own journey. When I brought up where we had been the year before, she switched tack.

"After your dad died was a tough time for me. Grandma and Grandpa moved out to BC a few months later. While the church had been a huge support when your dad was ill, our friends slowly pulled away after he was gone. I became the single woman; a threat to all the marriages around me. At a time when I needed support more than ever, they turned their backs on me, and I couldn't forget that. I regret that I lost that connection for you and your sister, but I ended up leaving the church. I was so angry and just couldn't forgive the minister and all those people who had supposedly been our friends.

What I did do though was join a grief support group, where I met Mary. She started as a grief counsellor but ended up as a huge support and good friend. She taught me to be strong for myself and helped to convince me to go back to school. She even encouraged me to share my story. I spoke at a conference and shared my experience as a young widow with two young children, someone who wasn't well represented in grief stories at the time."

She had walked the same damn path as me, only 30 years earlier. Young widows with young kids are still not well represented in the lexicon of grief. That's a good thing, but it makes for a lonely path when you don't see yourself anywhere. And I looked.

I had read every book I could get my hands on about grief in the Wellspring library. Any of the grief support groups I looked into were geared towards older adults, those who didn't have to worry about childcare or working around mealtimes. I couldn't do weekends and had given up finding a space where I felt like I belonged long ago. Even Wellspring, as incredible and healing a space as it was, was sometimes a difficult place to belong. More than once I struggled to walk in the door, knowing full well I didn't have cancer and no longer had anyone with cancer in my household.

Just so you know though, anyone I ever met there told me different.

"You belong here as much, if not more than me. We have all been touched and scarred by cancer. You need the space and healing. If it comes down to it, take my place! Stay as long as you need it." Ruddie insisted.

Ruddie no longer had salivary glands due to the radiation treatment that saved his life but left behind their mark in his cancer journey. With a constant bottle of water in hand and his wife by his side, he learned how to rebuild and renew his life. And darned if he was going to let me backslide on my own journey. His wife nodded in agreement as she squeezed my hand. They were a beautiful example of how we can all learn to live after trauma.

Our yoga instructor Emma was another incredible support for me too.

"You are doing awesome, Katherine," she insisted more than once. "Our bodies hold onto trauma, so regaining your core strength and health takes a long time. Every challenge you faced left its mark that your body needs to work through. Breathing and stretching form an important part of your recovery. You could add meditation to help you release even more blockages."

Another tool in my arsenal of recovery.

Emma knew all of her participant's stories and made modifications for everyone; from those with lymphedema who couldn't get up from the floor to me, who sometimes needed an extra squeeze with my tea after class. We were all touched, and scarred by our journey, and collectively needed the mental healing that this safe space offered, no matter your age, family dynamics, physical or mental health. We all had issues. For every stretch, drum circle, reiki session, or conversation I had behind Wellspring's doors, I released a few more of mine though.

I let go of my anger against 'old people'. They might have had more days than Brad was graced with, but they were just people all the same, with stories and journeys of their own.

I learned to breathe deeper and release into the power that the shedding of tears held. Those tears were no longer the heavy burden I had to suppress to be strong for Brad. They weren't a sign of weakness at his loss. They were cleansing. It took a ridiculous amount of them before I ever realized that though. When I inched towards Brad's death-aversary, then spilled beyond it, what I found on the other side was life.

That year down the road had been the hardest one of my life. But somehow, I survived.

PART THREE...
YEAR TWO & BEYOND

"When you are sorrowful, look again in
your heart, and you shall see that in truth
you are weeping for that which
has been your delight."

Khalil Gibran

Chapter 9: Hope

I would love to say it all gets easier at the end of the first year of loss. I really, really would. But that would be a lie. A wise woman once described grief to me like an ocean storm. In the beginning, there are waves, insurmountable waves that threaten to drown you constantly. They keep on coming and coming, crashing over you, and spinning you over and over in a tumult of disbelief. But ever so slowly, often imperceivably, those waves get a little smaller. They become more spaced apart, until you feel like your efforts at treading water are working and maybe you can start swimming again.

Until another giant wave hits you and you get smashed all over again.

The thing is, as time goes on you can anticipate those waves and come up with strategies to cope with their impact. The waves will never be as fierce or last as long as in those early days, even when they feel awful in the moment. It takes time, but I promise you will get there. In your own time.

In the interim, you will still get hit by those waves: days, weeks, months, and even years later. Sometimes you will see them coming and other times they will rear their ugly heads out of nowhere. I have gone back into counselling to work through issues years later and recognize that my loss will always impact me in some way or another. But I have a boat now. And a rudder I steer it with.

So no, I didn't wake up in September a newly reinvented woman. The sun didn't beam down on me for my happily ever after moment, just because I moved past my first year of mourning. In the Jewish faith, mourners sit Shiva for seven days, with an additional 30 days for Shloshim.[15] Only children are allowed to continue mourning for the first year. In Islam, there are three official days reserved for mourning in the immediate aftermath of someone's death. The widow is expected to stay in an extended period of mourning for an additional four lunar months, plus 10 days.[16] Both Hindu and Sikh religions believe in reincarnation, so their formal mourning periods are shorter: Hindus 13 days and Sikh only 10.[17]

Was I stretching things then by still feeling unmoored a year after Brad's death? Nope. Everyone grieves differently. And that's perfectly normal. My grief didn't swing into complicated or stuck grieving. I had moved through all the difficult firsts and grown a delicate new skin over this metamorphosizing life. I didn't have to please anyone with how I went about it. The trick was, I was still learning that, and my confidence was shaky at best.

What was the constant that gave me the drive to keep treading water though? The focus that had me getting up every morning whether I wanted to or not? My children. That little ten-month-old and precious two-and-a-half-year-old who also experienced loss but didn't have the words or mature comprehension to understand what had happened. I kept going for them.

On the day their father died, Taryn and Rylie were bit players in the saga that was my grief. They were on the sidelines at the funeral and were watchful observers as I waded through early grief. But they were not immune to the experience themselves. Their lives were just as affected and molded as mine. And they now had to not only move

---

[15] Shiva and other mourning observances, Chabad.org
[16] Islam: Periods of mourning, econdolence.com
[17] Cultural and religious issues professionals may encounter following a bereavement; Yunus Dudhwala, Barts Health NHS Trust, sudden.org

through life minus a parent, but their remaining parent was undergoing a huge transformation. While I felt the weight of that as I scribbled in journals at the end of the day, and understood it on another level, having experienced the same thing when my own father died at age five, I could not live or fix the experience for them. This journey was theirs to take too and it was no easier for them.

While children may not have the maturity or language to articulate what loss means, you can see it in how they carry themselves. Both myself as a child and both of my children became incredibly shy and removed from others. My girls had few males in their world, so shied away from them when they were exposed.

"I'm not afraid of them," Uncle Tony would say with a wink, as he scooped my girls up to take all four kids and cousins out to play when we visited my sister.

But it took time every visit for my girls to warm up to him.

Grandpa was little better, but trips for ice cream when we went out to fish and swim in his boat were a surefire way to bring them around when we visited him and my mom at their trailer.

As Denise and I grew closer and our families bonded, her husband Ben was another male presence that the girls analyzed, trying to decide how to behave around him. How could they resist being hoisted high overhead to reach the perfect apple while apple picking or snuggling in for their favourite activity in the world—story time. Ben had all the right moves and slowly won them over.

It was me who was the major player in their young lives though and I constantly felt like I was failing. I yelled when frustration got the better of me that I had to do it all myself. All I wanted was the nice house and to feel like I was providing for them, but always seemed to walk into rooms littered with toys and other items that didn't miraculously put themselves away at the end of the day.

That is a sign that fun was had there. Honestly, I couldn't see the life I was giving them, only the hole that was missing. There was so much love, but all I felt was loss in so many ways.

From the day they were born, I had read stories to my children. It was a special time for all of us to let go of the day, to let go of everything else that was going on around us, and to just cuddle and be together. We all loved it, me as much as them, and we voraciously read book after book, night after night. There was *Goodnight Moon, Monster Munchies, Guess How Much I Love You, The Very Hungry Caterpillar, Where the Wild Things Are, Brown Bear Brown Bear What Do You See, Love You Forever*, and so many more. They spoke of colours, numbers, feelings, and love, and for every time I felt like I wasn't enough, the moment we slipped under the covers, and I wrapped my arms around my little girls, it was all about love.

I picked books, like I chose meals.

"What do you want to read tonight?" was said as often as "What do you want for dinner?" We were a team and I tried desperately to please us all, Brad included. Meals were colourful, nutritious, and homemade most nights. Snacks were fruit, homemade cookies we baked together, and popcorn I shook up in an old copper pot on the stove. I strove for perfection, but failed to see that our life was pretty darn good, despite the losses we experienced.

A sunny summer day would arrive? I would pack a cooler bag full of cheese, crackers, kielbasa, and grapes, then grab towels, sand toys, and a beach umbrella, and head to the nearest beach.

If the days were cold and dark, and it felt like we hadn't been anywhere in forever? Everyone into the van for a road trip to Niagara Falls to wander around the Butterfly Conservatory to step out of the everyday, and release into the healing power of delicate wings flitting through the air around us, as the humid warmth reminded us that we would emerge from the cocoon of our winter eventually.

In need of another reason to feel alive? More snacks in the diaper bag and off we went to whatever local music festival or artisan show was playing in town. All three of us would dance, savour the sights and sounds, and interact with the world around us, as if we weren't wounded souls struggling to make our way in life. The girls took their cues from me, and I let the energy and vitality of the people who were in their best places remind me that life was a pretty special gift we were offered. You just had to look around to see it.

We also saw the wonders of the universe in walks through the woods, spring, summer, winter, and fall. The trees shed their leaves, grew new ones, and morphed through all the seasons, adapting to what life threw at them in a vibrant and colourful way. I breathed it in and pointed out all the miracles I saw to my girls as we walked along new paths to explore. Their enthusiasm to climb trees, scramble across downed trunks, and squat down into muddy or dusty hollows to discover new growth in the underbrush was transformative for us all. We always returned home breathing easier and hungry for the next adventure. I needed those moments to help me navigate the harder moments.

May 25, 2008
"I want Daddy to come home."
My heart broke tonight, as I tucked Taryn into bed.

"You took Daddy to the hospital and Daddy didn't come home. I wish Daddy could come home."

"I wish Daddy could come home too," I snuffled as tears poured freely and I hugged her with as much love as I could muster. "I would give anything to bring Daddy home."

"He can't come home," she recited from memory.

Is it sinking in? Oh lord, the pain and lack of understanding. She just wants her Daddy back. So do I. It hurts so much to say it again.

"Daddy was very sick, and he died. His body stopped working."

"But you took him back to the hospital," she said almost accusatorily.

"Daddy couldn't walk and had a hard time talking, and I couldn't help him. Mommy had to take him back to the hospital because I didn't know what to do."

I was terrified. He was dying, but I didn't know that. I didn't know what was going to happen and I knew I couldn't take care of him and the kids. Should I have left him here to die at home? I think he wouldn't have wanted the kids to see the worst of what went on.

Oh, I can't breathe.

There was nothing I could have done. The hospital was able to give him painkillers. But he spent some of his last hours in emerg where no one knew him. Maybe I shouldn't have left. They say people are conscious of their surroundings even in a coma. He

died alone in an empty hospital room. Oh lord. So
wrong. None of this should have happened. My
babies should have a father. I shouldn't have to try
to explain death to a three-year-old.
"You have lots of people around you that love and
care for you," I finally mustered.
Her response, "Yeah, like Victoria."
Crushing, knowing that in a month, her best friend is
moving away. Yes, she is a part of your life, but she
will be added to the long list of people you have lost
much too soon. Oh, heavy heart, why do you crush
me so?

Some days were harder than others. As days turned into weeks, months, and years though, we weathered the ups and downs together. Rylie learned to walk and developed amazing fine motor skills at an early age. When I was at my wits end with her taking off her diaper every time she went down for a nap or to bed at night, people stepped in to help.

While Lori, the supervisor at the daycare, tried to stop laughing after hearing my woes, she also rummaged in the closet behind her desk.

"Here," she said, as she handed me a roll of duct tape. "She won't be able to get that off."

I had been worried about Children's Aid stepping in and declaring me unfit, but those who held space for me knew how hard I was fighting to keep us afloat. Lori was one of my biggest champions and knew that my girls were well cared for. If it took a little duct tape to fix a problem, I wouldn't be the first one to benefit from its strength. And that seemingly large hurdle in the moment, was just a blip in time that my family weathered with no lasting scars.

It took time to see that though. And year two taught me that I now had time on my side. We weren't in a race to survive. Life was about slowing down to see the individual ripples and marvel at the beauty in the raindrops and budding flowers spread across my path.

So yes, I journalled and processed an enormous amount of mental energy. Processing Brad's illness, his loss, how that loss affected me, and my children was a massive undertaking that I gave plenty of space to. Ultimately, I had to reinvent my entire life.

That is what year two is about—year one is grieving the loss of your loved one, whereas year two is processing the loss of self. You go from a manic focus on the deceased to stepping back to see yourself in the equation. In a lot of ways, it felt worse. I may not have cried every day, like in the days after Brad died, but I still often felt overwhelmed and had little tolerance for stress. Any amount of it knocked me back and I floundered. It felt like I couldn't break free from its grip, even as I desperately tried to make headway into the new life I was building. This was my journey now. Brad might have been cheering and encouraging me on from the ethereal sidelines, but the path was mine. He lived on in memory and talked to me constantly— when you have been with someone long enough, you know what they would say in any situation—but the decisions and process were all me.

So, what else did year two hold?

A shallow relationship that often left me questioning myself and the validity of what I was doing with this man. In the weeks before Brad died, he recounted a conversation he had had with his palliative doctor. He said, "What kind of loser is my wife going to end up with?" That statement stuck with me.

While I could say, "he knew me too well" or "geez, how did he prophecy this?", instead I choose to think about that moment in a different light. What he was actually saying was, *"I should be the one with my wife, but I am going to die. She is going to be messed up and probably not thinking clearly. How is she going to recognize whether a new partner is treating her the way she deserves to be treated? Who is ever going to be good enough for her and my children?"* It was a cry of frustration at his loss and a kind of perceived failure on his part. He wouldn't be the one to be there for me like he promised when we were married. Not his fault, but a weight, nonetheless. And even though he was right about his fears—I did end up in a relationship with someone who wasn't looking for the commitment and family life I brought with me—he was also right about the magnitude of how much his loss affected me. I was blindsided by it and could not see.

That being said, you have to start somewhere, and this relationship was positive in its own way. It took a long time to recognize, but stepping into it reminded me that I was more than grief. I was a woman with needs outside of just mothering and surviving. In the areas where it was lacking, the relationship served as a painful reminder of all I had lost in Brad's passing—security, love, friendship, commitment—but in that way it became a measuring stick for what I should look for in future relationships. Because we are all worthy of love.

Sadly, year two also held other disappointments. My relationship with Brad's parents further eroded, which led to more guilt on my part for failing him. I had many conversations about this rift with several people though and slowly worked through my conflicted thoughts. I had feared this loss even before Brad died, knowing we were very different people. It wasn't my fault any more than it was theirs. It is incredibly hard to navigate grief and supporting others when you are hurting too is even harder. I wasn't the first to struggle in reconciling differences, nor will I be the last. Even still, it made me sad.

What this additional loss did accomplish though was that it pushed me to reach out to Brad's extended kin to hold on to some vestiges of family for my daughters. I fostered a relationship with his aunt and uncle, in hopes it would be enough of a tie for my children to their father's side of the family. I might not have been able to work through things with his immediate family, but it was the best I could do at the time.

This was a significant lesson that reinforced for me that everyone grieves differently in their own way, in their own timeline. The loss of Brad hit me and the rest of his family hard, and while for some it draws people together, for us, it worked the opposite. We couldn't bridge the divide that his loss created. Accepting that was a challenge that took me years to come to terms with and let go of, but my hope is that we all have our own version of peace that we attained. For me, I had to accept that I am only responsible for my path. We all travel our own routes.

In other notes, I congratulate myself for successfully re-entering the working world, if only on a part-time basis. Despite fears of not being able to juggle childrearing, household chores and maintenance, paying bills and work, I found that the busyness actually helped focus me. My new friend Denise was an incredible source of comfort and encouragement, which filled the many holes time had rent in me. We talked, cried, painted, laughed, and began to slowly blend our two families into a close friendship which I cherish even more every day that passes. The work, responsibility, and reminder that I was more than just grief was an incredible confidence booster which I needed then, more than ever.

If only those battles were enough. The monster that grief is continued to plague me, which meant a continuation in learning how to reach out for help when I needed it. Grief counselling came and went over year one and two. Sometimes it looked like emergency sessions with volunteer counsellors at Wellspring, but I slowly stopped beating myself up for what I thought of as weakness, as I recognized how intensive and far-reaching grieving is. And I took every opportunity I could to allow tensions to leak out of me on the table during reiki and therapeutic touch sessions. I tried everything, including yoga, drum circles, and whatever else was suggested. Nothing was off the table, as I always hoped whatever I tried might make the difference.

My journals captured so many words, tears, thoughts, and spasms too. Don't overlook the power that taking words out of your head, so you can inspect them on paper has. For me, it felt like a revelation to put to words what I was feeling. So often I felt like I was beyond understanding the world myself, but when I took the time to scratch out thoughts, heedless of spelling or grammar, it gave me a glimpse of me. I worked so hard to be strong and hold myself together while Brad was ill, never allowing space for my own thoughts or feelings, but in grief, it was all about me. It took a long time to reintroduce me to who that new person was. The journals helped. Seeing my words, I finally felt sympathy for the magnitude of my journey and put down the daggers I so often carried before.

That also gratefully meant that in year two, I slowly moved beyond feeling embarrassed for my grief and started to own it.

324

Honestly, there had never been a choice, so why run anymore? I was sad. I was adrift and uncertain of which way to turn or point myself. The life map that Brad had always seemed to have sketched out in his mind slipped away with him, and it was up to me to slowly scribble out a new path. What a revelation when I thought about planning a vacation like a normal person did by the time year three rolled around. Who did that? Me. After two and a half years of illness and being owned by doctor appointments, followed by two hard years of scouring the depths of my soul to figure out who I was and what direction I wanted to go in, owning my future was mindboggling.

What I didn't realize though until years later is that the journey never ends. Even if people had warned me, I couldn't have comprehended the magnitude of grief and the permanent scars it leaves behind. You are never the same after losing a loved one. But as sad as it is to lose that person, at some point you wake up and realize how blessed you are to have had them in your life at all. In subtle ways, your grief turns into the gift of joy, when you reflect on the good memories. Harder memories become lessons that you wear the badge of survival on. For every day you didn't want to get up, when you wanted to fling yourself into a moving river, or just STOP — you didn't. You woke up. You fed yourself. You walked away from the precipice and kept going. That is strength, the kind you never wanted or asked for but strength, nonetheless. And every day you push through until you close your eyes at night is a testament to your strength and love for the person who touched your life. Remember, they would be proud of you and love you all the more for the hardships you weather along the way. They wouldn't want you to punish yourself for losing them when that wasn't in your hands to decide. Live the life they would want you to have.

Be happy.

Happily, Ever After

So, where's my happily ever after? Did the white knight ever ride through the darkness and save me from a fate worse than death? Kind of. Who was it?

Me.

If I have learned nothing more important than this along this journey, it is that we need to be our own champions. We need to recognize our own strengths and honour the journey we are on in our own best way. You don't need anyone to save you. No one can ever turn back the clock to the before or make the hurt disappear. The real strength is that you wouldn't want anyone to.

You wouldn't want anyone to take away the pain, the tears, the sorrow. That would then also eradicate the joy, love, and laughter. Not a chance I would give that up.

Every tear reminds me that my loved one existed and that we had a relationship. That relationship wasn't perfect, but on reflection the lessons in it are invaluable. And going back and changing anything, changes life moving forward.

Are you willing to give up the walk through the woods when you spied a family of deer, the new friends you made when you pushed yourself to try something different on a good day, or the laughter that shook you so hard you couldn't breathe but that your loved one was never a part of? Or how about the understanding that you finally discovered when you realized that you've made good decisions all on your own and your loved one would be proud of how far you've come? No longer physically by your side but rooting you on in a new way regardless. I'm not. And that is the way it should be.

This is the new normal and as painful as it is, there is wisdom there too. Like the transformation of pottery fired at 2000 degrees, you too will come through the flames in different shape and form, so much water rent from you as to be miraculous. It looks different for everyone, with unique cracks, distinct colours, and new patterns you could never replicate. But there is beauty there too.

We all have our stories; many of them with sad chapters. I never remarried and admit that I probably guard my heart too closely. A lasting scar that I bump up against too often—my fear of loss. I know if you don't let people in, you don't get to experience the joy of love, but trust is a tough one for me.

I am not alone though. I have friends who would do anything for me and family who champion my every step. I'm sure you do too Sometimes we don't even realize they are there. Like the neighbour who plows your driveway after a storm because they know you have two little ones to take care of and are doing it all alone. Or the long-lost friend who is watching from the sidelines and rooting for you every step of the way, but only steps up on the rare occasion you ask for help. People want to help. They just don't always know how. And I know in the early days of grief it is so hard to know what you need and how people can help. Life in the early days of grief feels like too much. If you get glimmers though, Ask. Giving feels so good and receiving is just as rewarding. We all win when we help each other.

Today, my children have reached high school and university. They have so much living in front of them, including plenty of emotional journeys of their own. I remember my own grappling with life at their age and the questions that came with the turbulent teen years. As I contemplated who I was and what direction I wanted to head in, I couldn't help but look back and think about what might have been under other circumstances. Would I have been a different person if my father had lived? Perhaps more confidant, less hesitant to put myself out there, and try new things? Did my early loss leave a permanent scar that left the concept of change so terrifying that I would rather tread water and stagnate than embrace the bigger world and its mysteries? Would my children struggle with these self-same traumas having lost their own father and security at such a young age? I hope not, but I need to remember that they have their own journeys to make regardless. I don't sense the anger that bubbled under my skin as a teen in them. The glare I shot the high school Vice Principal when I sat across from them in their office.

"Who can we call to come pick you up," they asked sternly. "Your mother?"

"She's out of town."

"Your father?"

"He's dead."

There was venom in those words as I spat them out. I was in the office due to my own misdeeds, but seethed hearing the muddled "I'm so sorry for your loss" all over again. I heard it over and over again and it seemed a part of me. It was the armour I wore under the leather jacket meant to scare away anyone who couldn't be bothered to get me. To see beyond the loss and single parent status that was still so new in families back then. We were different. I was different. The clothes and friends with spiked and dyed hair felt safer than the solid two-parent families that still felt like the norm. Where I didn't fit in. My outward choices then just served to punctuate how different I felt inside.

As angry as I felt then though, I discovered that the people around me all had their own demons. The kids with two parents didn't necessarily have rosy home lives. There were other single parent families, some far more fragile emotionally and financially than ours. Other people experienced illness, loss, financial hardship, and emotional traumas that left their own scars. And we all had to work through them however we managed that. I befriended street kids, kids that drank and did drugs, kids that were promiscuous, and others who went to church youth groups. All of us held uncertainties, insecurities, hopes, fears, and dreams.

My children will too. Not just because they lost their father at an early age. Not because money hasn't always been plentiful. And not because there is anything wrong with them. We all experience the searching. We all need to figure out who we are and where we fit in. Where we belong. I think they are further ahead than I was at their age, but I don't need to put that on them. They have their stories, their scars and fears. I get it and will be there for them the best I can. They have their own journeys though. And mine isn't done yet either.

I survived year one. Year two was a different journey, easier in some ways, but more challenging in others. By year three, I had left behind the active grieving and started new paths. I packed my children into a van for a road trip to British Columbia and back: approximately 10,000 km and three weeks gone. Other roads trips took us to Maine with friends, and Nova Scotia with my sister. I dated. I started a career in social media management that I still tackle today. And throughout it all, I wrote. I am proud to report that this is the second book I have published. Major and minor milestones keep on piling up and my piles of stones becomes bigger by the day.

Had I survived? I had friends and family, a career, two well-behaved children, and new memories adding all the time. The years passed and I thought I finally had it all figured out. We had weathered grief. I had made it.

Until covid rocked the entire planet and brought everyone to a jarring standstill the likes of which my generation had never experienced. How was that for a new journey of its own? Ugh.

I'm not going to lie. That was a tough one and brought up loss issues all over again. We were asked to shelter in place and physical space was forcibly imposed. Where I had isolated myself years earlier while I processed my early grief, now everyone was told to steer clear of each other. It all felt wrong on so many levels. I reached out for counselling, as old grief waves washed over me. How could I still be hobbled over Brad's loss over a decade later? In fact, the loss of my father reared into view too. I didn't see that coming, but experience helped me understand what was going on. In the face of stress, loss steps in more often than I could ever have anticipated. Tears threaten, disbelief creeps in, and I question my every move again and again. The difference is that I know if I slow down, be kind to myself, and breathe, I will weather whatever storm arises.

So, I cried a few more buckets of tears. I sheltered in place, but also reached out to both give and ask for support. And we came out the other side once more. Eventually. With a booster or five behind us to help. Hallelujah.

What did that teach me? That even if waves grow, they recede too. And if they produce tears, so be it. It shows you have a heart full

330

of love, and that is beautiful. Infinitely beautiful. So don't be afraid. Don't be afraid to cry, as those tears were formed in love. Sorrow is born from laughter. And a period of stagnation is sometimes the best thing to sit in while you recover enough to begin to move forward again. Even if it feels like you are moving backward, each wave of grief moves you forward. Tread water. Paddle parallel to the shore. It is the only way to ever feel solid ground underneath you again.

And when you feel exhausted and like you can't go on anymore, **ask for help**. I promise you, there is an army of people waiting to dive in to be there for you. We are here to listen, to tread water with you, and to slowly paddle you to your new tomorrow. There is so much love out there. The more you are open to it, the more you give, the bigger your rewards.

So, is this "The End"? Not really. There is no end. But I am thankful you came on my journey with me. My father died 45 years ago. My husband has been gone 16. They will always be watching out for me because we took the time to love at some point on the path. So even though storms filled many of my days over the years, I know they created new paths and brought the gift of new experiences and people. My choice is to see the beauty in that. And the many people I have met who have also experienced loss over their lives seem to see that too.

Be grateful for the journey. There are gifts scattered everywhere on the path, some jagged, some smooth, but all with the power to heal, if you only sit with them and let them show you their magic. That magic is life.

This is the last stone on this pile. This is the last chapter of this book. But not the last stop in this journey.

Are you ready for the next chapter? Let's go.

Photo Credit: Luck and Lavendar Photography

NOT "THE END"...
BUT NEW BEGINNINGS

*"Don't cry because it's over.
Smile because it happened."*

Dr. Seuss

AUTHOR'S NOTE

This book was a long time in coming. That feels like the story of my life, but sometimes we need to get to a spot where we are truly ready before we can begin. And even if we do start, sometimes we need to go back and start over and over again until we get the story right. It goes beyond editing (believe me, there is plenty of that which goes on as well).

But now I have come to the end.

For me, this book was a challenge. I wrote it for me. I wrote it for the me who was scouring book stacks looking for answers in grief books in the months after Brad died. Finding the right words and the right tone were incredibly difficult. Diving back into Brad's illness and loss brought it all back to the surface. I'm not going to lie, there were tears.

There were many other reasons why I wrote this book though. Ultimately, it came down to people. There were those who reached out to ask how they could talk about and explain grief and death to their own children. The people who nodded silently when I said I was writing a grief book—the ones who had lost their own partners and knew how painful it was from personal experience and how important it is to not feel alone on the journey—I wrote it for them too. I wrote these words to say thank you to the warriors who walked my path with me—my counsellors, formal and informal—friends, family, and the professionals who believed in every step I took. And even though I changed the names of most of the characters in this book, I like to think that anyone can see themselves in any of these roles.

Thank you. You are my cheerleaders and I give thanks for you every day. You quite literally saved my life. But who were the biggest cheerleaders?

ACKNOWLEDGEMENTS

I have been blessed with so many cheerleaders. These folks helped get me to where I am today though.

My mother led the pack. Thank you for recognizing the path ahead of me, fearing the worst, but holding my hand to help me navigate as best as possible anyway. You had already walked a far too similar path of your own, and knowing that gutted me, but I couldn't have survived the journey without you. I love you for being with me every step of the way.

My sister Kerry is my best friend, biggest champion, and the greatest instigator of diving back into life whom I could ask for. You are always the first one to suggest the most questionable and fun adventures, and I couldn't have found life on the other side of loss without you. Know that I am always in for whatever adventure you suggest next! I am so incredibly blessed for the tears, fears, life, love, and laughter we have had along the way.

My babies, Taryn and Rylie, oh my babies. Your whole lives were wrapped up in my grief and I know that molded you. I apologize for all the times I wasn't strong enough to love you more but am incredibly proud of where you landed in this life we forged. You are smart, sensitive, and the most caring individuals I have the pleasure to know, and it is humbling to acknowledge my part in steering you to where you are today. I will always love you!

My publishing agent Marcia is the best cheerleader I could ask for to keep me going in this writing journey. She pushes me when

I need it, is always ready for the next chapter, and isn't afraid to join me on this voyage, even when the story turns dark. Thank you for all you do!

There have been so many others who believed in me when I didn't believe in myself, from counsellors to friends.

When I fell into the habit of beating myself up over perceived failures, you were my fiercest champion, Paul. I will be forever grateful that Mom brought you into our realm.

Thank you, Nancy, for working me towards a new normal in the form of family dinners, swimming lessons, and vacations, but more importantly, for reminding me of the power my words hold and encouraging me to use them to guide my way.

Leslie, you probably won't ever be ready to read this, but know that I recognize that you'll always have my back. Family is love, and grief pulled us together, regardless of the storm. We've got this.

And Corrie, oh my heart. You were the one who helped me to say I was a writer in the first place. Rediscovering you was the best thing that ever happened to me. Words have power lady! I love that we discovered how to wield them together and that we have both found how they heal and carry us forward.

I would be remiss if I didn't mention the incredible folks who attend weekly Shut Up and Write sessions too. When you need the encouragement to get words on the page, a writing group is your best resource. Find one or create a writing group of your own to build accountability!

Special thanks to Julie, Laura, Suzanne, Ryan, Heather, Daisy, and Daniel for being early readers of this book. Your suggestions and support helped make this book that much better and I owe you much gratitude.

And thank You for being part of my journey. There are so many more people who have asked about my journey, my words, and this story. I am forever grateful that I finally found my tribe and realized you were all right here with me all along.

ABOUT THE AUTHOR

Katherine Krige is a Freelance Writer and accomplished Social Media Manager. She is a graduate of York University with a B.A. in English, plus is completing several courses towards a Creative Writing Certificate in the Continuing Studies program at Western University. Having journalled from a young age, she put her writing skills to good use while travelling the world. Those journals proved integral for her bestselling travel memoir, *Roughing it in Africa*. They also helped her process and heal after the loss of her husband and directly led to writing the grief memoir, *Riding the Waves*. A widow in her early 30s, she raised two young children on her own and kept penning words for both herself and others. She currently lives in London, Ontario with her two almost-fully-grown children. You can find Katherine on Facebook, Instagram, LinkedIn, and at the local coffee shop when she has time to journal her way through another day.

www.katherinekrige.com

kkrige@katherinekrige.com

RESOURCES

Examples of What to Say or Do to Support Someone

- Tackle a household chore with or for them. Try to feel out if the task or company is most important and offer services accordingly.

  - ➤ *"Can I mow your lawn/shovel your driveway/rake your leaves?"*
  - ➤ *"I am going to help you paint the living room. Is there a day that works best for you?"*

- Ask if they would like to get together. This provides an opportunity to talk about their loved one, current challenges, or something completely unrelated. Sometimes an opportunity to socialize outside of day-to-day activities and routines is incredibly welcome.

  - ➤ *"Would you like to join me for a walk? I would love the company."*
  - ➤ *"Do you want to talk about your loved one? I remember when they did... (share a touching/funny/whatever story)"*

- Deliver a meal during a crisis, baked goods just because, or offer to share a meal so the person has company and conversation for a few hours.

  - ➤ *"I made a second lasagna for you while I was making one for me, because I know you love it. Feel free to eat it tonight or freeze it for later."*
  - ➤ *"I'm running to the grocery store. Do you need me to pick you up anything?"*

- Offer babysitting services for those with children, or pet care for those with pets, so they can tackle chores either at home or out of the house, without having to worry about taking their dependents with them.

> ➢ *"Let my daughter babysit, so you and I can go to the movies."*
> ➢ "The weather has been kind of crummy. Would you like me to walk your dog when I take mine out? Or go together for the exercise?" (exercise is good for mind and body for all)

- Step up for some of the harder parts. Be there for the everyday. Recognize that some days just feel heavier and need a little more support, however that looks like.

> ➢ *"When you are ready to go through your loved one's clothes, I will help you sort and pack them up."*
> ➢ *"I just popped by to say hi. If you don't feel like talking, don't feel you need to, but know I am here whenever you do."*

- Be thoughtful around holidays. Remember them in gift giving. It doesn't need to be big, as the thought really does count.

> ➢ *"My lilacs are just beautiful right now. I thought you might enjoy some too, so I cut you a bouquet from my garden. I hope you like them."*
> ➢ *"Would you like to join us for Thanksgiving? There's always room around the table for one more and we would love to have you."* (holidays and celebrations, especially firsts, are difficult for those trying to establish new normals)

Places & Organizations Mentioned in this Book

Canadian Cancer Society – https://cancer.ca/en/

"We offer a nationwide support system in the country for people with cancer and their family, friends and caregivers. Access free programs and services that can help manage life with cancer, including our supportive online community, our online and phone-based information specialists and much more."

Family Services Thames Valley - https://www.fstv.ca/

"For over 80 years, Family Service Thames Valley has offered counselling and support services to individuals and families. Whether it's relationship difficulties, adjusting to life transitions, or living with a developmental disability, we have programs to help."

Health Connect Ontario (Health 811) [formerly Telehealth] - https://health811.ontario.ca/static/guest/home or call 811

"Access safe, high-quality care and avoid unnecessary visits to the emergency room. This service is an easy way to get connected to care you or your loved ones need, but it does not replace your other touch point with your health care provider. In a medical emergency call 911 immediately."

Holmes Rahe Stress Scale - https://www.dartmouth.edu/eap/library/lifechangestresstest.pdf

"The body is a finely timed instrument that does not like surprises. Any sudden change stimuli which affects the body, or the reordering of important routines that the body become used to, can cause needless stress, throwing your whole physical being into turmoil.

Th(is) chart will give you some idea of how to informally score yourself on Social Readjustment Scale. Since being healthy is the optimum state you want to achieve, being sick is the state of being you most want to avoid."

Home and Community Care Access Services [formerly CCAC] - https://healthcareathome.ca/

"Ontario's 14 Home and Community Care Support Services organizations coordinate in-home and community-based care for thousands of patients across the province every day."

Victorian Order of Nurses (VON) Canada – https://von.ca/en

"We've been leading home and community care in Canada for over a century. We were among the first organizations in the country to offer home care and public health nursing and now, over a century later, we provide home and community support services to over 10,000 people every day across Ontario and Nova Scotia."

Wellspring - https://wellspring.ca/

"At Wellspring, you will find a range of programs designed to help provide connection and belonging, ease physical pain and emotional distress, build strength and mobility, and reduce fatigue. Specialized financial, workplace, counselling and other cancer-related supports are also available.

Wellspring programs are available across Canada online, and through centres in Ontario and Alberta, all at no charge, and without referral."

*Other Organizations to Seek Help**

Canadian Hospice Palliative Care Association: Grief and Bereavement Resource Repository - https://www.chpca.ca/resource/grief-and-bereavement-resource-repository/

"This repository of grief and bereavement resources is a collection of useful links and resources to help you and your loved ones cope with grief. Please note this page will be updated on regular basis with new and other suggested resources.

Canadian Mental Health Association - https://cmha.ca/

"With 330 community locations, CMHA is a nationwide organization that promotes mental health and supports people recovering from mental illness."

The Healthline - https://www.thehealthline.ca/

"Find local health and community services across Ontario."

Mental Health and Wellness: Services & Information
(Government of Canada) - https://www.canada.ca/en/public-health/topics/mental-health-wellness.html

"Links to services and information on mental health, mental illness, suicide prevention, post-traumatic stress disorder (PTSD), cannabis and mental health."

MyGrief.ca - https://www.mygrief.ca/

"MyGrief.ca is an online resource to help people move through their grief from the comfort of their own home, at their own pace. It can help you understand your grief and approach some of the most difficult questions that may arise. It was developed by people who have experienced the death of someone important to them and grief specialists. It complements existing community resources and helps address barriers to grief services. Many people working in healthcare use it as an education tool. It is also used by grief support groups and educators. The Canadian Partnership Against Cancer funded the vision and the original nine modules. Health Canada has funded the latest series of modules."

Ontario Funeral Service Association -
https://ofsa.org/grief_support_resources

"Grief Support resources"

Wellness Together Canada - https://www.wellnesstogether.ca/en-ca

"Wellness Together Canada is a collaborative project. Our mission is to provide high-quality resources for everybody. To help us do that, we are supported by a wide network of organizations, with decades of experience. Whatever the need, our partners are prepared to help.

Wellness Together Canada is designed to be used on demand. That means you get to choose what you need, when you need it. Our services range from basic wellness information, to one-on-one sessions with a counsellor, to community support. Whatever it is you're looking for, we're here to point you towards the best resources out there."

This list is far from exhaustive and is not meant to replace professional counselling or other health services. Descriptions are taken from their websites and are current as of 2023. Many of these resources have in-person, phone, or online contact information and help, and are meant to assist you in starting your search for care.

IF YOU ARE IN CRISIS, PLEASE REACH OUT TO SOMEONE FOR HELP.